# PONDS & LAKES
## OF THE
# WHITE MOUNTAINS

◆

*Upper Greeley Pond*

# Ponds & Lakes
## of the
# White Mountains

◆

## A FOUR-SEASON GUIDE
## FOR HIKERS AND ANGLERS

### STEVEN D. SMITH

BACKCOUNTRY PUBLICATIONS
WOODSTOCK, VERMONT

**An Invitation to the Reader**
If you find that conditions have changed along these walks, please let the author and publisher know so that corrections may be made. Address all correspondence to: Editor, Backcountry Publications, PO Box 748, Woodstock, VT 05091

Copyright © 1993, 1998 by Steven D. Smith
Second Edition

Published by Backcountry Publications, a division of The Countryman Press, Woodstock, VT 05091
Distributed by W. W. Norton & Company, Inc., 500 Fifth Avenue, New York, NY 10110

**Library of Congress Cataloging-in-Publication Data**
Smith, Steven D., 1953-
 Ponds & Lakes of the White Mountains : a four-season guide for hikers and anglers / Steven D. Smith. — 2nd ed.
  p.  cm.
 Includes bibliographical references (p.  346) and index.
 ISBN 0-88150-413-0 (alk. paper)
 1. Lakes—White Mountains (N.H. and Me.)—Recreational use—Guidebooks. 2. Hiking—White Mountains (N.H. and Me.)—Guidebooks. 3. White Mountains (N.H. and Me.)—Guidebooks. I. Title.
GV191.42.W49S64 1998
333.78'44'097422—dc21                                    97-47491
                                                              CIP

Extracts from the following works have been reprinted with permission: *Walks and Climbs in the White Mountains,* by Karl P. Harrington, copyright © 1926 by Yale University Press. *Lucy Crawford's History of the White Mountains,* ed. by Stearns Morse, copyright © 1978 by Appalachian Mountain Club; *Skyline Promenades: A Potpourri,* by J. Brooks Atkinson, copyright © 1925 by Alfred A. Knopf. All possible care has been taken to obtain permission from the copyright holders to reprint selections protected by copyright; any errors or omissions are unintentional and will be rectified in any future printings upon notification to the publishers.

Text and cover design by Ann Aspell
Maps by Richard Widhu, © 1993, The Countryman Press
Photographs by the author, except photos on pages 10 and 67 by Mike Dickerman
Cover Photos: Kinsman Pond (front) and Shoal Pond (back) by Steven D. Smith
Printed in the United States of America

10 9 8 7 6 5 4 3 2 1

*To Mom*
*To the Smith and Meguerdichian families*
*And to Dad, who couldn't be here.*

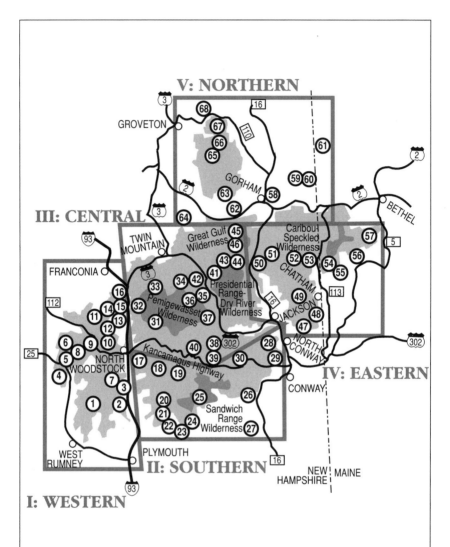

# PONDS AND LAKES
## OF THE
# WHITE MOUNTAINS

# CONTENTS

--------◆--------

## I. WESTERN WHITE MOUNTAINS

## II. SOUTHERN WHITE MOUNTAINS

### Sandwich Notch Road

## III. CENTRAL WHITE MOUNTAINS

## IV. EASTERN WHITE MOUNTAINS

## V. NORTHERN WHITE MOUNTAINS

# APPENDIX

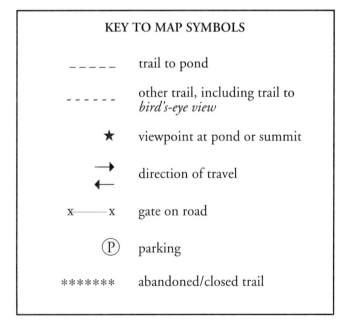

**KEY TO MAP SYMBOLS**

- - - - -      trail to pond

- - - - - -      other trail, including trail to *bird's-eye view*

★      viewpoint at pond or summit

→
←      direction of travel

x——x      gate on road

Ⓟ      parking

\*\*\*\*\*\*      abandoned/closed trail

# ACKNOWLEDGMENTS

First thanks should go to the dedicated stewards who manage the lands, trails, and waters of the White Mountains: the US Forest Service, Appalachian Mountain Club, New Hampshire State Parks, New Hampshire Fish and Game Department, and the various trail maintaining organizations.

Inspiration was provided by Bruce and Doreen Bolnick's engaging *Waterfalls of the White Mountains*, as well as Daniel Doan's two *Fifty Hikes* books, William V. P. Newlin's *Lakes & Ponds of Mt. Desert* and Barbara McMartin's *Discover The Adirondacks* series.

Many people went out of their way to provide information: from the New Hampshire Fish and Game Department, Paul Dest, Pat Locke, Larry Miller, and Fisheries Biologists Scott Decker and Donald Miller, who kindly reviewed a list of fish species for the individual ponds; Tom Chamberlain from the Maine Department of Inland Fisheries and Wildlife; Ned Therrien, Mike Seeger, Dave Govatski, and other helpful folks from the White Mountain National Forest; Carol Foss and Stephen Walker of the Audubon Society of New Hampshire; Alan Smith, Chocorua Lake Conservation Foundation; Philip Preston, Squam Lakes Association; Don Buso of the New York Botanical Garden Institute of Ecosystem Studies, who shed much-needed light on the complex issue of acid deposition; Elbow Pond enthusiasts Kathy Didier and Doc Cutler; Dr. Robert Averill, the authority on any matter concerning the Moosilauke region; Bob Berti of Forest Resources Consultants, managers of the Peaked Hill Pond area; Cindy King and Ginger Lang; Ray Welch; Thom Perkins, Jackson Ski Touring Foundation; Gene Daniell, peakbagging guru and editor of the indispensable *AMC White Mountain Guide*; and Associate Editor Jon Burroughs, whom I've never met, but who deserves recognition for remeasuring all the trails for the guide's 25th edition.

I'd like to thank Barbara McMartin and the estimable Dan Doan for their words of encouragement; Laura and Guy Waterman and Joe Bousquet for their thoughtful comments and concerns on the inclusion of bushwhack ponds; and Ray Evans, the legendary eightysomething hiker from Twin Mountain who shared his intimate knowledge of the Crawford Notch region. Also in Twin Mountain, the volunteer fire department has my eternal gratitude for their prompt action in response to an electrical fire, saving field notes and an early version of the manuscript from oblivion.

Special thanks are owed to David L. Nelson, whose enormous love and knowledge of the sport are clearly evident in his section on "Trout Fishing the Mountain Ponds."

An understanding boss is a priceless asset for a spare-time author, and Susan McHenry always gave me time away from The Mill at Loon Mountain when I needed it. Thanks also to Jim Meryman of Innisfree Bookshop for his title suggestion; Liz and Jim Lambregtse, for information on Mirror Lake, where they once lived; and Charlie Robie, Joe Trudell, and Jeff Perkins for inside stuff on ponds in the Lincoln area.

I owe a heartfelt thanks to my longtime hiking crony Mike Dickerman, reporter extraordinaire for the *Littleton Courier*, who has slogged with me to backcountry ponds in every season and who contributed several excellent photos for this book; also to Creston Ruiter, Roger and Peter Doucette, Bill Vecchio, John Dickerman, Harry Cunningham, and others with whom I've shared the joys and travails of exploring these wild and wonderful mountains.

The folks at Backcountry have been great! Editor-in-Chief Carl Taylor was an enthusiastic supporter from the start. Managing Editor Robin Dutcher-Bayer was helpful and gracious throughout, and copy editor Ruth Doan MacDougall (Dan's daughter) greatly improved the book with her deft editing and keen eye for detail. Production Manager Michael Gray worked wonders with disks, maps, and photos.

My family has been unfailingly supportive during the three year span of this project. Most everyone's joined me for a pond trek: Drew, Kate, Rachel, and Becky to Carter Ponds; Deb, George, David, Mike, and Mom (and Sammy), who walked the rocky way to Mountain Pond. This book is dedicated to them.

Though this book has been shaped by many persons, any errors of omission or commission are the sole responsibility of the author.

# INTRODUCTION

◆

*Nothing is more attractive in the mountains than the
presence of lakes.*

—Julius Ward
*The White Mountains*, 1890

Ponds and lakes add a touch of tranquility to the rugged White Mountain landscape. They mirror the moods of the skies, the colors of the forests, and the contours of the time-worn peaks. Whether glinting in sunshine, shrouded in mist, or armored in snow and ice, these watery openings are beautiful and interesting places to visit.

The still mountain waters appeal to outdoor lovers of all ages. They're the perfect antidote for a high-stress, high tech world. Here you can hike, fish, ski, snowshoe, watch birds or moose, swim, paddle a canoe, or simply tarry by a sunny shore. Even the casual tourist passing by a roadside pond may be moved to stop, look, and snap a photo.

Each of the White Mountains' hundred-odd ponds and lakes presents a distinctive personality. Their waters may be sapphire-blue or emerald-green, startlingly clear or murky as overcooked coffee. Some are somber, spruce-rimmed tarns shadowed by steep mountain walls. Others are encircled by hardwood hills, fringed with sand and pines, or bounded by bogs teeming with strange plants and unusual birds. (Hungry insects, too.) A handful nestle in craggy bowls amidst the very highest peaks.

This book is meant to be a celebration of the ponds' and lakes' varied beauties and an invitation to explore them and enjoy them, while leaving them unmarred for the delight of future visitors. In addition to describing how to get to these water bodies and what you might find and do there, this guide relates some of their natural and human history. Hopefully it will encourage you to make other discoveries of your own.

## THE PONDS AND LAKES

The ponds and lakes described here are mostly in the White Mountain

1

National Forest or adjacent State Parks and Forests. The few exceptions are on privately owned conservation lands or paper company woodlands traditionally open to responsible public use. Those with heavy residential development were generally excluded. The water bodies are split into five geographic regions, outlined on the map at the front of the book: Western, Southern, Central, Eastern, and Northern.

The effort required to reach the ponds and lakes varies widely. There are plenty of roadside beauties, some noted as aquatic playgrounds, others as picnic and photo opportunities. Several offer access to the physically challenged.

A number of ponds provide short and easy hikes suited for all ages. Others require a moderate commitment of time and energy, enough so that you know you're hiking in the mountains. And there are high, remote ponds whose admission price is a full day of strenuous endeavor.

Of course the old favorites—Lonesome Lake, Greeley Ponds, Lakes of the Clouds et al.—are here, and they are deservedly popular. But I also encourage you to seek out some of the trails and ponds in the less visited corners of the mountains.

Most of the hikes are on marked trails maintained by the White Mountain National Forest, the Appalachian Mountain Club, the NH State Parks, and other entities. A few trace routes over an assortment of logging roads, snowmobile trails, and unmarked anglers' paths. These should present no problems for hikers accustomed to using descriptions in combination with map and compass.

## POND NOMENCLATURE

As with *waterfalls* and *cascades*, there is no clear benchmark for distinguishing a large *pond* from a small *lake*. Webster's defines a pond as "a body of water smaller than a lake." A lake, in turn, is "an inland body of fresh water, larger than a pool or pond." The propensity of nineteenth-century White Mountain enthusiasts to dub even the smallest pocket of water a *lake* further muddles the nomenclature. (For example, Horseshoe *Pond* sprawls over 132 acres, while Hermit *Lake* occupies a basin of less than a half acre.)

In a general sense, ponds are thought of as smaller, shallower and warmer than lakes, with more aquatic plant growth. A relatively uniform water temperature is characteristic of many ponds, while lakes (and some deeper ponds) develop "thermal stratification," with a warmer layer of water on top in summer and a cooler layer in winter.

Since most of our White Mountain water bodies are on the small side, and for simplicity's sake, *pond* is the term most often used in this book.

## THE POND AND LAKE EXPLORATIONS

The information in each "exploration" will help you plan a visit that suits the ambition and interests of your party. Are you looking for a short hike with nice waterfront views? A roadside stop for a family swim or a leisurely paddle? A seldom-fished backwoods trout pond? A hot spot for birds or moose? A rugged hike to a high-country tarn? You'll find the options here. For quick reference, refer to the "Key to Pond and Lake Explorations" in the Appendix.

Briefly, each exploration includes:

- A summary of hiking facts, pond and lake statistics, activities, and fish species.
- An introductory overview.
- Road or trailhead access.
- A description of the trail to the pond or lake.
- Scenery and activities found at the pond or lake.
- Nearby viewpoints that offer a "bird's-eye view" over the water. Some of these can be visited as an extension of a pond exploration; others require a separate excursion.
- Notes on visiting in winter.

In encouraging you to visit these special places of the White Mountains, I make one urgent request: treat them with respect and the utmost care. Ponds and lakes are among our most fragile environments. Your consideration in not trampling vegetation, littering, polluting the water, disturbing wildlife, or camping too close to trail or shore will go a long way toward preserving the ponds in all their beauty and wildness for future generations to enjoy.

I wish you many happy, sunny days at the ponds.

# VISITING THE PONDS
# AND LAKES

---◆---

## Maps and Guidebooks

*US Geological Survey:* The most useful and detailed maps are the 7½ minute topographical quadrangles (with 20- or 40-foot contours) issued by the US Geological Survey. The appropriate map(s) for each exploration is listed, and the portion that shows the hiking route accompanies the text. The USGS maps are available at many sporting goods and outdoor stores, selling for $2.50-$3.00 per map in recent years, or from USGS Map Sales, Federal Center, Box 25286, Denver, CO 80225; 1-800-USA-MAPS.

Some older quads may show paths long since abandoned or may lack important new trails and logging roads. More up-to-date versions of the USGS maps are available from the US Forest Service at White Mountain National Forest headquarters: PO Box 638/719 Main St., Laconia, NH 03247; 603-528-8721.

AMC *White Mountain Guide:* The 25th edition of the "hiker's bible," issued in 1992, is the best yet, with revised trail descriptions and measurements. (Trail distances for the pond and lake explorations are taken from the AMC *Guide.*) The *Guide* also includes a set of excellent regional maps with 100-foot contours, good for trip planning and geographical overview.

*Delorme's Trail Map and Guide to the White Mountain National Forest:* About the same scale as the AMC maps but showing the entire National Forest on one map, with 100-foot contours and capsule trail descriptions on the back. A useful resource, and is widely available.

*AMC/Washburn Mount Washington and Presidential Range Map:* Ten years in the making, this cartographic classic developed by the eminent Bradford Washburn is the best available map for the Presidential Range. Though the 50-foot contours are a bit hard to read, the trails and other features are shown with great accuracy. It's available at bookstores and from the AMC.

## Hiking Facts

Roadside ponds and lakes are just that—you can drive, with a conventional vehicle, right up to the shore or to a parking area a short distance from the water's edge.

For water bodies accessible only by hiking, the trail mileage given is for the complete round-trip or loop walk. The vertical rise is the total amount of climbing for the hike, including ups and downs along the way and any ascent on the return trip.

Vertical rise, steepness, and roughness of the footway are as important as distance when gauging the difficulty of a hike. For example, the hikes to Kinsman Pond and Black Pond are about the same distance—7.2 versus 6.8 miles round-trip. Kinsman Pond, though, is a much more demanding trip, rising 2,300 feet over rough terrain. The stroll to Black Pond follows a wide, gentle railroad grade most of the way, with a modest 420-foot vertical rise.

Because hiking paces vary so widely, no time estimates are given for the hikes. A formula that can be used for comparative purposes is the "book time" used by the AMC *Guide:* one hour for each two trail miles, plus an additional half hour for each 1,000 feet of vertical rise. With these factors in mind, each hike is rated for relative difficulty:

*Easy* hikes range from very short up to about 3½ miles round-trip and offer level to gentle gradients, with a vertical rise under 500 feet. These can be accomplished in two hours or less and are excellent choices for families, beginning hikers, or experienced trampers looking for a mellow day.

*Moderate* hikes range from 3 to 7 miles, with a vertical rise up to 2,000 feet. These are good choices for a half-day outing.

*More Difficult* hikes include treks of 6 to 13 miles requiring a full day's commitment. Hikes in this category have a vertical rise over 2,000 feet, or have less arduous grades but run to the long side. These hikes are for experienced walkers. If you're just starting out, try some of the easy hikes first, then work your way up to more strenuous endeavors.

## Hiking Tips

- Plan your route carefully with the description in this guide, along with appropriate maps and the AMC *Guide*, and be sure it's suitable for the experience and physical abilities of your group. Allow ample time to get to your destination—and back. Leave word of your plans with friends or family, and notify them when you return.
- Obtain a weather forecast before setting out. White Mountain weather phones (area code 603) include Berlin, 752-2211; Conway,

447-5252; Littleton, 444-2656; or the AMC's Pinkham Notch Camp, 466-2727.

- Wear sturdy and broken-in footgear. Lightweight boots or even high-top sneakers are suitable for the gentler hikes and have less impact on the trails. You'll want medium-weight boots for the rougher hikes in the high ranges.
- Dress for the season and elevation of the hike. The regular hiking season in the White Mountains extends from late May to mid-October. Wintry conditions can occur in the lowlands before and after these parameters and at any time in the higher elevations. Wool and synthetics such as polypropylene are superior to cotton in warmth and insulating value, especially when wet. Layering your clothes allows you to regulate your body temperature.
- Bring a day pack with lunch, high-energy snacks, plenty of water, maps, compass, guidebook, pocket knife, watch, first aid kit, waterproof matches, sunglasses, toilet paper, bug repellent (in June and July), and flashlight with extra bulb and batteries. Carry extra clothing to cope with a range of weather conditions, including spare shirts, wool shirt or sweater, rain parka or poncho, and wind shell. If venturing above tree line, add sunscreen, long pants, winter hat, and gloves.
- A plastic garbage bag used as a liner inside your pack will keep your spare clothing dry. Bandannas have a thousand uses, and a walking stick is a welcome aid on rugged trails and at stream crossings. Binoculars and camera are worthwhile options.
- An overnight visit will, of course, require a larger pack, sleeping bag and other gear; consult an experienced friend, the staff at a reputable outdoor store, or one of the many how-to backpacking books.
- Set a steady, moderate pace that's comfortable for your slowest hiker, and keep your group together, especially at trail junctions.
- Watch your footing, particularly when the trail is wet. Tree roots, wooden "bog bridges," and rock ledges can be slick after a rainfall.
- Use caution at stream crossings, and don't put a brook between you and the road when heavy rain is forecast—it might be impossible to cross back.
- All surface water should be treated before drinking. That may be obvious at a tea-colored beaver pond, but the infamous *Giardia lamblia*, an intestinal parasite, has no prejudice against clear, cold water. Water can be made safe for drinking by boiling, treating with an iodine-based disinfectant, or using a portable filtration system. For day hik-

*On the trail to Flat Mountain Pond*

ers the obvious solution is to carry enough water to get you through the hike.

- All hikers should take great care not to contaminate water with human waste. The call of nature should be answered *at least* 200 feet from a stream, pond, or other water source, and waste should be buried in a hole six to eight inches deep.
- Stay as warm and dry as possible in cool, damp weather. Prevention is the best treatment for hypothermia, the "silent killer" that chills the body core to lethal levels. If someone shows early signs of hypothermia—shivering, clumsiness, slurred speech, apathy—he or she should be moved to shelter, changed into dry clothing, and given warm (not hot) sweet drinks. In the event of severe hypothermia or other medical emergency, one hiker should stay with the victim, keeping him or her as still and warm as possible, while one or preferably two persons hike out for help. (Hence the maxim that four persons make a safe hiking party.) A good emergency number is the New Hampshire State Police line, 1-800-852-3411.
- During a thunderstorm, stay away from pond shores, open areas, and solitary tall trees. If above tree line, get down to shelter, fast.
- Moose hunting season is in late October, and deer season is usually the last three weeks of November. Wear blaze orange at these times and stick to steeper, more remote trails.
- Unfortunately, there are sometimes break-ins at trailheads, a more likely prospect if you're out overnight. Remove all valuables from your vehicle.
- Bears are seldom seen on the trail. They can be a nuisance at some heavily used backcountry campsites; hang all food in a bear bag at least 10 feet off the ground between two trees. *Don't* bring any food or food-scented clothes into your tent.
- Moose are unpredictable but generally nonaggressive, though bulls can be ornery during the fall rutting season. Keep your distance.
- Poisonous snakes are not a concern in the Whites.
- In early summer the mountains—and especially the pond shores—are afflicted with blackflies, mosquitoes and deerflies. From late May through early July long sleeves and pants may be sensible even on the sultriest days. Talk to a dozen hikers and you're liable to get that many answers as to what concoction is best for keeping the little buggers at bay.
- As the AMC *Guide* notes, hiking is a sport of self-reliance, and therein

lies much of its appeal. Basically you're on your own in the woods. A little common sense goes a long way toward making your hike a safe and memorable experience.

## ACTIVITIES AT THE PONDS AND LAKES

### Picnicking

The text notes where there are good waterside "sitting rocks" or other spots accessible by trail or side path. Special emphasis is placed on shoreline views and viewpoints, for ponds illustrate the old adage that views *of* the mountains can equal the views *from* the mountains, especially if there's a reach of sparkling water between you and the peak in question. These watery rifts in the forest are especially exhilarating if you've tramped for miles through viewless woods.

### Camping

The AMC high country huts offer bunk room accommodations, hearty meals, and abundant cheer and camaraderie. Huts close to mountain ponds include Lonesome Lake, Greenleaf, Zealand Falls, Lakes of the Clouds, Madison, and Carter Notch. Reservations are strongly recommended; call 603-466-2727.

The WMNF operates developed roadside campgrounds at Russell, Basin, and Crocker Ponds. Reservations are available at the first two; call 1-800-283-CAMP. The NH Division of Parks runs a large campground at White Lake State Park.

Backcountry shelters are located at many mountain ponds; see the Appendix for a complete list. These are open-front wooden lean-tos usually maintained by the WMNF or AMC. Some have adjacent tent platforms, and a few have caretakers and fees. All are available on a first-come, first-served basis and are often jammed on summer and fall weekends. Packing a tent is a good insurance policy; you'll have to seek a campsite at least ¼ mile away from shelters in Forest Protection Areas. If you intend to camp, please read the section on "Protecting the Pond and Lake Environment" for a summary of camping regulations and tips on low-impact use.

### Swimming

In these pages you'll find out about the best swimming spots and which bog-stained ponds are best left to the patrolling beavers. Supervised swimming beaches are found at Echo Lake (Franconia), Echo Lake (North Conway), White Lake, South Pond, Forest Lake, and Jericho Lake. Other than that, you're on your own and you should use safe swimming practices, including the time-honored buddy system. Be prepared for the shock of chilly waters (though shallow, sun-warmed water can be comfortably tepid). Don't dive into unknown waters, where rocks or logs may lurk beneath the surface. Leeches are found in many of the muddier ponds. Wherever you swim, leave your soap behind; washing in ponds degrades the water quality.

## Birding

Good birding can be enjoyed at any pond or lake, but some water bodies are especially notable. Spring through midsummer and the early fall are the best times to bird. Some tips are offered in the section on the "Nature of the Ponds and Lakes."

## Canoeing

Opportunities are mentioned for ponds and lakes with a boat launch or accessible via a short carry. The AMC's *Quiet Water Canoe Guide*, by Alex Wilson, lists Long Pond, White Lake, Chocorua Lake, Mountain Pond, and Upper Kimball Lake as especially good choices. Many White Mountain ponds are either too small or too far off the road to excite the avid paddler. Motors are prohibited on all but a few of the water bodies in this book.

*Birding at Cherry Pond*

# PROTECTING THE POND
# AND LAKE ENVIRONMENT

◆

Ponds and lakes and their shores are among our most fragile mountain resources. Every visitor shares the responsibility of preserving this beauty through the use of low-impact hiking and camping techniques.

Overuse has been a thorny issue in the White Mountains since the early '70s, when a tidal wave of newly minted backpackers surged into the woods. This has been especially evident at popular backcountry camping areas: large clearings denuded of ground cover, rings of fire-blackened rocks, live trees hacked down for firewood, unsightly piles of trash.

In 1972 the WMNF implemented Forest Protection Areas (FPAs) to control camping in abused and fragile areas. The FPA regulations, now in effect year-round, prohibit camping and fires, except at designated sites, within ¼ mile of listed huts, shelters, roads, trailheads, streams, waterfalls, and ponds (including Black Pond and Sawyer Ponds). Along some trails the restricted area is 200 feet on either side. Certain fragile areas are entirely closed to camping. These include all terrain above tree line (where trees are less than eight feet high), the Cutler River drainage (Tuckerman Ravine), Greeley Ponds, Long Pond, and Spaulding Lake.

Happily, hikers have cooperated, and many areas are recovering. Some areas have even been removed from FPA status. The current list of FPAs can be obtained from WMNF headquarters in Laconia or any Ranger District office. Also, note that camping and fires are not allowed in NH State Parks except at official campgrounds. In the Mahoosuc Range, which is outside the WMNF, camping is permitted only at the shelters and designated sites along the Mahoosuc Trail. Never camp on private land without permission.

Here are some easily followed guidelines for low-impact, "no-trace" hiking and camping at the ponds and lakes. My belief is that with conscientious use, these places can bring pleasure to generations of pond-lovers to come.

- Carry out what you carry in! Better yet, pick up any litter left behind by less thoughtful visitors.

- Limit your hiking group to a maximum of 10 persons.
- When out on the trail, make it second nature to step on rocks, bog bridges, or roots in preference to vegetation or fragile soils. Minimize detours around mucky spots in the trail—that will only widen the mud holes. Don't shortcut switchbacks on trails that zig zag up a slope.
- Limit your hiking during the spring "mud season" (April 1 to Memorial Day), when trails are especially susceptible to erosion. If you do go, choose drier trails at lower elevations or on south-facing slopes.
- At the ponds and lakes, walk on the official trails or the well-established "anglers' paths" ("herd paths," in hiker's parlance) found behind the shores of many fishable water bodies. In this book such a path is occasionally mentioned as an access to a good viewpoint or fishing perch. Please don't make new paths of your own. Don't trample the shrubs along the shore or the fragile plants that eke out an existence in pond-side bogs.
- Refrain from picking flowers or otherwise disturbing trailside vegetation.
- Don't harass wildlife, and steer clear of nests, dens, and mothers with young. Canoeists should use special care at the few water bodies in this book that support nesting loons.
- The hardy plant life of the alpine zone is extremely vulnerable to damage from hiker's boots. Walk only on the trail or on bare rocks.
- Even if you're not in an FPA, camp at least 200 feet away from a trail, pond shore, or stream. It's best to choose from one of two types of campsites: a site that has seen fairly heavy use and won't suffer much from additional use, or a spot that has never been used and can be easily restored to its natural state to discourage future use. Don't dig ditches around tents, and build no bough beds or lashed lean-tos. Wear sneakers around camp to minimize trampling, and avoid repeated trips to water sources.
- The campfire, a traditional pleasure of a night in the woods, is becoming passé in today's heavily traveled mountains. Small backpacking stoves are more efficient for cooking and have less impact on the forest. If you must build a fire, use only dead and down wood, and don't leave an ugly fire ring behind. *Always* be careful with fire, and make sure it is completely extinguished before you depart.
- Wash yourself and your dishes well away from any water source. Practice good sanitation as noted earlier.

*Beaver Lodge at Lower Three Ponds*

You can give something back to the mountains by joining the Adopt-A-Trail program, a cooperative project of the WMNF and AMC. Adopters take over the basic maintenance for their chosen trail: brushing, blazing, clearing blow-down, removing litter, and cleaning drainages that protect the trail from erosion. For information, contact the AMC Trails Program, Box 298, Gorham, NH 03581 or WMNF Adopt-A-Trail program, PO Box 638, Laconia, NH 03247.

For more information on low-impact hiking and camping and other important wilderness issues, see *Backwoods Ethics* and *Wilderness Ethics*, both by Laura and Guy Waterman (Backcountry Publications).

Note: In the spring of 1997 the Forest Service implemented a new parking fee system at parking areas and trailheads on National Forest land. For more infomation, call the WMNF office at 603-528-8721, or one of the following Ranger Stations: Ammonoosuc, 603-869-2626; Pemigewasset, 603-536-1310; Androscoggin, 603-466-2856; Evans Notch, 207-824-2134; or Saco, 603-447-5448.

# THE NATURE OF THE PONDS AND LAKES

◆———

## POND AND LAKE ORIGINS

### Gifts of The Glaciers…

Flowing ponderously south from Canada, the great Ice Age glaciers sculpted the mountain landscape in a grinding display of power. Most natural water bodies in the White Mountains owe their existence at least in part to the bulldozing rivers of ice. The glaciers made their last retreat perhaps 12,000 years ago, so our ponds and lakes are, geologically speaking, very young features of the landscape.

Water bodies were fashioned by the ice sheet in several ways. Some occupy basins gouged from the bedrock. A classic example is Lakes of the Clouds in the Presidential Range, where, in addition to the ponds' striking rock bowls, many other examples of glacial artistry can be seen.

Other ponds were born in hollows amidst the till (a jumbled mix of clay, sand, and rocks of all sizes) that was deposited by the glacier. Pond-making was especially likely if the depression was underlain with a sealing hardpan of clay, or where drainage outlets were blocked by the glacial debris.

Before and after the great blankets of ice descended from Canada, small alpine glaciers were at work in the ravines of the Presidential Range. In addition to excavating such spectacular cirques as Tuckerman Ravine and the Great Gulf, the alpine glaciers plucked out the tiny basins that later became Hermit Lake and Spaulding Lake. Geologists call them "tarns," an appropriately beautiful name for these sparkling little gems of the hills. This term (from the Norse, *tjorn*, "a hole filled with water") is often used to refer to any small mountain pond, whether or not it was formed in a cirque.

Another glacial specialty is the "kettle pond," formed when a block of ice was stranded behind the receding ice sheet and buried in sand and gravel. Upon melting, the landlocked iceberg left a steep-sided depression.

If the bottom was below groundwater level or was lined with an impervious hardpan, a pond formed. Kettle ponds are frequent on sandy out-wash plains south of the mountains. They often have no inlets or outlets. Good examples include Echo Lake (North Conway), Heron Pond, and White Lake. Many of the region's interesting bogs and bog-ponds—such as the Black Spruce Ponds just west of White Lake—occupy glacial kettle holes.

More recent pond-making has occurred where a landslide slips off a steep slope and clogs a stream valley with rock and soil. Lost Pond near Pinkham Notch was formed at least in part by a postglacial rock slide off Wildcat Ridge.

## ...And The Engineers

In the genesis of mountain ponds, there are two notable exceptions to the glacial rule of thumb. The first is the artificial ponds and reservoirs created by human engineers for a variety of purposes. Basin Pond and Oliverian Pond were built primarily for flood control. Others, such as Long Pond and Durand Lake, were dammed at least in part for recreational uses. Little Bog Pond in the Nash Stream country was once a big water storage tank for downstream log drives. A few natural ponds, among them Flat Mountain Pond, Saco and Ammonoosuc Lakes, and Province Pond, have been enlarged or deepened by small man-made dams.

Far more common are water bodies crafted by "nature's engineer," the beaver. Though by 1900 excessive trapping had extirpated the beaver from New Hampshire, it has made a stirring comeback in the twentieth century and is now widespread and common in the mountains. The beaver's compelling urge to impound flowing water is demonstrated along (and sometimes across) many White Mountain trails, mostly in the valleys, but occasionally up to 3,000 feet or above. Their sturdy dams of sticks and mud may be only a few feet across, or spread for 100 yards or more. (The granddaddy of all beaver works was a ¾-mile-long dam with 40 lodges, reported from Berlin in the 1800s.) The pond thus formed provides protection from predators and a means to float food and building materials to the dome-shaped lodge.

Beaver ponds are generally small, murky, and peppered with the stark skeletons of drowned trees. Some existing ponds do not appear on the USGS topo maps, and new ones are forever being created even as abandoned ponds revert to meadows. They are important wildlife openings and serve as natural devices for flood control and aquifer recharge. The inquisitive angler might find native brook trout cruising the dark waters. Beaver ponds may provide excellent fishing for years if the water stays cool enough and free of excessive silt.

Extensive beaver works are on display at Tunnel Brook Ponds, Zealand Pond and No-Ketchum Pond. Look closely at the outlets to such water bodies as Lost Pond, Moss Pond, and Page Pond, and you'll see old beaver dams grown to grass, ferns, and shrubs. Beavers often stabilize or raise the water level in existing natural ponds. In fact, beaver sign may be found at a majority of ponds in this book, and there's always a chance of spotting one of the toothy dam-builders, especially around dawn or dusk. Aside from man, no other inhabitant of the mountains can alter the landscape so dramatically.

## POND SUCCESSION

Considered amidst the eons of geologic time, the lifetime of a pond is but a fleeting moment. Once a pond is formed, inexorable processes set to work reverting it back to dry land.

The water in a pond comes from some combination of springs, groundwater, precipitation, runoff, and inlet streams. In addition to delivering the precious liquid, the latter two agents slowly fill the pond from the bottom up with sediments and organic debris. Aquatic plants begin to take root around the edges, adding to the accumulation of decaying matter.

Over time emergent plants cover the entire surface, and the pond becomes a marsh, bog, or swamp. Eventually dry land appears in the form of a sedgy or shrubby meadow. If undisturbed, the process of pond succession usually culminates in a forest typical of the surrounding region. The whole progression may span less than a century for a small, shallow pond.

As you amble around the White Mountain ponds, you'll see water bodies in various stages of succession. Clear, deep ponds such as Sawyer Pond and Russell Pond will be around for centuries to come. Shallower, boggier ponds—Harrington Pond, Lily Pond, or Dream Lake for example—have shorter life spans ahead of them. Lily-choked puddles like Eagle Lake and Little Cherry Pond are nearing the end of the line.

## PLANT LIFE

The mood of a pond is set by its forest rim, whether it be the dark spires of spruce and fir, the majesty of tall pines, the feathery embrace of hemlock, the autumn fire of maples, or the grace of leaning birches. Alpine ponds are fringed only with the low-lying plants that have adapted to the stress of life above tree line.

Most every pond has a ring of shrubs beneath its wooded border. Many are members of the heath family, well-suited to wet, boggy, nutrient-poor conditions. Most common is leatherleaf, forming dense collars of brush around many a shore. Other common heaths are sheep laurel, bog laurel, rhodora, and labrador tea; they put on showy flowering displays in early summer. Sweet gale, mountain holly, and speckled alder are also prolific along pond shores.

A bog or bog forest is found beside many a pond. The bog is a unique wetland environment where there is little or no water circulation. The bog's water is acidic and poor in oxygen and nutrients. Organic matter decays with agonizing slowness. Peat, the progenitor of coal, forms beneath the surface.

The quintessential plants of the bog are sphagnum moss and the ubiquitous leatherleaf. Sphagnum has a tremendous capacity to absorb water (Native Americans used it for natural diapers) and often forms a floating or "quaking" mat at the edge of a pond, where black spruce and tamarack obtain tenuous footholds.

An unusual denizen of the bog is the pitcher plant, which gathers its nutrients from hapless insects that stray into its tubular, water-filled leaves. Its dark-red flowers have a weird, Star-Trekish look to them. Another carnivorous bog plant is the tiny sundew, whose rounded leaves are bedecked with sticky, bug-snaring hairs.

Plant life *in* the ponds is concentrated in the "littoral zone"—the area in which sunlight can penetrate to the bottom, permitting rooted plants to grow. The littoral zone is the food factory of the pond, teeming with insects, crustaceans, frogs, fish, and other aquatic life (anglers take note).

Ponds with an abundance of nutrients are said to be eutrophic ("richly nourishing") and support a prolific growth of aquatic plants. In shallow eutrophic ponds the littoral zone may extend from shore to shore. Ponds poor in nutrients are called oligotrophic ("scantily nourishing"). These are typically cold, clear, deep, and well-oxygenated waters, with the littoral zone limited to a narrow band along the shore.

Ecologists recognize several types of vegetation within the littoral zone. Common "emergent" plants include the purple-blooming pickerelweed, sedges, rushes, and the abundant pipewort, which bears buttonlike white flowers on slender stalks.

The most familiar "floating" plant is the yellow water lily, also known as spatterdock or cow lily. In late summer its flowers protrude on their

*Pickerelweed at Peaked Hill Pond*

stems above the water like unblinking yellow eyes. Lily pads and stems form a "micro-habitat" for many insects and other small pond inhabitants.

Deeper water is home to the "submersed" plants, which live completely underwater. Their feathery forms are familiar only to the avid pond-naturalist.

## ACID DEPOSITION

In New York's Adirondacks there are a number of ponds that look absolutely pellucid and pristine. But they are damaged ponds, their aquatic life severely impacted by acid deposition. This threat looms on the horizon for White Mountain ponds and lakes, too.

As you once learned in science class, the lower the pH number, the higher the acidity. A pH of 7.0 is neutral, neither acid nor alkaline. Each one-number drop in pH represents a ten-fold increase in acidity. Normal, unpolluted rainfall is naturally acidic, with a pH that ranges from 5.0 to 5.5. However, the average pH level of New Hampshire storms monitored since 1963 is 4.2—up to ten times more acidic than "natural" rainfall.

The state of New Hampshire has defined a pH status below 5.0 as critical for aquatic life. In the Northeast, where the calcium-poor bedrock provides little buffering capacity, ponds are especially vulnerable.

In a study of 51 remote high altitude trout ponds conducted around the state from 1981 to 1987, the NH Department of Environmental Services found that only three were at the "critical" stage, with pH below 5.0. (Two of these, Cone Mountain Pond and Bog Pond, are in the White Mountains.) But 29 ponds were in the "endangered" category, with pH between 5.0 and 6.0, and could suffer further acidification. Only 19 ponds—those apparently less vulnerable to acidification—had a "satisfactory" pH greater than 6.0

A major contributor to acid deposition (which includes acid rain, snow, fog, and suspended aerosols) is the combustion of fossil fuels, whether it be the towering smokestacks of coal-burning power plants or the exhaust gases from millions of automobiles. The sulfur dioxide and nitrogen oxides emitted from these sources combine with water vapor, forming sulfuric and nitric acids. Unfortunately, expensive and politically difficult solutions to this complex national and international problem may be years away. By then many more ponds and lakes may be impacted.

## BIRDING

Birdwatchers will find ponds and lakes to be among the most rewarding destinations in the White Mountains. Pond shores are "edge" habitats, where the forest meets meadow, bog, swamp, marsh, and open water, ensuring a good variety of species.

Birding is best from mid-May to mid-July, when the birds wear their bright breeding plumage and give forth their most exuberant song. Early morning and late afternoon are the most active times.

Around lower elevation waters fringed with northern hardwoods you'll find scarlet tanagers, wood thrushes, red-eyed vireos, redstarts, and ovenbirds. If the shore is edged with softwoods there may be winter wrens, dark-eyed juncos, white-throated sparrows, hermit thrushes, purple finches, solitary vireos, and a variety of colorful wood-warblers.

Swamp and song sparrows, yellowthroats, alder and olive-sided flycatchers, northern waterthrushes, common grackles, and red-winged blackbirds call from the pond-side swamps, bogs, and meadows. Tree swallows dart over the water, cedar waxwings lisp and flutter, and spotted sandpipers teeter along the shore. You might see a great blue heron flap by with ponderous wing beats. Belted kingfishers patrol the waters, giving their belligerent rattling call.

Summer water birds include black ducks, wood ducks, and hooded mergansers. Mountain Pond, Long Pond, Horseshoe Pond, White Lake, Cherry Pond, and South Pond are often host to pairs of the threatened common loon. (Take pains not to disturb loon nesting activity.) Canada geese and other waterfowl can be seen during spring and fall migration.

At higher elevations you'll find birds typical of the boreal forest and bogs of the great northwoods: rusty blackbirds, golden and ruby-crowned kinglets, blackpoll and bay-breasted warblers, Swainson's thrushes, boreal chickadees, and yellow-bellied flycatchers. With luck, you might encounter the absurdly tame spruce grouse or the brazen Canada jay. Juncos and white-throated sparrows are abundant. The sad, clear whistle of the white-throat is the theme song of the high, wild mountain ponds.

Especially good birding spots include Elbow Pond, Tunnel Brook Ponds, Guinea and Black Mountain Ponds, Flat Mountain Pond, Zealand and Zeacliff Ponds, Nancy and Norcross Ponds, Church Pond, No-Ketchum Pond, and Cherry Ponds.

## MOOSE WATCHING

Any White Mountain pond exploration may be enlivened by the appearance of a moose, especially in the northern region. Abundant in precolonial times, the moose was hunted to near-extirpation in New Hampshire by the mid-1800s. Its recovery in the last two decades, to the point that a hunting season was reopened in 1988, is truly amazing.

Moose are by far the largest animals in the White Mountains. A mature bull tips the scales at well over 1,000 pounds. Though they look awkward, moose are capable of running over 30 miles per hour. Their long legs enable them to amble through the muckiest bogs and deepest snows with ease. Moose are strong swimmers and are also the region's heavyweight mountaineers, ranging over the ridge tops and more than once startling hikers and tourists on the summit cone of Mount Washington.

Ponds provide moose with great jawfuls of slimy water plants, a delicacy that is consumed with gargantuan relish. A 1,200-pound moose will munch 35 pounds of vegetation daily. The water also offers the moose relief from swarms of blackflies and mosquitoes.

With luck, you may be able to watch a moose forage and frolic in the water, oblivious to your intrusion. (Always keep a respectful distance from these unpredictable giants.) Most impressive, perhaps, is the sight of a huge antlered head shedding buckets of water as it breaches the surface. Even if you don't have that thrill, you'll surely see moose sign along the trail—great

*Moose swimming in Moss Pond, Mahoosuc Range*

cloven hoofprints, big "cow pies" in summer or mounds of brown pellets in fall and winter, and shoulder-high incisor scrapes on young hardwood trees.

# VISITING IN WINTER

$\blacklozenge$

For those who would know the ponds and lakes in all their moods, winter may be the finest season. The frozen water bodies become exhilarating open roads for the snowshoer or cross-country skier. Even the boggiest, brushiest pond is open for a leisurely inspection. The winter pond-traveler is rewarded with splendid snowy vistas denied to the summer visitor.

A snow-season trip requires more planning, equipment, and attention to safety than a summer afternoon lark. But if you're properly clothed and equipped, you can travel in relative comfort through the cold and snow. The best way to learn about winter travel is to go forth with experienced friends or join in an organized trip or workshop geared to novices, such as those offered by the AMC. (Several excellent books on winter outdoor travel are listed in Section I of the Bibliography.)

You have two choices for traveling through the snow: snowshoes and cross-country skis. The snowshoe is sturdy, reliable, and easy to master. The high-tech aluminum versions are durable, light, and maneuverable, with excellent traction. Warm, insulated boots are a must. A ski pole is very helpful for balance.

Many lower elevation ponds are accessible to the intermediate cross-country skier, and some trips are suitable for novices. Several White Mountain pond excursions are described in Roioli Schweiker's *Twenty-Five Ski Tours in New Hampshire*. The book also contains helpful pointers on equipment and technique.

The key to winter clothing is layering, preferably with wool, synthetics such as polypropylene, and a warm and windproof parka. Cotton clothing is a no-no. Wear fewer layers when you're on the move, more when you stop and cool off. Hats, mittens or insulated gloves, and warm socks are essential. Gaiters will keep snow out of your boots.

You'll need a spacious day pack to carry extra clothing, high-energy snacks, and a thermos or a water bottle wrapped in a wool sock to prevent freezing. Make an effort to drink fluids, even though you may not be thirsty; dehydration is a real problem. Sunglasses will protect your eyes

*Winter at Garfield Pond*

from the blinding glare on a sunny day. Goggles, scarf, and face mask may be helpful on a wide and windy pond.

Checking the weather forecast is exceedingly important in winter. Rain and 40 degrees is a recipe for hypothermia. Subzero readings can freeze exposed flesh on a windswept pond. If the weatherman predicts sunny skies and temperatures in the 20s, count your blessings.

Road access and parking are major considerations. Many Forest Service roads are unplowed, necessitating long approach treks for what would be short jaunts in summer (e.g., Sawyer Pond, Zealand Pond, Mountain Pond). Parking at some trailheads is very limited. Specifics are included in the individual pond notes.

In addition to the length and steepness of your chosen trail, you must consider snow depth and conditions. The higher you go, the deeper the snow, except in windswept sections of the alpine zone. (Only experienced, fully equipped winter hikers should venture above the trees. To protect alpine vegetation, camping is allowed only where the snow is at least two feet deep. Camping on frozen pond surfaces is prohibited. In areas with little or no snow cover walk only on the trail or on bare rock.)

Following a trail in winter can be difficult, as blazes and other signs of the footway are hidden by the snow. Breaking trail is arduous work, and should be rotated frequently. The return trip can be rapid and exhilarating.

Approach all winter stream crossings with caution. Stream crossings can range from easy to impossible in winter. In good conditions snow and ice "bridges" span many watercourses. Always cross with care, especially in early winter, after a thaw, or in boggy country. Heavy winter rains can open streams up and swell larger ones to dangerous levels.

During snow droughts or after thaws—conditions all too prevalent in some years—some trails may be icy, and instep crampons will prove useful. (This also holds true for late fall/early winter hiking, before the snows come.) And remember that darkness comes early during winter's shorter days.

Please use courtesy on the winter trails—do not walk in ski tracks, and don't ruin a good snowshoe track with "postholes." Don't stomp on shrubs or other fragile vegetation. Be prepared to share many lower-elevation trails and ponds with snowmobiles.

## SAFETY ON THE ICE

The traverse of an open expanse of white is one of the great pleasures of a winter pond excursion. Like any activity in the woods, this is not without its risks. You should approach any pond ice with respect. A dunking in the frigid waters can be life-threatening within minutes. The keys to a safe visit are caution, common sense, awareness, and experience. If in doubt, don't go out on the ice.

The reason pond ice forms from the top down is a little miracle of nature: water reaches its greatest density at 39.2°F (4°C). It is lighter at higher and lower temperatures. When it cools to the freezing point, water rises to the surface and changes to ice. If this were not so, ponds would freeze from the bottom up.

Listed below are a few tips I can offer after several winters of exploring the ponds. Specifics are included with individual pond notes.

- The NH Fish and Game folks consider five inches to be a minimum thickness of ice for general use. Above 2,000 feet I've found the ice to be sound, on the average, from New Year's through mid- to late March. At larger and/or lower ponds this may be trimmed by a couple of weeks on either end. Be aware of recent weather patterns.
- Pond surfaces have many looks during the winter. An early deep freeze forms "black ice," clear and hard. Midwinter ice—often a foot

*Harrington Pond in Winter*

or more thick—is generally hard and gray. Depending on wind exposure, snowfall, and elevation, the ice may be snow-free and slick, covered with a wind-rippled crust, or buried under several feet of snow.
Ice-out usually occurs in late April, though at higher elevations ice
may persist into May.

- Use a ski pole to tap and test the ice ahead of you. Good ice should
  respond with a solid thunk. If the ice sounds hollow, make a careful
  retreat.
- Single pressure cracks are usually OK, but steer clear of places where
  multiple cracks meet.
- Avoid the ice after a heavy rain and thaw, when it can be greatly weak-
  ened. A layer of slush and water may form atop the ice.
- The thickness of ice may vary throughout a pond. The edges freeze
  first, and ice may be thinner in the middle. There is likely to be thin
  ice around inlet and outlet brooks. Other potential trouble spots include springs under the ice, and places where beavers are active. Give
  all of these a wide berth.
- Skirt any ice that appears discolored, dark, or slushy. Avoid projecting rocks or stumps and slumps or depressions in the surface.
- Beware of deep, heavy snow over early ice.

- Recent snowmobile tracks usually indicate safe passage on foot.
- At times the ice gets vocal with booms and rumblings. While this can be very disconcerting, it usually means the pond is "making ice." The expansive force of winter's ice presses rocks around the shores of many ponds, a phenomenon revealed in summer.
- Snowshoes or skis will spread your weight and lessen any chance of breaking through. Some authorities recommend loosening bindings when crossing ice; if you did break through with snow shoes or skis, they could get caught under the ice. If you're bare-booting, place your feet wide apart and shuffle across the ice. Keep your group spread out.
- If you do fall in, spread your arms on the ice, kick free of the water, and roll onto firmer ice. Rescuers should crawl spread-eagled on the ice and carefully extend a rope, ski pole, or hand to the victim. Anyone who has fallen in should obviously be gotten out of the wind and into dry clothes and warmed posthaste.

## ICE FISHING

A few of the more accessible ponds and lakes are popular for ice fishing, a time-honored North Country winter pursuit. Before going ice fishing, you should consult the list of ponds and regulations issued by the state Fish and Game departments. For the latest and most complete information on ice fishing tactics and equipment, consult Jim Capossela's *Ice Fishing: A Complete Guide ... Basic to Advanced* (The Countryman Press, 1992). This comprehensive book offers an excellent summary of ice characteristics and safety precautions.

# RECOMMENDED WINTER POND EXCURSIONS

Notes on trail access, parking, views, potential danger spots, and other items of interest to the winter visitor are included for most of the pond explorations. Ponds with no winter notes were (subjectively) deemed to be of less interest to the winter explorer.

The following ponds offer rewarding easy to moderate excursions for snowshoers (S) and/or cross-country skiers (XC).

| | | |
|---|---|---|
| Three Ponds | S | XC |
| Peaked Hill Pond | S | XC |
| Wachipauka Pond | S | |
| Elbow Pond | S | XC |
| Tunnel Brook Ponds | | |
| (from south) | S | XC |
| Beaver Pond | S | XC |
| Long Pond | S | XC |
| Lonesome Lake | S | |
| Profile Lake | S | XC |
| Russell Pond | S | XC |
| Greeley Ponds | S | XC |
| Hall Ponds | S | XC |
| Heron Pond | S | XC |
| White Lake | S | XC |
| Echo Lake/N. Conway | S | XC |
| Falls Pond | S | XC |
| Black Pond | S | XC |
| Ethan Pond | S | |
| Ammonoosuc Lake | S | XC |
| Hermit Lake | S | |
| Province Pond | S | XC |
| Mountain Pond | S | XC |
| Lost Pond | S | XC |
| Basin Pond | S | XC |
| Shell Pond | S | XC |
| Virginia Lake | S | XC |
| Durand Lake | S | XC |
| Cherry Pond | S | XC |
| South Pond | S | XC |

# TROUT FISHING THE MOUNTAIN PONDS

## BY DAVID L. NELSON

◆

There's a time during the tedium of February when the dedicated fly fisher drifts with the memory of fly rods and mountain ponds. It's a time when you'd gladly trade winter's white flakes for June's swarming blackflies, in return for just one more hike into a backcountry trout pond.

Memory quickly conjures up the mirror finish of a pond come early evening, dimpled only by the leaping of hungry trout feeding on a multitudinous hatch of insects. You dream of a 16-inch squaretail cruising just below that glassy surface, lazily gulping mayfly emergers until it comes to one particular fly that is somehow different, yet the same. Caution aside, the fish surges ahead and bam! The dream mind's fly rod tightens. The line leaps from the water as this bulldog battler dives for the bottom, until the fine thread connecting fish and angler is broken by the scraping of the snowplow outside the window. Such is the fortune of the February fly fisher.

Dreams and imagination must, however, yield to reality when one considers these mountain ponds with fly rod in hand. They are not easy to get to, and they are not easy to fish. Detailed planning should prevail.

Let's consider the ponds themselves for a moment. Most of the water bodies in this book are capable of supporting the brook trout, otherwise known as the squaretail or speckled trout. This celebrated fish is somewhat of a fussbudget, but it can flourish as long as its basic requirements are met: a year-round supply of cool, well-oxygenated water, and gravel beds on which to spawn in late fall. It cannot survive prolonged temperatures over 68 degrees, which is why trout ponds are referred to as cold-water ("salmonoid") ponds.

Depth alone does not determine a pond's suitability. Trout can get by even in shallow ponds warmed to bathwater temperatures by the summer sun—if there are springs, inlets, or deeper holes where they can find cold water. They can even survive in beaver ponds if the water stays cool enough and is free of excessive silt.

Once you arrive at a trout pond, the easy thought is to slide into a pair of waders, rig the rod, and step in. To do so can produce wet results. Over the course of centuries a deep layer of organic material has been deposited on the bottom of many mountain ponds. A stroll along the shore will reveal few, if any, places where the bottom is solid. At any time the next step may put you in over your head, or mire you in heavy mud. Consider also that forest growth will be tight to the shores, leaving little or no room for back casting.

With these two problems in mind, the obvious solution is to arrive with a flotation device of some sort. Many of these trout ponds are in deep, along hiking trails that simply do not accommodate the hauling of a 50- to 75-pound canoe. Instead, the use of a float tube (locally known as a "bellyboat") is highly recommended, a 10- or 12-pound package that can be equipped with a backpack harness. A good pair of neoprene waders is essential, because these waters can be ice-cold.

The fly rod and the float tube spell trout success. In no way is the spinning gear worked along the shore to be belittled; spin casting requires less gear and can be very effective. However, the very existence of these fish depends on the insect life, and their feeding lanes are not frequented by flashy lures or gobs of worms hanging on hooks. Trout are keyed to the hatches of various insects, and at times they pay little attention to anything else.

A question often asked about these waters is the "when" query. This brings to mind the old-timer leaning against a tree saying that since the time you spend fishing is not counted against you, any time is a good time to fish. However, considering that it is often a long, gear-laden hike into these waters, a close look at timing is important.

We all get the itch to fish in April, and many of these waters are trout ponds designated by the NH Fish and Game Department, which permits an opening day on the last Saturday of April. (Check the law book; the dates can change.) A heartbreaker can be to arrive at a remote pond on opening day, only to find it still locked tight in ice. In the mountains, the general rule is that you'll find access to the water during mid-May.

Even then the water can still be too cold to support much insect life. So once again we bump the date ahead, understanding that the calendar to watch is the insect's calendar and that the old-timer leaning against the tree will stay there until he sees the first hatch of a size 18, brown-colored mayfly during the last days of May or the early days of June. When this delicate insect dance unfolds, the action begins.

By the end of June and throughout July, the air will be full of mosquitoes, mayflies, dragonflies, and caddis, and the fish will be at the height of their feeding activity. Also active at this time are the ever-present crayfish and bloodsuckers making their way along the bottom. These are tasty morsels for the larger trout who have learned that survival depends on a simple equation: The energy expended in obtaining food must not exceed the energy derived from the food.

All of this heightened feeding activity will continue until the dog days of August. Now the sun has warmed the waters to the point where fish will spend most of their time lounging on the bottom near the cold-water spring areas. Fishing is generally poor during this month.

Next come the cooler nights of September and October, a time when many experienced fishermen will declare that the year's best fishing has arrived. It's almost as if a light switch were turned on in mid-September. In fall trout are driven by the urge to bulk up for winter and also by the approach of the spawning cycle. The need to feed is intense, and will continue past mid-October's closing of the fishing season.

Yet the real key to success lies not so much with the "when" as with the approach to these ponds. Actual technique will not vary that much from fishing methods used on any other waters. But understanding the feeding

*Fishing at Speck Pond*

patterns of mountain trout is paramount. In rivers trout will hold in feeding lanes and wait for food to be presented to them. In the ponds they must cruise, and knowing these cruising lanes can mean the difference between hot dogs in the frying pan and a trout feast.

There is a band of water often, but not necessarily, along the shore into which sunlight can penetrate to the bottom, allowing rooted vegetation to grow. The depth of this lane will be determined by the clarity of the water. It is within the plant life of this "littoral zone" that the preponderance of insect life will develop. Without sun on the bottom there will be no vegetation and no insect life, and trout do not shop in grocery stores with empty shelves. The search for this littoral band is critical to success, and the race for the middle of the pond "where the big ones are" is like getting dressed up for the party and showing up on the wrong night.

My advice is to spend your first half hour at a pond examining the water from the shore and studying carefully where the insect life is active. Watch for the dimples on the water created by insect hatches, watch for the rises of trout and the direction of their movement, and watch for the telltale presence of the swallows as they flit about over the hatching bugs. This can really be the most productive time of your trip.

Consideration should be given to types of equipment. This subject always brings up a proverbial image: the angler equipped with thousands of dollars of sophisticated gear getting skunked by the youngster using his granddad's hand-me-down metal telescopic rod, with one fly that's the strangest-looking beast you could imagine. The moral is, the fancy gear is not needed. Basically, there are five varieties of flies in four different sizes and two or three colors that will catch all the trout you could wish for. A simple five- to-six-weight fly rod is ample in a seven-and-a-half- to eight-and-a-half-foot length.

The key to the catch is using this gear with gentle presentation and short cast in mind. The gentle presentation will be aided greatly with the use of proper leader materials. If there is one area where the decision on equipment is crucial, this is it. Nine-feet-long six X and seven X leaders are a must, for these waters are generally clear and these trout are savvy. Even a sloppy cast can be effective if the fly is left on the water long enough for the ripples to disperse, but if the fly is attached to a bulky leader the fish will see it as a neon sign that says go away.

Remember also the suggestion for the use of a float tube. This will allow you to kick gently through the littoral lanes, making a long cast unnecessary. Seldom will you need more than a gentle 30-foot cast and a sharp eye for the cruising patterns of rising trout.

Combine these thoughts with the fly pouch that contains the nymph to dun forms of the mayfly in sizes 14 to 18, the nymph to adult forms of the caddis fly in these same sizes, and the much-needed size 16 to 22 midge patterns, and you will have action that is just reward for the effort. Augment this excellent collection with two or three sizes of the woollybugger in a variety of shades and two or three sizes of the hornberg, and you can consider yourself well-equipped. To reiterate, keep the gear simple and the approach watchful, and your fishing on the backcountry ponds will be productive and enjoyable.

As you learn about these ponds, it becomes obvious that these precious places are a fragile resource. Thankfully, from that old-timer to the new arrival there lives a spirit of concern that gives us hope that these ponds may provide enjoyment for generations to come. The responsible angler will tread softly on the pond environment. He or she will not litter, cut live wood, pollute the water, camp too close to the shore, or trample the plants of the shoreline and the littoral zone.

Any backcountry angler relishes the thought of a pond-side trout feast. It's exquisite when done in butter laced with garlic and tarragon. (Remember that a portable stove has much less impact than a fire.) There's nothing wrong with taking an occasional trout for a backwoods lunch, but we suggest that an undisciplined killing of the fish for the sake of sport will eventually destroy the environment you are about to experience.

The angler who practices catch-and-release will find that barbless hooks are a wise alternative to the traditional barbed variety. The barbless hook will penetrate deeper and therefore hold better. More importantly, it will make it far easier to release the fish properly. There is seldom any need to remove the fish from the water as you can easily hold the fish under the surface and simply slide the barbless hook out. Be sure to wet your hands before handling a fish out of the water, and when slipping the hook out, turn the fish upside down to calm it.

Ponds designated as trout ponds by the NH Fish and Game Department have limits on the number of fish you may have in possession. (Consult the annual "Freshwater Fishing Digest" for the rules and limits that pertain to specific ponds.) Fish and Game enforcement personnel are dedicated to the conservation of these mountain ponds, and they are not known to be tolerant of those who refuse to obey the laws.

Without the annual stocking by the Fish and Game folks, there would be little if any trout fishing in many of these ponds. On its own the trout cannot reproduce prolifically enough to keep up with the fishing pressure.

In the White Mountains spring stocking takes place in May—by truck for the more accessible ponds and by helicopter and backpack in the backcountry. The exact dates and locations of stocking are closely guarded secrets. The department is also developing a new program of fall stocking of fingerling trout. These fish have the winter months to adapt to their environment. In the spring it's often a savvy and healthy fish you'll encounter, measuring six to eight inches and occasionally growing into a real lunker.

You'll need three items and a little time to locate the better fishing ponds. The first is this book, perhaps accompanied by the appropriate US Geological Survey topographic map. The second is a good road map. The third is a copy of the current Fish and Game "Freshwater Fishing Digest."

After reviewing the regulations, refer to the stream and pond coding section. Each pond has a coded designation that defines its trout pond designation, its fish limit, and whether the water is fly-fishing only. Most ponds have a five-fish or five-pound limit; pay special attention to those that have a two-fish limit. Some anglers spend the winter poring over maps and lists of ponds, searching for two or three new productive trout waters to be field-researched in the spring. In a few years an angler will get to know his or her way around the mountain ponds, though this information may be shared only under duress.

Once you have taken the time to assemble the gear, make the plan, research the location, and hike into one of these backwoods jewels, if you find that you will be sharing the spot with another angler using a camouflaged float tube and swinging a little three-weight fly rod, go over and say hello. It's a sure thing that there will be a swap of fish stories, an exchange of ideas and tips about catch-and-release, and a heartfelt wish that your biggest problem in life be the big one that got away.

*David L. Nelson hooked his first fish—a bass—at the age of five on Massabesic Lake in Manchester, NH. In nearly five decades of fishing he has cast into waters across New England and the United States. Nelson has hosted a television show about the New Hampshire outdoors and operates an equipment and fly-rod instructional service in the White Mountains. A real estate broker by trade, he lives with his wife and two children in North Woodstock, NH.*

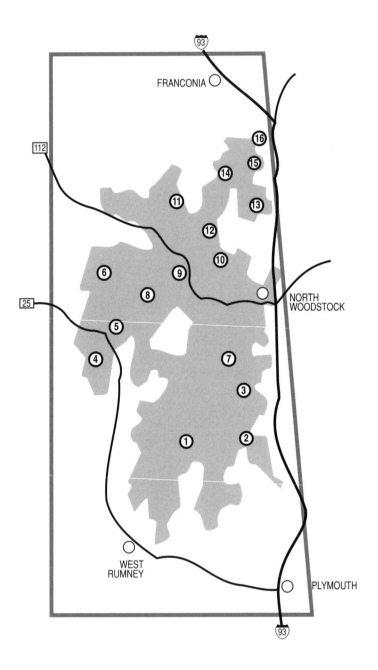

*Trail signs at Lonesome Lake*

# I. WESTERN WHITE MOUNTAINS

◆

THE WHITE MOUNTAINS west of I-93 harbor a diversified assemblage of scenic mountain ponds. There are roadside beauties, short-hike favorites, and remote, wild ponds cradled by high ridges.

The southern third of the western Whites is a complex of wooded ridges in the 3,000-3,500-foot elevation range, including Mounts Carr, Stinson, and Kineo. Sprinkled amidst these modest peaks are the pretty Three Ponds and plaintive Peaked Hill Pond. This country is off the beaten track for most hikers. Two larger water bodies—Ellsworth Pond and Stinson Lake—are road-accessible but have shorelines that are partly or wholly privately owned. Farther north is roadside Mirror Lake, a favorite swimming spot.

Dominating the center of the western region is the bald, massive dome of 4,802-foot Mount Moosilauke, a deservedly popular hiking objective. The ponds in this area offer varying perspectives on the great mountain, whether it be from afar at delightful Wachipauka Pond, peculiar Elbow Pond, and aptly named Long Pond, or the more intimate looks from roadside Beaver Pond and the chain of beaver impoundments in Tunnel Brook Notch.

To the north a half-dozen high mountain ponds are strung along the east side of rugged Kinsman Ridge: wild Gordon Pond, tiny Harrington Pond, sprawling Bog Pond, trailless Mud Pond, cliff-faced Kinsman Pond, and the ever-popular Lonesome Lake with its stunning view of Franconia Ridge. At the northern tip of the range, beside the Franconia Notch Parkway, are the beautiful Profile Lake and Echo Lake. The two Franconia Notch ponds have been favorite resorts since the early 1800s and are perhaps the most visited ponds in the White Mountains today.

Two other ponds in the western Whites, man-made Oliverian Pond and Easton's hidden Mud Pond, appeal primarily to anglers in search of lightly-fished waters.

At press time for this second printing, a 3,400-acre addition to the SW corner of the WMNF was planned as part of the 5,000-acre Lake Tarleton project, a unique public-private conservation partnership. This would include most of the shoreline on beautiful 315-acre *Lake Tarleton*, located beside NH 25C in Warren and Piermont; all of roadside, undeveloped *Lake Katherine* (37 acres); some frontage on partially developed *Lake Armington* (142 acres); and all of *Lake Constance*, a pristine 9-acre backcountry pond nestled in the hills to the north and accessible only via old, unmarked logging roads. This area is covered by USGS 7½' Warren and East Haverhill quads. The state of New Hampshire plans to develop a visitor center by the beach on the west shore of Lake Tarleton.

# CHAPTER 1

# THREE PONDS

◆

**Location:** NE of Carr Mountain
**Hiking Facts:** 5.5 miles round-trip, 550-foot vertical rise, moderate
**Map:** USGS 7½' Mount Kineo

|  | **Middle Pond** | **Upper Pond** |
|---|---|---|
| **Area:** | 13 acres | 12.5 acres |
| **Elevation:** | 1,725 feet | 1,740 feet |
| **Avg./Max. Depth:** | 6/10 feet | 4/10 feet |

**Activities:** Hiking, fishing (brook trout), picnicking, camping (lean-to)

――――――――――――――――◆――――――――――――――――

*Over on the east side of Mount Carr two bright gems*
*gleam in the greenwood...*

—William Little
*History of Warren, N.H.*, 1870

The Three Ponds are cradled in a beaver-haunted basin between the wild, wooded ridges of Carr Mountain (3,453 feet) and Mount Kineo (3,313 feet). The easy, slightly muddy woods-walk to the ponds is one of the nicest half-day jaunts in the mountains. You're treated to attractive forests, a tumbling brook, beaver meadows, and pretty waterside picnic spots with wide views. Originally known as the Glen Ponds, they have been locally famous for their trout fishing since the 1800s. A lean-to overlooking Middle Pond facilitates a comfortable overnight backpack.

## Access

Turn off I-93 at Exit 26 and drive 7 miles west/north on NH 25. Turn right (north) on Stinson Lake Road. Pass through Rumney Village and at 4.9 miles from NH 25 keep straight at the foot of heavily developed Stinson Lake, where there is a boat access ramp on the right. The road winds along the west shore, with good views. The surface changes to dirt and at 6.8 miles you'll see the hiker symbol and parking for Three Ponds Trail on the left.

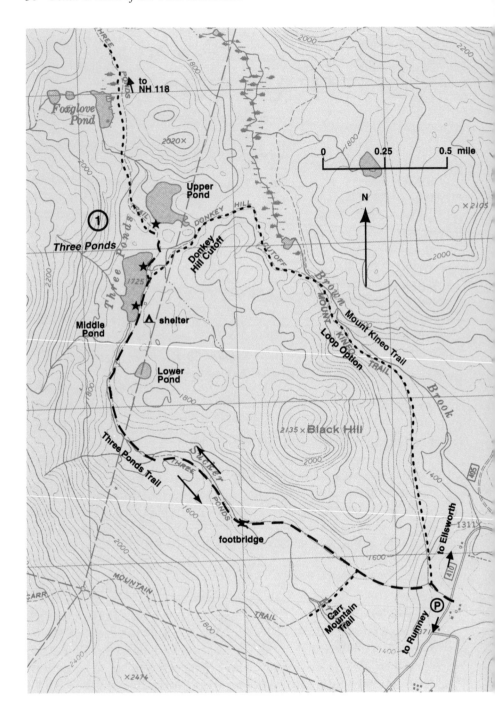

The trailhead can also be approached from Exit 28 off I-93 via NH 49 and the Ellsworth-Rumney road. Distance from I-93 is 8.4 miles.

## The Trail To Three Ponds

The trail crosses a wet spot on bog bridges and climbs easily past the junction with Mount Kineo Trail right at 0.1 mile. A steeper pitch follows; look for a huge lightning-scarred maple thrusting a trident of trunks to the sky. The footway levels and rolls through mixed woods past the Carr Mountain Trail on the left at 0.5 mile. (The summit of Carr Mountain, with excellent northern views, is 2.9 miles and 2,000 vertical feet away.)

You descend gently past a small swamp, skirt a beaver meadow on your left, and bear left to cross Sucker Brook on a footbridge at 1 mile. Turn right onto an old logging road on the far bank of the boulder-strewn brook and follow its curve at a gentle grade. A swing to the left brings a steeper grade for a short distance. At 0.2 mile relocation loops to the right alongside Sucker Brook, bypassing a mucky section of the old road.

Soon you cross a stony tributary brook on a sturdy bridge. You make your first of three unbridged crossings of Sucker Brook 100 yards beyond. If the step stones are submerged, scout upstream (left) for an easier passage.

Easy climbing follows, with the rock-choked brook now on your left. Fine hardwood forest blankets the slopes on either side of the stream. At the crest of the grade, 2 miles from your car, you confront the final two crossings, with 100 feet of dry brook bed between.

Just beyond, beaver flooding has prompted a 0.2-mile trail relocation on higher ground to the right. You quickly step over the rivulet that drains from trailless, 2½-acre Lower Pond, located a short distance upslope. (See *Gazetteer.*) The trail rolls along above the flooded section, then swings left and descends, with views of Middle Pond through the trees.

## At Middle Pond

The relocation returns to the original footway near the SE corner of Middle Pond. If the water level permits, hop a few yards left on rocks and weathered logs for a long, gorgeous view north down the pond to rounded Whitcher Hill (2,565 feet). Brilliant hardwood hillsides make this vista a stunner in foliage season.

The trail tracks along the east shore behind a veil of shrubs. In a few yards the south end of a short loop trail angles right and up to Three Ponds Shelter. The wide lean-to has a limited view down to the water. Continuing 150 feet on the main trail, you break into a grassy shoreside clearing fringed with broken rock. This picnic spot soaks up the afternoon sun and offers a wide view of the pond. The long north ridge of Carr Mountain presides over the peaceful scene. A lone sentinel pine towers over the fringe of shrubs on the opposite shore.

Two centuries ago a settler named Carr was not prepared with a picnic lunch when he attempted to cross over the sprawling mountain between Ellsworth and Warren. Surprised by a fierce storm, he was forced into an unplanned two-night sojourn in the woods. It's said he sustained himself by dining on frogs he nabbed around the shores of the Three Ponds. When he finally made it safely to the village of Warren, the townsfolk granted his name to the mountain that almost took his life.

The trail forges on behind shoreline trees and shrubs. Patches of American yew, a low, scraggly evergreen shrub, crowd the footway in places. You make a little jog to the right and soon meet the north end of the shelter loop trail. In 10 feet a side path leads a few steps left to a sloping, sun-warmed rock that faces SW across the water to Carr Mountain.

At the next split in the main trail, bear right on a rooty relocation that skirts bushy swampland and quickly comes to the junction with Donkey Hill Cutoff, 2.5 miles from your car. The Cutoff swings right while your route on Three Ponds Trail forks left to cross a recently refurbished beaver dam. Depending on current activity, this traverse can be a cakewalk or a tricky balancing act.

Across the dam you climb over a wooded knoll to an opening at the NE corner of Middle Pond, beside an old overturned rowboat. This angle gives you a broad perspective on Carr Mountain looming over the pond. A tall snag on the east shore adds a picturesque touch.

## At Upper Pond

The trail proceeds gently north through attractive woods along an ancient logging road. In 0.2 mile, at a double yellow blaze, the Three Ponds Trail swerves left. Continue straight ahead on the unsigned spur trail to Upper Pond, which curves right to a grassy clearing, then angles left through a thicket of firs to the SW corner of the pond.

Step out over water-slicked logs to a flat-topped picnic rock with an expansive view of the pond, a rounded dogleg rimmed with tall spruce and lowly leatherleaf. To the north a scalloped hardwood ridge wraps around the pond's basin. The dark evergreen crest of Mount Kineo peers over on the right. Though a bit short on sun exposure, this perch is a delightful resting or fishing spot.

*Middle Three Ponds*

Beyond the side trail to Upper Pond, the longer and less-used northern link of Three Ponds Trail continues 4.5 miles to Hubbard Brook Trail, 0.2 mile from NH 118. Just west of the trail, 0.5 mile north of Upper Pond, lies a water body known as *Foxglove Pond* (elevation 1,900 feet). It is not nearly as fetching as its name, consisting of a couple of acres of stagnant water dotted with shrub-islands and breastworks of dead trees.

*Loop Option:* Upon returning to the junction of Three Ponds Trail and Donkey Hill Cutoff by the beaver dam, you may opt to return to your car via a loop around the latter trail and the lower Mount Kineo Trail. This return route is 2.8 miles, only slightly longer than the 2.5 miles back on Three Ponds Trail. Highlights include a vast beaver swamp with interesting views of Mount Kineo, and a splashing cascade on Brown Brook.

*Winter:* This is a delightful ramble on snowshoes or skis. Trailless Lower Pond is much more accessible. The views of Mounts Carr and Kineo from Middle and Upper Ponds are excellent, and you can explore boggy Foxglove Pond and two tiny beaver ponds to the west. Stinson Lake Road is usually plowed to the trailhead. The parking lot may be plowed; otherwise find a safe place to park beside the road. The Ellsworth road approach is usually unplowed.

CHAPTER 2

# PEAKED HILL POND

◆

**Location:** Thornton, west of I-93
**Hiking Facts:** 3.4 miles round-trip, 450-foot vertical rise, easy
**Map:** USGS 7½' Woodstock
**Area:** 16 acres   **Elevation:** 1,180 feet
**Avg./Max. Depth:** 6/13 feet
**Activities:** Hiking, fishing (brook trout), picnicking, birding

◆

Though it's only a mile and a half west of busy I-93, Peaked Hill Pond is less frequented than other equally accessible White Mountain ponds. An oblong sheet of water with boggy shores, it lies quietly amidst low, wooded hills.

The walk to Peaked Hill Pond is not a stroll through an untamed forest. The surrounding land has been worked for many years, first by hardscrabble farmers whose stone walls crisscross the forest, later by mechanized loggers, whose rough road provides your hiking route to the pond. Nevertheless, it's an interesting and undemanding excursion ending at a sun-washed shoreside resting spot, ideal for picnicking and summer afternoon lazing.

## Access
The Peaked Hill Pond Trail is marked by a National Forest sign on the west side of US 3, 2.1 miles north of I-93's Exit 29 and 4.1 miles south of Exit 30. Driving north, turn left on a rough paved side road between Valley Brook Cottages and the 93 Motel. Drive uphill under both lanes of I-93. At 0.4 mile bear right at a fork and proceed 0.15 mile farther on a gravel spur road that parallels I-93. Park off the road on the left before you reach a steel gate.

## The Trail To Peaked Hill Pond
Walk past the gate and bear left and uphill on the logging road. In 0.1 mile look for a gargantuan white ash on the right. With bony arm thrust out from massive, furrowed trunk, it has the look of a leafy character from J.R.R. Tolkien's Middle-earth.

Beyond the Ent-like tree, you climb easily through open, brushy country favored by ruffed grouse. At 0.4 mile, just before the National Forest boundary, there's a new logging yard on the left. At 0.6 mile the road levels amidst a fine hemlock stand and comes to the edge of a weedy field on the left. This former logging yard is mowed annually to maintain an opening for wildlife. Walled in by a triangle of old field pines, the opening is flooded with goldenrod in late summer.

Just south of the clearing is a shrubby bog encircling *Mud Pond* (elevation 980 feet), which shows as a considerable body of water on the USGS map. For a glimpse of Mud Pond, walk left (south) along the east edge of the field. From the SE corner a short path leads ahead to the edge of the bog, an expanse of leatherleaf, sedges, and weathered snags. The central pool of open water—two or three acres at most—is largely hidden from view. It's more accessible in winter, when the bog is frozen and snowbound. However, inveterate summer pond-explorers can make their way about 0.2 mile southward behind the east shore, partly following overgrown skid roads, and down to a fine west-facing sitting rock overlooking the pond itself. Be prepared to get scratched by brambles if you venture this way!

Follow the track leading west through the field to its NW edge. Beyond, the road climbs through mixed woods, with Bagley Brook downslope to the right. Depending on recent logging activity, the road may be muddy underfoot. At 1 mile from your car, with a large boulder on the right, the road/trail swings 90° left as a less-used road continues ahead. A rare yellow blaze up-slope to the left marks the turn.

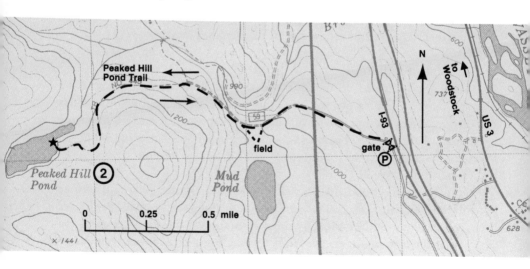

*Peaked Hill Pond and Peaked Hill*

You climb more steeply for 0.2 mile, then the grade slackens. Ignore yellow blazes that lead right off the road into the woods; that former trail route has been abandoned for years. At 1.5 miles follow the road as it arcs around an old logging yard on the right, or cut directly west across the clearing. Once back in the woods on the far side, bear right at a fork. (The left-branching road parallels the south shore of the pond, but offers no access.) The road/trail curves right and downhill for 0.1 mile, ending at a heavily used campsite amidst tall spruce, hemlock, and pine.

## At Peaked Hill Pond

Walk a few steps left to the SE shore of Peaked Hill Pond. Rock seats are sprinkled in front of two upturned root balls. This spacious opening offers a wide water view and a warm afternoon sun exposure. Westward across the pond is Peaked Hill—a pyramid of billowy hardwoods—looming 1,000 feet above you. The actual 2,340-foot summit is behind and to the right of the nearer peak.

The pond's shores are rimmed with hemlock, spruce, pine, and a fringe of leatherleaf and sweet gale. Drowned stubs along the shore hint at beaver activity. Pickerelweed and tiny water lilies speckle the water. Around the corner the eastern outlet cove backs up to a bushy meadow and old beaver dam. (A mill and homestead were once located near the outlet; the old dam was partly man-made.) A large pitted boulder a few yards to your right offers a more elevated perch for surveying the pond. Water level permitting, it's reached via a short, overgrown path from the campsite clearing.

The wooded shores are alive with birds in early summer—vireos, thrushes, sparrows, and warblers, lots of warblers. Once I listened to dueling winter wrens trade songs back and forth across the water. Fishing may also be a profitable activity; the pond is stocked with trout. Swimming, however, will not come to mind—the bottom is mucky and infested with wriggling leeches.

The walk back is an easy ramble of 45 minutes or less. At the trailhead you may find it easier to back your car the 0.15 mile to the fork rather than attempt a turnaround in the narrow road.

*Note:* The south shore of Peaked Hill Pond (including the viewpoints) and parts of the trail are on private land. The owners have graciously allowed continued access, assuming that hikers observe proper etiquette. No camping or fires, please. The north shore of the pond is on National Forest land.

*Winter:* The side road off US 3 is usually plowed to a level spot with limited parking before the I-93 underpasses; otherwise park safely on the shoulder off the highway. The trail is often used by snowmobiles. The rolling water bars are easier to negotiate on snowshoes than skis. Winter is the time to explore bog-ringed Mud Pond partway in. From the SE corner of the field, a snowmobile trail slices south through the bog, then bears west at the north edge of Mud Pond. Peaked Hill Pond is sunny and sheltered, perfect for a snow-season picnic. There are bonus views of Mounts Tecumseh and Osceola from the west end.

CHAPTER 3

# MIRROR LAKE

———————◆———————

**Location:** Woodstock, west of I-93
**Hiking Facts:** Roadside
**Map:** USGS 7½' Woodstock
**Area:** 37 acres   **Elevation:** 700 feet
**Avg./Max. Depth:** 17/30 feet
**Activities:** Swimming, picnicking, canoeing, fishing (smallmouth bass, chain
    pickerel, horned pout, yellow perch; rainbow trout stocked since 1991)

———————————————◆———————————————

Mirror Lake is a placid sheet of water on the fringe of the National Forest, just west of I-93. Although there are several private residences on the west shore, most of the pond is undeveloped. The National Forest acquired much of the north and east shoreline in 1987, and the town of Woodstock maintains a public beach on the south shore.

This pond has a long history of human use, detailed in an article by Gene E. Likens in *Appalachia*. At various times in the 1800s there were sawmills, tanneries, farms, a soda bottling works, and a dance hall at or near the shore of Mirror Lake. The pond's name metamorphosed from McLellan's Pond to Hubbard Pond to Tannery Pond to its present title. After several decades of forest regeneration, Mirror Lake looks much more natural today than it did in turn-of-the-century photos.

The Forest Service's Hubbard Brook Experimental Forest is just up the road. Long-term ecosystem studies of that drainage have produced a 400-page research tome focused on Mirror Lake, edited by Professor Likens.

For the pond visitor, Mirror Lake provides swimming, canoeing, and warm-water fishing in a pretty setting.

## Access
Mirror Lake Road leaves the west side of US 3 4.5 miles north of I-93's Exit 29 and 1.7 miles south of Exit 30. Drive 0.7 mile, passing under I-

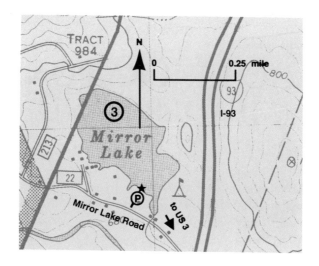

93, and look for a "Public Beach" sign on the right. A short loop road leads into a small parking area.

## At Mirror Lake

The pond is lined with slender, leaning birches and overlooked by a low, rounded hump of a mountain. The water of this glacial kettle pond is clear with a gravelly bottom in front of a small beach. It's a nice place to combine a swim and a picnic. With a canoe you could paddle to sunny ledges fronting the peninsula along the east shore. From the beach area the houses on the west shore (to the left) are unobtrusive. The closest house is behind the parking area, hidden by a high fence; please respect the owners' privacy. Also, note that research equipment from Hubbard Brook Experimental Forest should not be disturbed.

*Winter:* Mirror Lake is locally popular for ice fishing and snowmobiling. Skiers and snowshoers can follow a snowmobile trail to the east shore, starting on the north side of Mirror Lake Road (roadside parking) just west of I-93. Round-trip, including a traverse of the pond, is about 1 mile.

CHAPTER 4

# WACHIPAUKA POND (MEADER POND)

◆

**Location:** Warren, west of Oliverian Notch
**Hiking Facts:** 5 miles round-trip, 950-foot vertical rise, moderate; add 1.4 miles,
600 feet for Webster Slide Mountain.
**Map:** USGS 7½' Warren
**Area:** 22 acres   **Elevation:** 1,494 feet
**Avg./Max. Depth:** 12/30 feet
**Activities:** Hiking, picnicking, fishing (brook trout, horned pout), swimming

◆

*High up in the N.E. corner of Warren is situated a pretty
little sheet of water. The Indians called it Wachipauka,
but the later generations of our mountain hamlet delight
to term it Meader Pond.*

—William Little
*History of Warren, N.H.*, 1870

Wachipauka is a pond with a past. Set in picturesque fashion beneath the cliffs of Webster Slide Mountain, it was a popular stop on a backwoods travel route during colonial days. In his engaging (if occasionally fanciful) town history, William Little unrolled a colorful cast of characters who reputedly sojourned by the shores of Wachipauka, often on the way to or from some bloody errand.

The pond was named by the Native Americans who came there to fish and hunt. Translated, the Abenaki word means "mountain pond." This was said to be a favorite camping spot for Waternomee, a chieftain whose name is preserved on a spur of Mount Moosilauke.

Perhaps the first white men to encamp there were the Massachusetts rangers of Capt. Thomas Baker, who passed through in 1712 en route to a raid on the Pemigewasset villages near present-day Plymouth. Among those killed in the surprise attack was Waternomee.

The tables were turned four decades later as a party of St. Francis warriors from Canada, with white captives in tow, stopped at Wachipauka Pond on the way back from *their* raid on Franklin, NH. The famed Roger's Rangers paid a visit in 1756 while headed for an engagement at Lake George, NY. Settlers built a more permanent camp on the shore in 1767. They later applied the name of one of their own, Paul Meader, to the pond. (Historian Roland Bixby tells of a legend that the pond was formed in the crater of a fallen meteor and hence was known as *Meteor* Pond.)

In the late twentieth century Wachipauka Pond remains an enchanting place, a fine destination for a half-day hike. Despite its former notoriety, today it's off the beaten path in a less-visited corner of the National Forest. Other than Appalachian Trail "thru-hikers" in late summer, you'll probably have little company at Wachipauka. The walk's objective is a sunny, breezy clearing with a sweeping view over the water. The trip can be extended to the 2,184-foot summit of Webster Slide Mountain, where ledges provide a startling down-look at the pond.

## Access

The north end of Wachipauka Pond Trail, a link in the Appalachian Trail, is marked by a brown hiker symbol but no sign. It leaves the SW side of NH 25, 0.5 mile north of the village of Glencliff and 100 yards south of the Warren/Benton town line. A large pull-off provides parking.

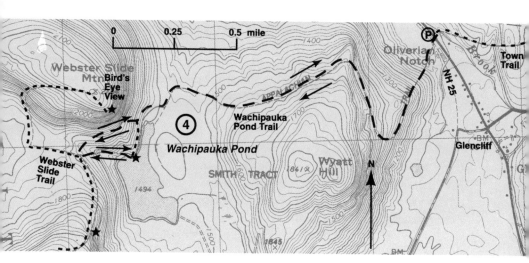

## The Trail To Wachipauka Pond

The trail starts on a dirt road at the south end of the parking area, marked by a white blaze nailed to a post. In 50 feet you cross an old railroad grade and take up a footpath a few steps left, again indicated by a white blaze. Climb up wooden steps and follow the trail's undulations through second-growth hardwoods.

In about 0.5 mile a sharp right turn leads you into a steep ascent. The pitch eases as you skirt a ledgy knob on the right. Moderate to easy climbing through a deep hardwood forest ensues, bringing you to the high point of this traverse over the slope of Wyatt Hill at 1.2 miles. Through most of the summer the monotonous song of the red-eyed vireo will accompany you on this walk—an endless series of short, clipped phrases, rising and falling from the treetops.

A gradual descent of 0.6 mile leads to a braid of log cribbing spanning a swampy area; then you trend left (south) to drier ground. At about 2 miles you swing around between the base of Webster Slide Mountain and the boggy northern finger of Wachipauka Pond. As the footway becomes rockier, a side path leaves left to parallel the west shore of the finger. (This former route of the trail, though starting to get overgrown, provides an alternative to the longer route described below.)

Keeping ahead on the white-blazed Appalachian Trail, you soon pass a big double-trunked ash, then turn right where another path continues straight. The Appalachian Trail struggles up a short steep pitch and swings left to slab the slope above the pond. A slight dip at 2.3 miles drops you at a four-way trail junction in a grove of tall hardwoods.

Ahead, the Appalachian Trail continues 2.6 miles southward to NH 25C, passing an outlook east in 0.4 mile and the wooded summit of Mount Mist (2,230 feet) in 0.8 mile. To the right, marked by a sign, is the spur trail to Webster Slide Mountain. The unsigned trail descending to the left leads to the shore of Wachipauka Pond.

## At Wachipauka Pond

Marked with the orange-black-orange blazes of the Dartmouth Outing Club, the side trail descends for 0.2 mile through a lovely hardwood glen, with the water shining through the trees. Near the shore you pass a campsite on the right, then the path levels between clumps of bracken and emerges at a clearing beside a towering white pine.

Located on a point where the northern finger joins the main body of the pond, this spot commands an expansive view south over the water and gathers sun through the day and into early evening. The great pine shades root and rock seats. To the right Mount Mist rises in a graceful sweep of hardwoods. Spruce, pine, and hardwoods edge the distant shores. The long, wavy ridge of Carr Mountain looms on the horizon.

Rock and gravel line the pond bottom in front of the clearing, so a swim can be enjoyed on a hot day. Anglers will find stocked trout for the catching.

## Webster Slide Mountain

If you have most of the day at your disposal, I'd recommend the short (0.7 mile) but stiff (600 vertical feet) climb to Webster Slide Mountain for a dazzling *bird's-eye view* of the pond. From the shoreline clearing, follow the side trail back up to the junction and keep straight ahead, crossing the Appalachian Trail.

The Webster Slide spur trail climbs briefly to a flat col, then swings right on the level to a Dartmouth Outing Club sign that marks a former junction on the Appalachian Trail. You bear right here and begin to climb steeply, circling the back side of the mountain through small maples, birches, and oaks. After ¼ mile the grade lessens and spruces mix into the forest. You meander over the summit plateau and dip to a clearing in spruce

*Wachipauka Pond from Webster Slide Mountain*

woods where the former Wachipauka Pond shelter was set.

From the clearing a path angles down to the right, then veers left and drops very steeply through red pines to sun-warmed, slanting white ledges. Use caution, as the footing is a bit tricky atop the cliffs. From this airy perch you look straight down on the pond, which takes the shape of a giant, shimmering stingray floating in a deciduous ocean. The distant view includes Mounts Cushman, Kineo, and Carr, bald, tower-topped Mount Cardigan, and Mount Cube far to the right.

Tradition avers that the mountain received its name from an incident involving a hunter named Webster. The man's dog was hot on the tail of a deer or moose when both pursuer and prey came suddenly to the edge of the cliff and tumbled to destruction.

Retrace your steps to the Appalachian Trail for the return trip. You'll have a 200-foot climb back over the side of Wyatt Hill. The round-trip to both pond and mountain is 6.4 miles with a vertical rise of 1,550 feet.

*Alternate Approach:* A rough jeep road provides an alternate access to the pond from the south, starting on Swain Hill Road in Warren. Driving in from NH 25, take the left fork at 1.3 miles. You pass the marshy Weeks Crossing Pond on the right at 2.1 miles. Park at the three-way fork at 2.5 miles and walk up the rough middle road, sometimes chewed up by four-wheel-drive vehicles. Bear left about 1 mile from the parking spot. You'll reach the outlet at the pond's SE corner at about 1.5 miles. Rocks at the shore offer beautiful views across the water to the steep, cliffy faces of Mount Mist and Webster Slide Mountain. No trail connects this route with the trail on the opposite shore.

*Winter:* Wachipauka Pond makes a fine half-day snowshoe trip from NH 25. There's ample roadside parking. Out on the pond you'll find great views of Mount Moosilauke and the cliff-faced hulk of Webster Slide Mountain. Snowmobiles sometimes come in via the jeep road on the SE.

# CHAPTER 5

# OLIVERIAN POND

◆

**Location:** Benton, on north side of NH 25
**Hiking Facts:** Roadside
**Map:** USGS 7½' East Haverhill
**Area:** 28.5 acres   **Elevation:** 850 feet
**Avg./Max. Depth:** 5/8 feet
**Activities:** Fishing (brook trout), canoeing, picnicking

◆

Oliverian Pond was created in 1962 with the construction of a large flood control dam on Oliverian Brook. It's a popular locale for boating and trout fishing, though the 46-foot-high dam looming over the west shore takes some of the sparkle from the setting. The area does provide good views of Owls Head (1,967 feet), an impressive cliff at the south end of the Benton Range.

### Access
The National Forest access road to the Oliverian Pond boat launch leaves the north

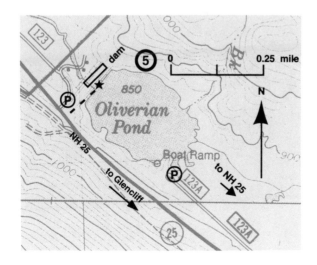

side of NH 25, 1.6 miles west of Glencliff. The paved 0.5 mile road ends at a parking loop and the boat ramp. Beaten paths lead from the right side of the parking area to boulders overlooking the pond and the dam beyond.

## At Oliverian Pond

The only option Oliverian offers for walkers is a short, pleasant stroll along the grassy top of the dam. Park by the entrance to a gated road off NH 25, 0.8 mile west of the boat launch road. A few yards to the right a metal plaque lists the technical specs of the dam (122,000 cubic yards of fill) and the watershed (6,784 acres). Walk left past a line of boulders on a narrow footway through a garden of field-and-roadside wildflowers. From this elevated perch there's an open vista over Oliverian Pond to the great dark cliff of Owls Head, in some years a nesting site for peregrine falcons. Spruce-clad Blueberry Mountain (2,662 feet) is on the left, and the south ridge of Mount Moosilauke is on the right. Far to the west (left) you can see the Granite Hills in Vermont. You might even be tempted to linger for a picnic. (Note: The former WMNF Oliverian Campground has been closed.)

# CHAPTER 6

# LONG POND

◆

**Location:** Between Benton Range and Mount Clough
**Hiking Facts:** Roadside
**Map:** USGS 7½' East Haverhill
**Area:** 124 acres   **Elevation:** 2,181 feet
**Avg./Max. Depth:** 4/8 feet
**Activities:** Picnicking, canoeing, fishing (brook trout, horned pout)

◆

Finger-shaped Long Pond is one of the White Mountains' hidden roadside treasures. Stretching a mile across a wooded plateau amidst trailless ridges, this spruce-fringed highland lake has a remote and wild feel to it.

## Access

The picnic area and boat launch at the north end of Long Pond are served by a National Forest access road off the gravel North and South Road (FR 19) between Benton and Glencliff. From the south, take NH 25 to the tiny village of Glencliff. Turn north onto Sanatorium Road and in 1 mile steer left onto the North and South Road. In another 4.1 miles, much of it an uphill pull, you have a glimpse of Long Pond to the left, with ledgy Black Mountain (2,830 feet) on the horizon. At 4.7 miles turn left (west) onto the access road for Long Pond.

To approach from Benton on the north, follow NH 116 south from its western junction with NH 112. In 1.6 miles the North and South Road departs left, marked by a sign for Long Pond. You'll reach the access road on the right in 2.5 miles.

## At Long Pond

The narrow side road to the pond twists through hardwoods and dense conifers for 0.5 mile, ending at a loop parking area near the boat ramp and the birch-shaded picnic grove. (This is a day-use area only; camping is not allowed.) The northern third of the pond opens southward between fir-

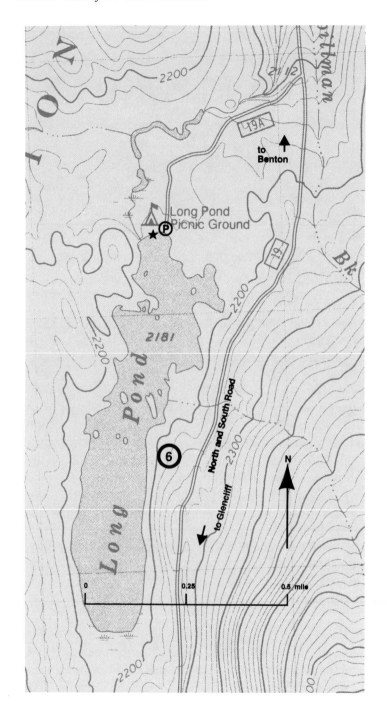

dotted Mount Clough (3,561 feet) on the left and a sweeping ridge known as the Hogsback (highest point, Jeffers Mountain, 2,994 feet) on the right. The Hogsback is the tallest of several mountains in the low but very interesting Benton Range. Several clear-cuts have torn its forest cloak; this is busy logging country.

Walk to the right along the grassy embankment toward the concrete dam at the far end. Here you'll find a nice look left at bald-topped Mount Moosilauke, the region's giant, rising above the water. Several boulders offer picnicking and fishing perches in front of the embankment.

The dam was first constructed in 1933 by the Civilian Conservation Corps, expanding what was apparently a rather swampy water body. The CCC also built the access road and established the Long Pond Forest Camp (since abandoned) on the shore.

Long Pond is stocked with brook trout, and horned pout are plentiful at times. It is best explored by canoe. In his *Quiet Water Canoe Guide*, Alex Wilson considers this to be the very best paddling pond in the White Mountains. A pleasurable afternoon can be spent poking around the coves and the rocky, spruce-clad islands, which might tempt you to abandon ship temporarily for a sunny picnic stop. Note: Loons are found at Long Pond; please take care not to disturb any nesting activity.

Walking opportunities are limited at Long Pond. From the picnic area, an unmarked angler's path winds SE behind the shore, passing several confusing forks. In about 0.15 mile, a final right branch leads out to a small grassy spot on a point with a nice view south down the island-dotted pond. Exploring along north and south roads, you may find other obscure paths leading to vantages along the east shore of the pond.

*Winter:* Easiest access is from the north end of unplowed North and South Road at NH 116 in Benton; limited parking. The steadily ascending road, packed by snowmobiles, can be walked or skied to the Long Pond side road. The round trip to the north end of the pond is 6 miles with an 800-foot vertical rise. The pond is windswept and wonderfully desolate in winter, with fine views of the surrounding mountains. As you weave among the snowy, spruce-topped islands you might fancy yourself in the lake country of Maine or Minnesota. Avoid the ice by the outlet near the dam.

CHAPTER 7

# ELBOW POND

◆———————◆

**Location:** Woodstock, SE of NH 118
**Hiking Facts:** Elbow Pond North—1.4 miles round-trip, minimal vertical rise,
   easy. Elbow Pond South— 2.4 miles round-trip, unmarked and muddy.
**Maps:** USGS 7½' Woodstock and Mount Kineo
**Area:** 56 acres  **Elevation:** 1,414 feet
**Avg./Max. Depth:** 8/32 feet
**Activities:** Hiking, fishing (largemouth bass, chain pickerel, yellow perch,
   horned pout), birding, picnicking

———————————————————◆———————————————————

A large, bulbous pond spread across a swampy plateau, Elbow Pond is little
known to hikers. It's more often visited by anglers in four-wheel-drive
vehicles, who jounce over the rough dirt road that leads in from NH 118. In
winter it's a popular destination for snowmobilers. But Elbow Pond also has
much of interest for the pond-hiking enthusiast.

Elbow Pond is actually two ponds in one. Elbow Pond North is a shallow and swampy arm, with abundant growth of lily pads and pickerelweed.
Elbow Pond South is a 25-acre saucer of deeper water. The two are linked
by a narrow strait between bushy peninsulas. According to Robert and
Mary Hixon's *Place Names of the White Mountains*, a settler named Thomas
Vincent spotted the pond while hunting on nearby Mount Cushman in the
1780s and noted its elbow-like shape.

The walk in to Elbow Pond North is a short, easy jaunt along the last
stretch of the jeep road, the bed of a former logging railroad. Intrepid explorers can make a muddy trip to Elbow Pond South along old roads and
trails.

The environs of Elbow Pond are so flat that the USGS map shows no
contour lines in the area to the west. This swampy tangle is a haunt for
moose, deer, bear, and a myriad of birds. (As you would expect, it's a very
buggy place in early summer.) The various shores provide warm-water fishing (the state has recently stocked largemouth bass) and broad views of the

surrounding ridges. These include Mount Cushman (3,221 feet) to the SW, Mount Cilley (2,227 feet) on the east, and the high southeastern arm of Mount Moosilauke known as the Blue Ridge (3,770 feet) on the west.

## Access

For years the dirt road (FR 156) into Elbow Pond North was accessible only to four-wheel-drive vehicles. In 1994, though, the Forest Service built a new bridge over Jackman Brook and refurbished the first 0.8 mile of the road in conjunction with a timber sale. Conventional vehicles can now drive to within 0.4 mile of the pond.

From US 3 in North Woodstock, drive 2.5 miles west on NH 112 to its junction with NH 118. Turn left here and after 2.5 miles of bumpy, uphill

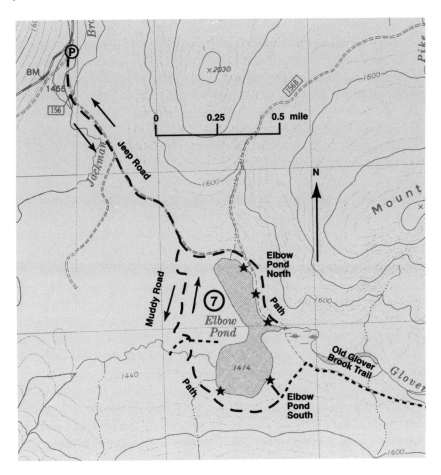

driving, look for an unmarked dirt road on the left. Turn left here, passing a winter and mud season parking area on the left. Cross the bridge and drive up the rough but sound road. At 0.8 mile, just past a muddy side road on the right, park in an open area to the right. At this point a new logging road forks left and uphill, while the main road continues ahead, but much rougher.

## The Trail To Elbow Pond North

The Elbow Pond Road was once a busy branch of the Gordon Pond logging railroad. According to C. Francis Belcher's *Logging Railroads of the White Mountains*, this line was laid out by lumberman G. L. Johnson, a "shrewd old cuss" from Monroe, NH, starting in 1908. The spruce growth in the Elbow Pond–Mount Cilley area was said to be so thick "you had to take a candle to see your way through." This was no virgin forest, however. Settlements had been established at Mount Cilley and Elbow Pond in the 1820s. Following their abandonment in the 1860s, the clearings quickly reverted to old-field spruce. Johnson's crews skinned this forest, along with thousands of nearby acres, in less than ten years. Today the woods in this area are once again dense—a hodgepodge of hardwoods and conifers choked with bushes and laced with blow-down.

## At Elbow Pond North

Walk up the continuation of the main road, skirting several mud holes churned out by four-wheel-drive vehicles and passing a small swamp on the left. At 0.4 mile from the parking spot, the road ends at a clearing near the NE corner of Elbow Pond North. A muddy spur leads 100 feet right to the water's edge and a long vista south down the pond, with a view of Mount Cushman straight across and the Blue Ridge to the right. In midsummer the shallow water sprouts ranks of purple-blooming pickerelweed.

An unmarked footpath leads south along the east edge of the pond. This was once part of the WMNF Elbow Pond Trail and served several private camps before the land was purchased by the Forest Service in the 1970s. Debris from the camps is still found in places along the path, but nature is slowly reclaiming her own.

The path runs in the open to a sunny, grassy clearing, a very nice picnic spot with a fine view over the pond to Blue Ridge. The footway continues through shrubby woods and across a sloping, lichen-cloaked ledge. Look for the showy blooms of blue flag in early summer; in August a blueberry feast is yours for the plucking all along the shore. As you pull even with the channel that joins the two ponds, you get birch-framed glimpses of distant Elbow Pond South. There's a fine pondside ledge shaded by a sturdy white pine. A bit farther on another waterline ledge in front of a ruined camp makes a nice resting spot and a logical turnaround point, 0.7 mile from your car. (Beyond here the old path is swallowed by a bushy bog.)

## The Route To Elbow Pond South

To visit this beautiful circle of water, walk south on the muddy road that branches right just before the parking spot (0.8 mile from NH 118). Undertake this side-venture *only* if you are an experienced pond-explorer comfortable with unmarked routes and muddy boots. Be sure you have a compass and the USGS Woodstock 7½' quad. The trip is easier in winter, when the wet sections are frozen.

The side road is very mucky, and in places submerged, in its first ¼ mile. (In seasons of abundant rainfall you may have to scuttle this mission entirely.) In 0.1 mile it curves left, then shortly right. Here you'll have to pick your way along the edge of the soggy road. At the right turn cut the corner through the woods and emerge where the footing is merely muddy and not underwater. The road soon improves and provides drier walking.

At 0.5 mile from the main road your route bears left and comes to a three-way fork. Bear right on the middle and most-used road. In 100 yards you come to a grassy clearing on the bank of a brook. By bushwhacking 50 feet right you'll find an easy crossing on rocks. On the far bank, bushwhack left through hobblebush to pick up the route again, now more a well-defined path than a road. Farther on you skirt a mudhole and cross a boggy spot on an iron pipe.

## At Elbow Pond South

At 0.8 mile from the main road you cross a small rocky stream and come to a side path that leads left 100 feet to a camp clearing. An extension runs to the SW shore of Elbow Pond South for a view across the water to Mount Cilley, with a glimpse of Mounts Osceola and Tecumseh to the east.

Return to the main path, which, like the path beside Elbow Pond North, is part of the old Elbow Pond Trail. Abandoned in the 1950s, it traced a wide horseshoe around the pond and connected with several other now-obscure trails. You continue SE and east around the shore, with glimpses of the water through the trees. You pass two more ruined camps on the left and make a slight ascent and descent. After some mucky footing, the path cuts back into the woods away from the pond.

At 1.2 miles from the main road you come to a junction. The main

*View from shore of Elbow Pond North*

path bears right; this is the former Glover Brook Trail, a pretty woods route that descends 3 miles to Potato Hill Road off US 3 in Woodstock. (This path starts on private land, but efforts are underway to secure a legal right-of-way for hikers.)

Turn left here on the side path and walk 100 yards, through a small, bushy camp clearing, and on to a small grassy spot on the SE shore of Elbow Pond South. The reward for your perseverance is Elbow Pond's finest vista. The water spreads wide to distant shores thick with shrubs and red maples. The eastern massif of Mount Moosilauke sprawls across the horizon: the Blue Ridge, Mount Jim, and Mount Waternomee. The lovely view is enhanced by the remote feel of this less-visited shore.

For the return trip, retrace your steps 1.2 miles to the main road. Remember to bushwhack left a few yards to make the brook crossing.

*Winter.* The road to Elbow Pond North is an easy and pleasant ski or stroll over a packed snowmobile track. A parking area off NH 118 is usually plowed. It's fun to traverse the wide, frozen pond, but beware of soft ice near the NW corner of Elbow Pond North and at the channel between the ponds.

# CHAPTER 8

# TUNNEL BROOK PONDS

◆

**Location:** Tunnel Brook Notch in Benton
**Hiking Facts:** 4.2 miles round-trip, 400-foot vertical rise, moderate
**Maps:** USGS 7½' Mount Moosilauke
**Area:** Variable   **Elevation:** 2,220–2,260 feet
**Activities:** Hiking, birding, fishing (possible native brook trout), picnicking

◆

The sharp, slide-scarred notch between Mount Moosilauke (4,802 feet) and Mount Clough (3,561 feet) is a showcase for the work of *Castor canadensis*— the proverbially industrious beaver. The Tunnel Brook beavers have more than lived up to their reputation, fashioning a remarkable chain of dams, ponds, and meadows extending for ¾ mile between the steep mountain walls.

The mellow hike into the gap on Tunnel Brook Trail is a fascinating half-day outing. Within the pass you'll enjoy frequent views of the ponds, the beaver works, the slides, and the enclosing mountains. The variety of habitats makes this an excellent locale for studying bird and plant life. Local anglers say some of the eight beaver ponds may harbor native brook trout. The largest and southernmost impoundment is known as *Mud Pond*. Its boggy shore presents a close-up view of Mount Moosilauke's South Peak (4,523 feet) crowning the massive wooded ridge on the east side of the cut.

## Access

The Tunnel Brook Trail traverses the notch from north to south. The north trailhead provides the shorter and easier route. From US 3 in North Woodstock, drive 10.3 miles west on NH 112 to where Tunnel Brook Road leaves on the left. This is 0.3 mile before the eastern junction with NH 116. The surface changes to gravel at 0.7 mile, and at 1.4 miles you turn left at a junction (the right fork is the Noxon Road, which leads 2.7 miles to NH 116 in Benton). Proceed past the Benton Trail at 2.9 miles to the parking area at the road's end, 3.7 miles from NH 112.

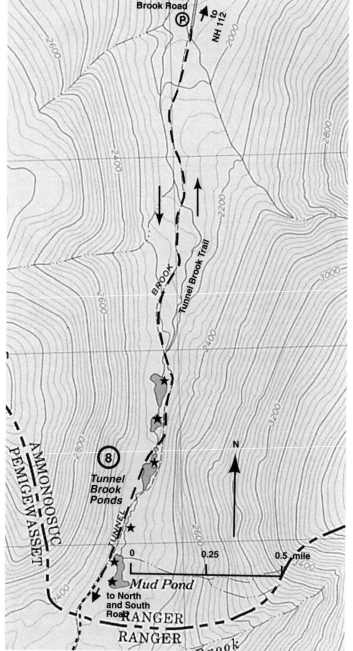

## The Trail To Tunnel Brook Ponds

The gentle north approach guides you along an ancient roadbed through a lovely northern hardwood forest dominated by large yellow birches. In some sections the footing is as smooth as any you'll find on a White Mountain trail. The road once connected Benton, Wildwood, and Easton on the north with Glencliff and Warren on the south. It was closed by landslides in the 1920s; it's said that a Ford Model T was the last car to make it through the Notch.

The trail rises gradually, crossing two small brooks, then levels and runs briefly along the east bank of Tunnel Brook. You cross two more small streams, pass the site of an old logging camp on the left, and bore through a conifer thicket beside an alder swamp. The trail meanders upward through varied hardwoods, then crests a rise and, with rougher footing, undulates through gravelly, scraggly woods at the base of an old slide on the west side of the notch. The way through the scrubby birches is marked by cairns, including one squared-off beauty that is a museum-quality presentation of this trailside art form. The path curves and dips to the left and hops back to the east side of Tunnel Brook at 1.3 miles. Soon you emerge from the woods into the open country of the notch.

*Alternate Approach*: Take Tunnel Brook Trail from the south, off the North and South Road 1.2 miles from Glencliff; 6.0 miles round-trip, 900-foot vertical rise, moderate. The trail has easy grades with one moderately steep climb of 0.5 mile. (See Daniel Doan's *Fifty More Hikes in New Hampshire*.)

## At Tunnel Brook Ponds

The brushy opening borders the first and northernmost of the beaver ponds, Pond #1 for easy reference. Two overgrown side paths depart on the right for a grassy spot by the pond's curving beaver dam. In spring and early summer you'll be greeted by a whistling ensemble of white-throated sparrows. Toward dusk spring peepers envelop the Notch with their shrill pipings.

Beyond the dusky water the great slides of Mount Clough fan out across a broad front. Landslides occur when heavy rainstorms saturate the ground on steep slopes (generally 25 to 35 degrees). Soil, rocks, and trees roar down the mountainside, leaving a swath of stones and gravel tapering to smooth ledges near the top of the slide. Revegetation happens only slowly, with legions of scruffy white birches in the vanguard.

The main trail runs southward amidst gloomy firs; then the woods brighten beyond a huge, lightning-scarred yellow birch. There's a glimpse of Pond #2 down through the trees. In recent years its water level has been down, exposing mud flats and bleached tree trunks. You pass by Pond #3, a small shrub-fringed pool, then dip to rock seats by the dam containing Pond #4, a pretty one fringed with shapely firs. A beaver lodge is stacked against the south shore. The trail twists along the east bank, with views over the water to the widest Clough slide and at least five others.

At 1.6 miles you cross to the west side of Tunnel Brook on a small beaver dam; hiker signs mark the way on either end. The footway leads through a gravelly, brushy area dotted with slender birches, then weaves among deep firs alongside Pond #5. This elongated pool is peppered with bony snags and flanked by a wall of hardwoods.

After a mucky stretch alongside the swampy brook, a heavily camped clearing opens on the left (1.9 miles). Step out to a grassy spot for a view up to Moosilauke's South Peak over Pond #6. In 1991 this was an unsightly morass of mud and small snags. A year later it was a pond again, thanks to a refurbished beaver dam. The landscapes and waterscapes of Tunnel Brook Notch can change quickly and dramatically.

A slight rise takes you into a corridor carved through dense firs on a bank above Pond #7. A narrow outlook over this pool has been hacked through the firs. You pass by a mini-pond (call it #7-a), then dip to the NW corner of Mud Pond, the 8th and final impoundment in Tunnel Brook Notch. From an opening just beyond you see the northern lobe of this hourglass-shaped pool, dwarfed by the slide-scarred ridge of Moosilauke.

The trail crosses a clearing sprinkled with slide out-wash and marked with a blue-painted cairn. In another 100 yards, at a small dip in the trail, a side path leads 150 feet left to the SW corner of Mud Pond, fringed with tall grasses. This earns one hiker's vote as the neatest spot in the Notch. The massive south ridge of Moosilauke presides over the pond and its sedgy meadows, rich in avian and amphibian life. The hidden ravine of Slide Brook displays a necklace of gravel slides. A weathered old blow-down provides a passable seat. Savor this wild scene for a spell before retracing your steps 2.1 miles to your car.

*Bird's-Eye View:* On another day you can enjoy a terrific aerial view of the notch and the southernmost ponds from the bare South Peak of Moosilauke, reached via a side path near the junction of Glencliff Trail and the old Carriage Road. A splendid viewpoint in its own right, South Peak sees far fewer visitors than the main summit a mile up the ridge.

*Winter:* The north approach is much longer in winter because Tunnel Brook Road isn't plowed; the southern route is a better choice. It's a moderate snowshoe or fairly difficult ski trek. Park beside Sanatorium Road at the entrance to North and South Road; this adds 0.2 mile each way to the

*Tunnel Brook Pond #4*

summer distance. The views of the Notch from frozen Mud Pond are excellent. It's possible to traverse several of the beaver ponds, but be wary of soft ice where the brook flows in and out and near dams and lodges.

# CHAPTER 9

# BEAVER POND (BEAVER LAKE)

◆

**Location:** Kinsman Notch
**Hiking Facts:** Roadside; optional hike, 0.2 mile round-trip, easy
**Map:** USGS 7½' Mount Moosilauke
**Area:** 9 acres  **Elevation:** 1,850 feet
**Avg./Max. Depth:** 7/12 feet
**Activities:** Picnicking, canoeing, fishing (yellow perch, horned pout), hiking

◆

Kinsman Notch, the glacier-carved pass that snakes between Mount Moosilauke and Kinsman Ridge, lacks the notoriety of Franconia Notch, its near neighbor to the northeast. Aside from the remarkable Lost River Reservation, you'll find few tourist amenities. But there's plenty of wild and rugged scenery along twisting NH 112, including one of the prettiest roadside ponds in the mountains.

Beaver Pond rests just north of the high point of the Notch (1,870 feet). This little flat, once known as Beaver Meadow, marks a great bend in the pass, splitting the drainages of the north-flowing Wild Ammonoosuc River and the east-flowing Lost River.

Beaver Meadow bustled with logging camps in the early 1900s. The Fall Mountain Company and G.L. Johnson lumber firm took turns stripping the timber from every feasible slope. In 1915, as the logging drew to a close, the state opened the automobile road through the notch. Since then the area has recovered remarkably from the devastation wrought by the lumbermen.

Beaver Pond owes its existence to a small concrete dam at its north end, where Beaver Brook tumbles northward to join the Wild Ammonoosuc. (In its 2,000-foot plunge above Beaver Pond the brook presents a dazzling waterfall display—see Bruce and Doreen Bolnick's *Waterfalls of the White Mountains*.) The dam apparently dates back to the early 1900s.

## Access

Drive west on NH 112—the Lost River Road—from US 3 in North Woodstock. After passing the junction with NH 118, the highway climbs steadily into the Notch. The ledgy walls close in as you pass the entrance to Lost River 5.5 miles from US 3, and the Appalachian Trail crossing 0.4 mile farther, at the height-of-land. Just beyond, Beaver Pond suddenly appears on the left. At the north end of the pond, just before the road starts to descend from the Notch, there is a new paved parking area on the left marked with signs for "Beaver Pond Scenic Area." Use caution when entering or exiting, as there is a steep curve in the road at the turn-off.

## At Beaver Pond

From the parking area beside the pond you're treated to a postcard-quality view across the water to the high, graceful ridge formed by Mount Waternomee and Mount Jim. These wooded satellites of mighty Moosilauke close in the notch on the southwest. At the height of foliage season—late September/ early October—this vista is a photographer's delight.

On the right a wild, dark crag divides the precipitous ravines of Beaver Brook (left) and Stark Falls Brook (right). Forest historian J. Willcox Brown told how James "Jakey" McGraw, walking boss for G.L. Johnson, conspired to reap the virgin spruce that stood tall and seemingly out of reach behind this imposing crag. The resourceful McGraw cut a logging road around the cliff and up into the steep valley of Stark Falls Brook, then devised an ingenious scheme for sliding the logs down to the meadow below. For this feat, noted Brown, McGraw earned a place in the logging hall of fame. (See J. Willcox Brown's *Forest History of Mount Moosilauke*.)

Also prominent in the view across Beaver Pond is a whaleback ledge that juts out like a jetty from the western shore. It's one of the great sitting-and-sunning rocks in the mountains. (Swimming is not allowed; the pond is a public water supply for the town of Woodsville.) Follow a footpath a few yards from the parking area to the dam at the pond's north end. If there are no step stones across the breach in the dam, a path right leads down to ledges where you can step over the sluice-like brook.

Clamber up the opposite bank and pursue the path left on a somewhat mucky course through dark conifers. In 100 yards bear left out to the great ledge for an exhilarating vista south over the pond to the mountain wall beyond. The rock itself is a striking tongue of Kinsman quartz monzonite, a member of the granite family, wrapped with a white vein of quartz. It has the "sheep-back" shape typical of glaciated ledges—moderately sloped on

*Beaver Pond*

the north side, nearly sheer on the south, where it plunges 10 feet to the dark water. Geology buff or not, you'll appreciate the ledge's terrific view and balmy southern exposure.

If you put in a canoe at the north end parking spot, you can investigate a narrow spruce-clad island near the NE corner or try some warm-water fishing around the pond. Beaver Pond was supplied with trout for years, but the state suspended stocking because of high acidity levels in winter and spring.

*Winter:* This is a nice winter mini-hike or ski tour, with best access from a plowed parking area for the Beaver Brook Trail a short distance south of the pond. A pleasant hardwood ramble brings you to the pond's south end. The views of the Notch are great, and it's fun to explore the little island near the north end of the pond. From the SW corner of the pond there's a view to distant South Kinsman Mountain, but watch for soft ice near the boggy inlet.

CHAPTER 10

# GORDON POND

———————◆———————

**Location:** Kinsman Ridge, south of Mount Wolf
**Hiking Facts:** 7.2 miles round-trip, 2,250-foot vertical rise (1,500 inbound, 750 outbound), more difficult
**Map:** USGS 7½' Mount Moosilauke (Page 68)
**Area:** 3 acres   **Elevation:** 2,567 feet
**Activities:** Hiking, picnicking, fishing (brook trout)

———————————————◆———————————————

You can choose the low road or the high road to Gordon Pond, a wild little water body cupped in a pocket of conifers under the steep slope of Mount Wolf (3,500 feet). With a fine shoreside picnic rock and an impressive view of the mountain, the isolated pond makes a nice objective for a full day's hike.

The low road, longer and easier, is the Gordon Pond Trail, a pleasant woods walk up the valley of Gordon Pond Brook. The shorter but tougher high road is the Kinsman Ridge Trail, an Appalachian Trail link that traces a roller-coaster route over the ridge from Kinsman Notch. Though the pond is a mere 700 feet higher than the starting point in the notch, you'll have climbed three times that before the day is done.

I prefer the elevated approach for its beautiful high-country forests and the surprise view that opens eastward to distant mountains around the valley of the East Branch. An added bonus is a day's-end visit to *Beaver Pond* just up the road from the trailhead.

## Access

The white-blazed Kinsman Ridge Trail leaves NH 112 in the heart of Kinsman Notch, 5.9 miles west of the US 3 stoplight in North Woodstock. Driving west, you'll find parking for Beaver Brook Trail on the left, 0.4 mile beyond Lost River. Walk a short distance up NH 112 to a sign for Kinsman Ridge Trail across the road.

## The Trail To Gordon Pond

There's no gentle warm-up to this hike. The first half mile is a cruncher that lifts you 600 feet above the floor of the notch, spiraling skyward through a white birch forest. Countless rock and log steps testify to the herculean efforts of trail crews in stabilizing the steep grade. When the pitch eases, you cross an interesting ridge-top bog on split-log bridges, then ascend moderately to a junction right with the Dilly Trail at 0.6 mile—a *long* 0.6. (There's an outlook over Kinsman Notch 0.1 mile and 100 vertical feet down this trail.)

From the junction, Kinsman Ridge Trail climbs over a knob, then drops sharply to the right, zigzagging through mossy ledges. The 200-foot descent continues into a dreamy glade of beech and yellow birch. Beyond the col you meander upward through yellow and white birch mixed with red spruce and balsam fir. Hobblebush, with paired heart-shaped leaves suspended on long tendrils, dominates the understory. Parklike glades give an open look to the forest, typical of many ridges at this 2,500–2,800-foot elevation.

Soon you're walking along the crest of the ridge through a darker, mossy growth of conifers. After some pleasant ridge-running, you descend to a birch-forested col and climb to the trailside outlook ledge, 2.4 miles from the highway. The balsam spires in front are slowly blotting out the seated view, but standing you can see the lower Franconias, Hancock and Carrigain, Scar Ridge and Osceola, and the western peaks of the Sandwich Range.

Beyond the view you climb easily over a hump, traverse a pretty fir-forested col, and surmount one final 3,009-foot knob—the highest on this southern arm of Kinsman Ridge. Now you head down toward Gordon Pond, descending at first along the ridge line, then angling down the east slope through open woods. You step across two small streams and climb the final 50 yards to the junction with the Gordon Pond Trail, 3.3 miles and a good two hours from the road.

*Alternate Approach:* Take Gordon Pond Trail from NH 112 across from Govoni's Restaurant; 9.4 miles round-trip, 1,600-foot vertical rise. This is a climb in three stages: 1) easy walking on the bed of the old Gordon Pond logging railroad; 2) moderate climbing through hardwoods on old logging roads; 3) the final approach from Gordon Fall, a minor cascade, across a boggy plateau of spruce and fir. (See Daniel Doan's *Fifty More Hikes in New Hampshire*.)

*Gordon Pond and Mount Wolf*

## At Gordon Pond

From the Kinsman Ridge Trail, turn right (SE) onto the blue-blazed Gordon Pond Trail, which leads gradually downhill. In 0.2 mile you pick your way across a mud wallow and weave through a fir glade, where the trail appears to split. The main trail branches right; here you can take a well-worn side path left for a first look at Gordon Pond from its mucky SW shore (bear right at a fork 100 feet in).

The best shoreside lunch spot is found by continuing ahead on Gordon Pond Trail. You pass through a thicket of young conifers where the trail may be overgrown, then drop down a bank and rock-hop across the dark outlet brook. At a blue blaze on the opposite bank, bear left on a beaten path that leads to a spacious campsite. Swing right at the far corner on a path into dense conifer growth. Overgrown and soggy in places, this side path leads 100 yards to the stony, grassy south shore of Gordon Pond.

A hundred feet to the left, by the outlet cove, is a low, flat, whitish rock at the water's edge. This tailor-made picnic seat puts the sun at your back and opens a great view of the pond and the imposing, forested mass of Mount Wolf shooting up from a little notch in the ridge.

The dense spruce and fir growth around the shore gives Gordon Pond a wild and remote aura. Several clues tell you that a higher water level, managed by beavers, once prevailed here: a meadow peppered with snags at the pond's north end; the wet, exposed shoreline; and a curving old beaver dam at the outlet around to the left. If the beavers return, they might put the picnic rock under water. (There's a higher rock seat a few yards to the right.)

On a summer day you'll hear green frogs twanging and a lively bird chorus—white-throated sparrows, dark-eyed juncos, winter wrens, magnolia warblers, solitary vireos and several more. The uncommon rusty blackbird sometimes nests here, along with the familiar grackle. Listen for the rusty's ascending, squeaky "song." The pond has been aerially stocked with trout by the state, and because of its remoteness there is little fishing pressure.

On the return trip over Kinsman Ridge, you'll face about 750 feet of climbing, with the major 450-foot rise coming at the outset. Take your time, and enjoy the ridge walk.

*Winter:* This is an especially wild spot in winter, with imposing views of Mount Wolf and a glimpse of Moosilauke. The Kinsman Ridge route is a challenging snowshoe trek; the Beaver Brook Trail parking area is usually plowed. The lower Gordon Pond Trail is used by snowmobiles; limited parking near Govoni's Restaurant.

# CHAPTER 11

# MUD POND (EASTON)

———————◆———————

**Location:** Easton, east of NH 116
**Hiking Facts:** 0.2 mile round-trip, 100-foot vertical rise (outbound), easy
**Map:** USGS 7½' Mount Moosilauke
**Area:** 4 acres  **Elevation:** 1,260 feet
**Activities:** Fishing (brook trout), picnicking, hiking

———————◆———————

This quiet pocket of boggy water, one of four Mud Ponds in the western White Mountains, resides in a depression west of Kinsman Ridge only a stone's throw from NH 116. It's hidden by a screen of forest and a steep drop, so drivers negotiating the curves of this country highway would never suspect there's a peaceful trout pond close by.

## Access
Drive north on NH 116 from its eastern junction with NH 112. In 1.4 miles the road begins a sharp bend to the right. At 1.6 miles it straightens briefly before making an abrupt leftward curve. The path to Mud Pond is on the right along this straightaway, just past a yellow highway sign. Best parking is on the wide shoulder before the next curve.

## The Trail To Mud Pond
You'll find the unmarked path by a "Public Water Supply" sign. The well-trodden footway runs level a few yards, then drops steeply 0.1 mile through a shady hemlock grove to a clearing midway along the pond's north shore.

## At Mud Pond
Small sitting rocks offer a good view of this somber four-acre oval completely enclosed by spruce, fir, and hemlock. It's a nice spot for a picnic or just a quick, quiet interlude away from the road. Visit in the evening and you may be greeted by the loud warning slap of a beaver's tail on the water. Obscure paths lead along the shore in either direction to other vantages.

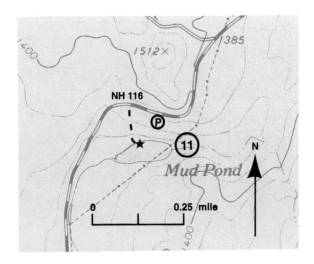

Signs by the road and shore note that Mud Pond is a public water supply; swimming and boating are not allowed. Fishing, however, is permitted,
and stocked brook trout ply the murky waters.

The 100-foot climb back to the road will have you huffing a bit when
you return to your car.

*Winter:* The road is usually plowed wide enough for parking before the
leftward curve. If you're passing by, Mud Pond is worth a quick stop for the
unique view of South Kinsman Mountain from the west half of its frozen
surface—but keep away from the boggy outlet.

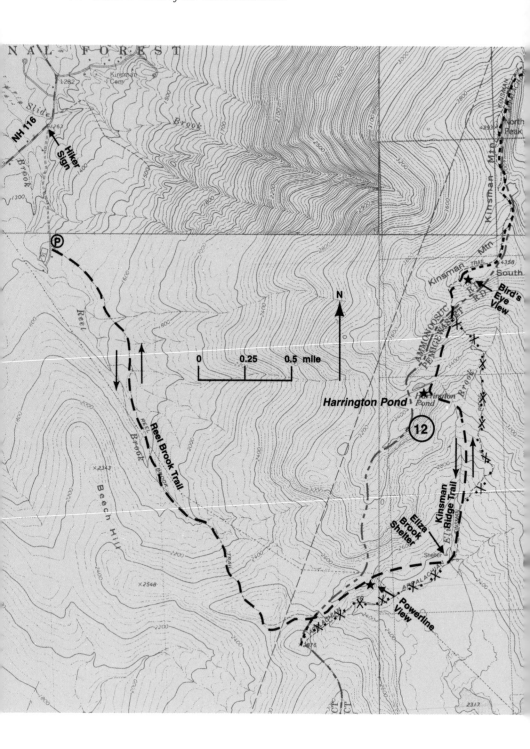

# CHAPTER 12

# HARRINGTON POND

———————◆———————

**Location:** Shoulder of South Kinsman Mountain
**Hiking Facts:** 10.6 mile round-trip, 2,400-foot vertical rise, more difficult
**Maps:** USGS 7½' Lincoln and Mount Moosilauke; (Franconia and Sugar Hill)
**Area:** 1.5 acres   **Elevation:** 3,380 feet
**Activities:** Hiking

——————————————◆——————————————

*It was to this little Harrington Pond that a frog piping
his nightly serenade guided the writer through the dense
darkness, when first a trail was roughly blazed along this
hitherto inaccessible ridge.*
—Karl P. Harrington
*Walks and Climbs in the White Mountains,* 1926

A mile south of South Kinsman Mountain the tangled ridge crest parts to reveal a tiny pond wrapped in a boggy mat of shrubs and sedges. Karl P. Harrington, AMC trail-builder extraordinaire of the early 1900s, came upon his namesake pond while laying out the rugged Kinsman Ridge Trail in 1917. Now, as then, this little lakelet enjoys a picturesque setting amidst ragged ledges and twisted firs.

Though the Kinsman Ridge Trail edges the soggy meadow encircling Harrington Pond, it provides no picnic seats and no access to the water. Still, experienced trampers making the long and rugged southern approach to the Kinsman summits will treasure a visit to this remote and wild place.

### Access
The hiking route to Harrington Pond utilizes the 2.9 mile Reel Brook Trail and a 2.4-mile link of Kinsman Ridge Trail. The trailhead is found on a dirt road leading 0.6 mile south from NH 116, 3.7 miles north of NH 112; look for a hiker symbol beside NH 116.

## The Trail To Harrington Pond

The blue-blazed Reel Brook Trail climbs at easy to moderate grades up the hardwood-forested valley, with several brook crossings. The northbound stretch along the white-blazed Kinsman Ridge Trail crosses a power line in the "original" Kinsman Notch (good views east to Bog Pond and distant mountains) and dips to Eliza Brook Shelter. The trail winds up the valley of Eliza Brook—a chain of cascades and pools strung through a wild fir forest—then swings left for a steep climb to the shelf that holds Harrington Pond.

## At Harrington Pond

Bog bridges lead you to the meadow on the east side of the pond, which is guarded by a wide fringe of shrubs and overlooked by a line of SE-facing cliffs. To the right the long, rocky ridge rises a thousand feet to the scrubby summit of South Kinsman (4,358 feet). Interesting bog flora abound, including pitcher plant, leatherleaf, labrador tea, and pale laurel. Listen for highland birds like the ruby-crowned kinglet, blackpoll warbler, and yellow-bellied flycatcher. As there's no place to sit, you'll have to stand atop the logs to survey the pretty Harrington Pond scene. Please don't walk on the fragile vegetation.

If you're going on to South Kinsman, you face a grueling mile's climb, one of the tougher stretches of the Appalachian Trail in the Whites. You can pause between scrambles to enjoy views down the Eliza Brook valley to Bog Pond. As you approach the open summit, ledges just right of the trail offer a *bird's-eye view* of Harrington Pond, in Karl Harrington's words "a wee mirror of water set in its little cup far below, reflecting over the treetops a shimmering glint." The summit supports a mini-alpine zone; enjoy the wide views, but please walk on the rocks and not the fragile vegetation. If you've spotted a car, you may continue along the ridge to North Kinsman and descend to NH 116 via the Mount Kinsman Trail. The full traverse is 11.4 miles with a 3,300-foot vertical rise; add 0.6 mile and 200 feet of climbing for a side trip to Kinsman Pond.

*Winter:* Harrington Pond is for serious winter trampers only. Wind-packed snowdrifts and rime-frosted firs rim this tiny frozen teardrop. You'll get a dramatic close-up of the cliffs rising above the north shore. The trail is seldom broken out, and you must add a 0.6-mile walk in each direction on the unplowed side road. There's usually room to park on the shoulder of NH 116.

# CHAPTER 13

# LONESOME LAKE

◆

**Location:** West of Franconia Notch
**Hiking Facts:** 3.2 miles round-trip, 1,000-foot vertical rise, moderate
**Map:** USGS 7½' Franconia
**Area:** 14 acres   **Elevation:** 2,740 feet
**Avg./Max. Depth:** 5/8 feet
**Activities:** Hiking, swimming, fishing (brook trout), picnicking, AMC hut

◆

*Lonesome Lake commands all that is desirable
in a mountain retreat.*
—Julius H. Ward
*The White Mountains*, 1890

From May through October you'll seldom lack for company at this somewhat misnamed tarn set on a plateau high above Franconia Notch. But there's good reason for the popularity of Lonesome Lake. It is, unquestionably, one of the finest short hikes in the White Mountains—or anywhere.

Why? Start with the pond itself, a sparkling basin rimmed with spruce, fir, and tamarack. Add superb shoreline views of Kinsman's twin summits, Cannon's rugged ridges, and especially the gaunt, slide-scarred facade of Franconia Ridge. Spice with leaping trout, singing birds, and fascinating bogs. Wrap with an encircling trail that offers waterside viewing rocks, a swimming dock, and a nearby AMC hut. Lonesome Lake is a winner, sure to please every member of the hiking family.

The pleasures of Lonesome Lake have been savored for well over a century. Early on it was called Tamarack Pond, then Moran Lake. In 1876 two avid anglers—William Bridges and William C. Prime—built a log cabin on the east side of the pond. Prime, a famed author known as "America's Izaak Walton" for his classic *I Go A-Fishing*, applied the name Lonesome Lake to his beloved retreat. (Small wonder he liked the place; on his first visit he snared 45 trout!) Among his favored guests was Gen. George B. McClellan of Civil War fame.

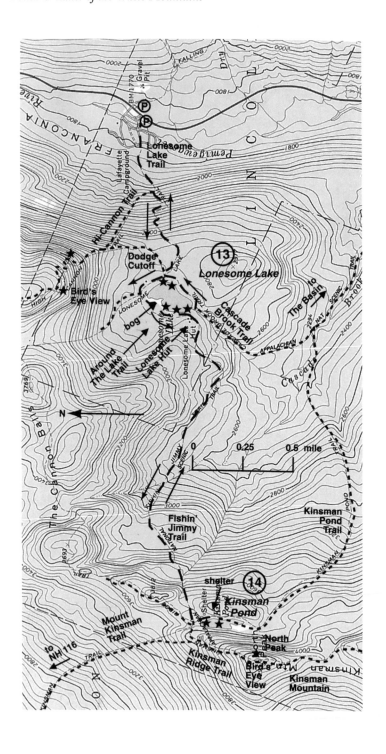

In 1929 the state of New Hampshire acquired Lonesome Lake as part of the Franconia Notch reservation. The AMC was invited to operate the former Prime cabins as part of its chain of high huts. In 1963 the state tore down the decaying old buildings and built the current AMC complex in the woods above the SW shore. The hut accommodates 46 hikers and is open from early May to mid-October, with full service June through Labor Day. Its easy access makes it the most popular hut with families.

## Access

The shortest and most-used route is the Lonesome Lake Trail, starting at Lafayette Place Campground on the west (southbound) side of Franconia Notch Parkway between Exits 1 and 2. Hiker parking is available on either side of the highway. A pedestrian underpass provides access from the east side lots. The trail, marked by a state sign, leaves from the SW corner of the southernmost west-side parking area. The entire hike is within Franconia Notch State Park, and camping is prohibited except at the campground.

## The Trail To Lonesome Lake

The yellow-blazed Lonesome Lake Trail spans the Pemigewasset River on a footbridge and proceeds up through the sprawling campground, crossing three gravel roads. Beyond the campsites you rise easily through a northern hardwood forest boasting some ancient specimens. Swinging left, you clomp across two plank bridges and pass the Hi-Cannon Trail on the right at 0.4 mile.

The trail now undertakes two long, slabbing switchbacks—left, then right—on a gravelly footway, largely following the route of an old bridle path that once served guests from the nearby Profile House. The grade is moderate but steady, for the lake is a full thousand feet above the floor of the notch. White birch, red spruce, and balsam fir mix into the forest as you ascend. The second switchback ends at the brink of a ravine, where you bear left for the final rocky ascent to the tableland. The rumble of the parkway traffic recedes as you climb into a wild wood of birch and evergreen. You pass a blow-down opening left, surmount a final rise, and dip to a four-way trail junction near the east shore of Lonesome Lake, 1.2 miles from your car.

The Cascade Brook Trail leaves left, the upper Lonesome Lake Trail departs right, and the Dodge Cutoff to Hi-Cannon Trail (an alternate descent route) diverges sharp right. Look back at the yellow-blazed trail you came in on and fix it in your memory for the return trip.

*Alternate Approach:* Take the Basin-Cascades and Cascade Brook trails from the Basin; 5.4 miles round-trip (including circuit of lake), 1,200-foot vertical rise. This longer, gentler route displays outstanding brook scenery. It comes in at the outlet on the south shore of the lake. Combined with the Lonesome Lake and Pemi trails it makes a nice 6-mile loop.

## At Lonesome Lake

A few steps left of the four-way trail junction a side path right leads down to the viewpoint on the east shore. There's a serene vista across the spruce-fringed pond to the rolling, green-carpeted Kinsmans: North Kinsman (4,293 feet) on the right, spotted with ledges; South Kinsman (4,358 feet) to the left. A pair of logs provides a low-slung seat where you can soak up the view and the sun, which pours down on this opening all afternoon and evening. Summer music is performed by a high-country chorus of white-throated sparrows (a clear, plaintive whistle) and Swainson's thrushes (a liquid upward spiral).

From here you can circle the lake in either direction on Around-Lonesome-Lake Trail, which coincides with bits of three other trails. Returning from the viewpoint side path, the quickest way to the hut and swimming dock is right (south) on the Cascade Brook and Fishin' Jimmy trails for 0.3 mile.

I prefer to amble the longer route around the north shore. To do this, turn left (north) on the upper Lonesome Lake Trail. You pass through a clearing where William C. Prime's cabins once stood and follow a parade of plank and topped-log bridges through a boggy conifer forest. In 0.2 mile, amidst a rooty, muddy clearing, bear left on the blue-blazed Around-Lonesome-Lake Trail. (To the right, Lonesome Lake Trail climbs to Kinsman Ridge Trail in Coppermine Col.)

Bog bridges and roots lift you over an inlet stream that flows from old beaver ponds on the right. More logs lead you into an open bog, thick with sedges and leatherleaf and fringed with feathery tamaracks. There's a long view left to the craggy peak of Mount Liberty (4,459 feet) and a veiled glimpse of the higher Franconias. Please give the fragile plant life a break and stay on the bog bridges. After crossing two bog channels, the trail winds behind the shore through a congregation of bog shrubs: sweet gale, leatherleaf, mountain holly, sheep laurel, rhodora, and others.

In about 0.1 mile look for a fine shoreside sitting rock (capacity two persons) tucked into the shrubs 8 feet left of the trail. On a day of sun and shadow the vista across the water to the barren ramparts of Franconia Ridge

*Lonesome Lake and Franconia Ridge*

is so beautiful it's almost surreal. Every detail of ridge and ravine is revealed. Arrayed left to right are the knobby North Peak and sharper main summit of Mount Lafayette (5,260 feet), Mount Lincoln (5,089 feet), and Little Haystack Mountain (4,760 feet). You can easily spot such landmarks as Shining Rock Cliff (below Little Haystack) and the jagged ledges of the Knife Edge (just right of Lincoln). With binoculars you can watch hikers striding along the open ridge. Figures that don't move are cairns marking Franconia Ridge Trail.

There are beauties close at hand, too, including a colony of the tiny, insectivorous sundew amidst the sphagnum in front of your seat. The slender stems of pipewort poke from the shallows. Buttonlike flowers give them a more descriptive name, "hat pins."

Beyond the rock there are more views, then you cut through softwoods to the dock area. Here's the place for a dip in the chill waters of Lonesome Lake, which are at their deepest in this SW corner. The wooden platform also provides a gorgeous view of the Franconias. It's a popular resting and picnic spot. The hut, with an octagonal central building and outlying bunkhouses, is found up in the woods along Fishin' Jimmy Trail. Day hikers can stop in for lemonade and a candy bar.

To complete the circuit, bear left beyond the swimming area. You briefly join the Fishin' Jimmy Trail/Appalachian Trail to cross the outlet, shored up with boulders and planks to stabilize the water level. The bridge opens a view left to Coppermine Col, a U-shaped gap gouged by the glacier and flanked by Northeast Cannon Ball (3,769 feet) and the ledgy southern buttress of Cannon Mountain. Bear left at a junction onto the short, muddy upper section of Cascade Brook Trail. (Its lower section, part of the Appalachian Trail, splits right.)

In 0.2 mile, just before you complete the loop, a short side path leads left to a sloping sitting rock with its roots in the water. From this sun-soaked boulder you gain a wide view of the pond, the Kinsmans, and the Cannon ridges. Anglers use this perch to cast out to deeper water where brook trout lurk. Back at the four-way junction you have an easy 1.2 mile descent to your car on Lonesome Lake Trail.

*Bird's-Eye View:* Outlook ledges on Hi-Cannon Trail provide an aerialist's perspective on Lonesome Lake. If you have time and energy for this rugged side trip, take Dodge Cutoff from the four-way junction. In 0.3 mile turn left on Hi-Cannon Trail. Rocky climbing leads 0.4 mile to a nice view east across the notch. The trail bears sharp left here and scales a rough slope, aided in one spot by a nerve-testing ladder. In 0.2 mile you come to the first of three sloping ledges on the left, elevation about 3,500 feet. The third, located at a right turn in the trail, offers the best view of the lake nestled below in the forest, with the Franconia Range to the left, the Kinsmans on the right, and a wide vista to the south. Use caution if the ledges are wet or icy. With this side trip thrown in and a descent via Hi-Cannon Trail, your total hike would be 4.7 miles with a vertical rise of 1,800 feet.

*Winter:* Lonesome Lake is one of the best snowshoe trips in the Whites, with an equable grade and a great reward at the top. The hiker parking areas are usually plowed on both sides of the parkway. The trail from Lafayette Place is heavily used by snowshoers and bare-boot hikers; it's too steep for most skiers. Views are outstanding from the frozen pond, especially toward the snowy Franconias. Avoid the ice near the southern outlet and at the boggy inlet area along the NW shore.

CHAPTER 14

# KINSMAN POND

◆

**Location:** Kinsman Ridge, east of North Kinsman Mountain
**Hiking Facts:** 7.2 miles round-trip, 2,300-foot vertical rise, more difficult; add
   1.2 miles and 550 vertical feet for North Kinsman Mountain.
**Map:** USGS 7½' Franconia (Page 82)
**Area:** 5 acres   **Elevation:** 3,740 feet
**Activities:** Hiking, camping (lean-to), fishing (brook trout), picnicking

◆

The ledgy wall of North Kinsman Mountain forms a dramatic backdrop for narrow Kinsman Pond, highest of the Kinsman Ridge tarns. This high-country hideaway was discovered in 1871 by two Dartmouth graduates, A.A. Abbott and A.M. Bacheler, during research for Charles H. Hitchcock's geological survey of New Hampshire. The opening of the AMC's Kinsman Ridge Trail in 1917–9 and the construction of a shelter near the shore in 1921 brought Kinsman Pond within reach of the hiking public.

The pond remains a remote but popular destination for backpackers and day hikers today. No less than four trail routes can be used for the approach. None is easy, but each has its unique rewards. Perhaps the most-used access is the Fishin' Jimmy Trail from Lonesome Lake. After absorbing the impressive views from the rocky east shore, many hikers will want to slog up to the 4,293-foot summit of North Kinsman for long-range vistas and a bird's-eye look at the pond. The features in this area were named for Asa (some sources say Nathan) Kinsman, who, with his hardy wife, settled in the wilderness of Easton in the 1780s.

### Access
The hike begins on the Lonesome Lake Trail at Lafayette Place Campground. See *Lonesome Lake.*

### The Trail To Kinsman Pond

Follow the Lonesome Lake and Cascade Brook trails for 1.5 miles to the junction with Fishin' Jimmy Trail by the outlet at the south end of Lonesome Lake. Proceed on the Fishin' Jimmy Trail past the swimming dock and the AMC Lonesome Lake Hut. (As the AMC guidebook notes, the odd name of this trail comes from a character in a story by regional author Annie Trumbull Slosson.) For 0.3 mile beyond the hut the grades are gentle through a salt-and-pepper forest of birch, spruce, and fir, giving no hint of the rough terrain to come.

Climbing in fits and starts, the trail works its way along the southern slopes of the Cannon Balls. You make several brook crossings and a couple of disheartening descents. There's an uphill surge of about 400 vertical feet, rocky and rooty through thick firs. The trail levels on a boggy, mossy flat at 3,200 feet, then resumes the attack.

The next pitch features wooden triangular steps pinned to the steepest ledges. Another breather, then you tackle a winding, bouldery pitch spotted with more wooden steps. The final approach to four-way Kinsman Junction is an easier walk, partly over bog bridges through a sphagnum bog thick with fir and black spruce.

At the crossroads, turn left on the Kinsman Pond Trail. (Straight ahead is southbound Kinsman Ridge Trail to the Kinsman summits; right is the same trail northbound for the Cannon Balls.) This path winds for 0.1 mile through thick firs, with many bog bridges, to Kinsman Pond Shelter and nearby tent platforms at the north end of the pond.

*Alternate Approach:* One option is to start at the Basin and follow the Basin-Cascades Trail for 1 mile, the Cascade Brook Trail for 0.5 mile, and the Kinsman Pond Trail for 2.4 miles. Total round-trip is 7.8 miles with a 2,200-foot vertical rise. This approach offers fine brook and waterfall scenery and a pretty stand of old-growth conifers in the wild basin east of the Kinsmans. The downside is that the upper mile of Kinsman Pond Trail is wet and rough, coinciding with a brook bed in places. A loop could be fashioned by descending Fishin' Jimmy Trail to Lonesome Lake and taking Cascade Brook Trail back down to Basin-Cascades Trail.

Other day-hike approaches can be made from the west via the Mount Kinsman Trail from Easton, and from the north over the Cannon Balls.

### At Kinsman Pond

Just south of the shelter the Kinsman Pond Trail dips by the east shore of the pond. A side path leads a few steps right to a line of rocks and one of the more spectacular pond-and-peak views in the mountains. Across the water the cliffy, scrubby wall of North Kinsman rises almost sheer from the rocky western shore. Look closely at the ledge crowning the left (south) end of the ridge and you may spot hikers looking down at you from the bird's-eye perch near the summit. To the left, beyond a ledgy peninsula at the south end of the pond, you see South Kinsman's flattened dome. Choose from several fine, flat sitting rocks if you're inclined to enjoy the view for a while. On a nice summer day they're in the sun through much of the afternoon.

For different perspectives on the pond, you can follow the Kinsman Pond Trail south along the east shore. It alternately runs close by the water and ducks up into the dense, scruffy firs on the slope above the pond, with rough, bouldery footing. The pond's outlet is at its south end (though the USGS map shows it draining NE). Old cuttings and a weathered lodge indicate that high-altitude beavers were once in residence at Kinsman Pond.

Years ago a small plane crashed in the fir woods just SE of the pond. In 1982 I took a picture of one of the wings at rest in the trees, but I've been unable to locate the spot on recent visits.

If you're camping at Kinsman Pond (shelter or tent platforms only), keep in mind that the tea-colored water is not fit to drink unless boiled or effectively treated. By the same token, it's not especially inviting for a swim. The pond has been aerially stocked with fingerling brook trout by New Hampshire Fish and Game. The 12-person wood plank lean-to was recently treated to a new roof. It is reputed to harbor an especially fierce tribe of mice.

## North Kinsman Mountain

To enjoy those summit views, return to Kinsman Junction and bear left on the southbound Kinsman Ridge Trail. Several ledgy steps lead up to a junction with Mount Kinsman Trail on the right in 0.2 mile. From here to the summit it's a steady, rocky grind of 400+ feet in 0.4 mile. The high point is a peaked boulder left of the trail, after which you come to the side path left to the viewpoints (sign).

Drop down two ledges and cross a muddy patch to the first viewpoint, a rock table featuring a grand broadside prospect of Franconia Ridge. To view the pond you must scramble down to the next outlook. Leave the first viewpoint on a path at its left (north) end. Drop carefully down an almost sheer six-foot ledge (there are convenient footholds), cross a muddy spot, and emerge on open rocks.

The lower right ledge offers the best view of the pond, looking almost

*Kinsman Pond from North Kinsman*

straight down on its dark surface and the shelter roof. In this aerial view the pond, with its two southern prongs, has the shape of a slender arrowhead or a watery Long Island. Farther east, to the right of the Cannon Balls, Lonesome Lake rests placidly on its forested plateau. Often you'll see gliders playing in the drafts around the ridge.

*Winter:* Kinsman Pond is spectacular in its snow-crusted garb under the frosty cliffs of North Kinsman. Fishin' Jimmy Trail is often packed out by Kinsman peak-baggers, but several steep pitches can be icy and difficult. The Kinsman Pond Trail route has more even grades, though the Basin-Cascades Trail can be treacherous if icy.

CHAPTER 15

# PROFILE LAKE

◆

**Location:** Franconia Notch
**Hiking Facts:** Roadside; optional hike, 1.2 miles round-trip, 100-foot vertical
rise, easy
**Map:** USGS 7½' Franconia
**Area:** 15 acres   **Elevation:** 1,940 feet
**Avg./Max. Depth:** 8/14 feet
**Activities:** Old Man viewing, fishing (brook trout; fly-fishing only), picnicking,
canoeing, hiking

◆

*...as though Nature would provide for her creation an*
*appropriate mirror...*
—Samuel C. Eastman
*The White Mountain Guide Book*, 1867

Cast in the shadow of the Old Man of the Mountain, New Hampshire's most
famous citizen, Profile Lake is probably seen and visited by more persons than
any other White Mountain pond. The green-tinted tarn is photogenically set
between the naked rock faces of Eagle Cliff and the huge eastern buttress of
Cannon Mountain, whose cliff-top ledges form the Old Man. Though it may
seem to be secondary to the Granite State's top attraction, "The Old Man's
Washbowl" is first and foremost with many a pond devotee.

In the late 1800s and early 1900s guests of the nearby Profile House
came here to enjoy picnics, walks, band concerts, boating (the hotel kept a
"little navy of dainty boats" on hand), fishing, flirting, and contemplation
of the scenery. The Profile House burned in 1923, but with the exception
of the music, the 1990s visitor can still indulge in these pleasures. Hikers
can savor a lovely walk along the west shore of the pond, and anglers will
find excellent fly-fishing.

## Access

The Franconia Notch Parkway curves along the east shore of Profile Lake and provides access at both the north (200-yard walk) and south ends. There are no roadside pull-offs along the shore, and stopping is dangerous and illegal. The more popular north (Old Man) end can be accessed from either side of the parkway at Exit 2 (Cannon Mountain Tramway).

The south-end parking area, 0.6 mile south of Exit 2, is available only to southbound drivers and is marked by a "Trailhead Parking" sign. There's a convenient boat launch for anglers and canoeists. A short path leads to a bench with a gorgeous view north up the pond with Eagle Cliff towering on the right. This side of the pond is quieter than the Old Man scene and is a great spot for a picnic.

## Profile Lake Trail

Leaving the parkway at Exit 2, head west toward the Cannon Mountain Tramway. The prominently marked Old Man access road departs left before the tramway parking lots and makes a one-way loop (0.2 mile each way) to parking areas and rest rooms. From here there are two walking options down to the lake.

Most everybody follows the crowds along the 200-yard paved walkway, dubbed the "Profile Lake Trail," which departs by the rest rooms. This descends a fairly steep pitch and then runs level to the Old Man viewing area at the NE corner of the lake. Visitors in wheelchairs can use a designated parking area off the outbound loop road and follow a level, paved spur that bypasses the steep grade.

There are several points of interest along the Profile Lake Trail. About halfway along, the Notch bike path leaves left through an underpass to the east side of the Parkway and passes the outlet of *Breeding Pond* (1 acre, max. depth 2 feet). This small, artificial pond was associated with a trout-breeding operation at the turn of the century; it is currently closed to fishing. Some consider Breeding Pond to be the ultimate source of the Pemigewasset River. You can get a closer look by hopping out on the outlet boulders. (The bike path continues south, passing the east-side Old Man viewing area, and provides nice tree-framed vistas over Profile Lake before ducking back under the parkway to the parking area at the pond's south end.)

The Profile Lake Trail continues past a small nature center and several interpretive displays. As the lake comes into sight ahead, look left up to Eagle Cliff for a view of the Eaglet, a remarkable needle of rock detached from the main crag. The walkway ends at a paved cul-de-sac with waterside boulder-seats and a battery of coin-operated binocular viewers. A Braille tablet installed by the local Boy Scout troop enables unsighted visitors to enjoy the setting.

There's also a plaque honoring Rev. Guy Roberts and Edward H. Geddes, whose efforts early in this century helped save the Old Man from a possible demise due to frost action and weathering. Today it's partly held together by an amazing system of cables and turnbuckles and is inspected annually by its longtime caretakers, the Nielsen family. Legend holds that the Profile was discovered in 1805 by two surveyors, Luke Brooks and Francis Whitcomb. Stopping to draw water from what was then known as "Ferrin's Pond," Brooks looked up and spotted the stony face, declaring it to be a likeness of President Thomas Jefferson.

Over a century later, after the Profile House burned, "Saving the Great Stone Face" was a rallying cry for conservationists. The Society for the Protection of New Hampshire Forests led a fund-raising campaign to keep the 6,000 acres owned by the hotel out of the lumberman's hands. The notch was acquired by the state in 1928.

From the end of Profile Lake Trail the Old Man is in clear view, 1,200 feet above you. The vista southward down the pond to the converging ridges of the Notch is quite picturesque. But don't expect solitude unless it's raining or in the dead of winter. In the morning or evening you'll often see fly-fishing enthusiasts chest-deep in the water off to the right. This is a superior trout pond, with a two-fish limit and a season open from the fourth Saturday in April to October 15.

## Pemi Trail

The nicest walk at Profile Lake is provided by the Pemi Trail along its west shore. This path begins at a sign and stone stairway at the tip of the north-end loop road. It climbs easily through leafy hardwood forest and makes a sharp left turn where an unmarked side path splits right. You bend left again at a sign marking another fork; the right-hand path is a rock climbers' path used for descent from theCannon Cliffs. The Pemi Trail descends gradually to the NW corner of Profile Lake. (At the bottom a side path drops left to follow and cross the inlet brook, joining the Profile Lake Trail near its midway point.)

The Pemi Trail rolls along the rugged, rocky bank above the west shore through an attractive wood of yellow birch, the reigning tree beside Profile Lake. Frequent views open left across the water, and there's an occasional sitting rock. Halfway along the shore the trail breaks into the open amidst pointed boulders and the scattered sticks of an old beaver lodge.

Continue another 200 feet to the best trailside sitting rock, directly across from Eagle Pass, a deep cut in the east wall of the notch. From here you can see nearly the whole spread of the pond to left and right. Across the water the ragged, rocky ridge of Eagle Cliff stretches to the left. A slide-scarred buttress of Mount Lafayette carries the ridge line southward beyond Eagle Pass. The only demerit for this spot is the nearly constant roar of traffic on the parkway by the east shore.

This pleasant walk can be extended to the south end of the pond, 0.6 mile from your car. Look for a fresh beaver dam across the outlet brook, close by the boat launch on the opposite bank. Come in the evening and you may see these waterborne engineers tending to their handiwork.

The Pemi Trail continues south, reaching Lafayette Place Campground in 1.4 miles and the Basin in 3.3 miles. For a novel approach to Profile Lake, consider walking *up* the Pemi Trail from Lafayette Place—a 3-mile round-trip with about 300 feet of climbing to the mid-shore sitting rock. It's a mellow woodsy stroll, shadowing the Pemigewasset River through tunnels of hardwoods. About 0.3 mile north of the campground, where the trail briefly splits, a brushy area to the left provides a unique view of the Cannon Cliffs and Eagle Cliff. No roads or buildings disturb the foreground. It's like stepping back in time to the days when the first pioneers probed this wild mountain pass.

*Winter:* Profile Lake can be traversed as part of a ski or snowshoe tour of the notch. Nearby parking is found at the northbound Old Man viewing area, the tramway, or the south-end parking area by the boat launch. The Old Man parking area at the pond's north end is not plowed. Access is via the bike path (used by snowmobiles) or Pemi Trail (reserved for cross-country skiing). The frozen surface provides grand views of the mountain walls and the Old Man. Avoid the inlet and outlet areas, where the ice may be soft. A moonlight ski or stroll is a special treat, with the moonbeams glinting off ice-draped Eagle Cliff.

CHAPTER 16

# ECHO LAKE
# (FRANCONIA)

◆

**Location:** Franconia Notch
**Hiking Facts:** Roadside; optional short walks along shore or to Artist's Bluff
**Map:** USGS 7½' Franconia (Page 92)
**Area:** 28 acres   **Elevation:** 1,940 feet
**Avg./Max. Depth:** 15/39 feet
**Activities:** Swimming, picnicking, fishing (brook trout), canoeing, bicycling, hiking

◆

*...a sweet and perennial symbol of purity and peace.*
—Thomas Starr King
*The White Hills,* 1859

Franconia Notch's Echo Lake is a broad, sun-kissed mountain pond, blessed with clear, deep water and a magnificent setting in the shadow of Eagle Cliff and Cannon Mountain. Tourists and anglers have made their way to its shores since the first road was pushed through the notch in the early 1800s.

In 1853 the opening of the famed Profile House between Echo and Profile Lakes ushered in an era of grand hotel gentility in the great mountain pass. The hotel's well-to-do guests found serenity and amusement at Echo Lake. Here they could rent rowboats, tour the pond aboard a mini-steamboat named *Ida,* or for 50 cents have a small cannon fired, to be answered by "a whole park of artillery" booming off the ragged crags of Eagle Cliff.

Echo Lake is an equally popular playground today, highly visible and easily reached from the Franconia Notch Parkway. At its north end is a superb swimming beach. The quieter south shore hosts a boat launch and fishing beach. From either end you can enjoy a short stroll along a lakeside path by the west shore. Bicyclists can cruise a paved trail beside the east shore. Canoeists and sailboarders come to ply the breezy waters. Hikers strike off for the short but steep pilgrimage to nearby Artist's Bluff, earning a dazzling bird's eye view of the lake and notch. This is a pond the whole family can enjoy.

## Access

Echo Lake is served by two exits off the Franconia Notch Parkway. For the boat launch at the south end of the pond, use Exit 2 (Cannon Mountain Tramway). Follow the access road 0.2 mile north past the tramway parking lot. Bear right at a "Boat Launch" sign and drive 0.1 mile to the gravel boat ramp on the right. Park on the shoulder of the access road.

Use Exit 3 (0.6 mile north of Exit 2) for access to the north end. Drive 0.1 mile west on NH 18 to the large Echo Lake Beach parking area on the left.

## At Echo Lake

The majority of visitors come to Echo Lake for the fine state-operated swimming beach, open daily from mid-June through Labor Day, 10:00 A.M.–6:00 P.M. In 1992 admission was $2.50 per person, free for children under 12. A gravel walkway descends from the ticket booth past the bathhouses to the beach, a strip of sand 100 yards across. A lifeguard stands watch over the roped-off swimming area. The water is clear and invigorating and quite shallow near the shore. Refreshments are served, with picnic tables available behind the beach. This side of Echo Lake is a busy, busy place on a hot summer day. One way to escape the hubbub is to rent a canoe, rowboat, or paddleboat and explore the pond afloat.

In early morning or evening, or during the off-season, the beach has a quieter aspect, well-suited for a leisurely stroll. Starr King, Sweetser, Ward, and others urged their Gilded Age readers to visit Echo Lake at the turning hours of the day, for then the colors would be at their richest. The impressive views include the many-headed ridge of Eagle Cliff on the left, the cut lines of the notch south over the water, and bulky, ski-trailed Cannon Mountain on the right.

## The Lake Path

A recently upgraded path affords a pleasant walk along the west shore of the lake, 0.8 mile round-trip to the south end and back. There are many fine views of Eagle Cliff across the water.

At the right (west) end of the beach a sign, "Echo Point Megaphone," indicates the start of the path. It leads 100 yards south through birches and alders to the big green horn. Originally used by guests of the Profile House, the megaphone was removed after the 1938 hurricane but was restored to its lakeside stand in 1981. Youngsters and adults alike delight in bouncing shouts off the rock faces of Eagle Cliff to the east. Listen closely and you'll hear at least two separate echoes peel off the mountainside. It's said that Native Americans of the area believed the echoes to be the war whoops of the gods.

Continuing south, stone fill and bog bridges guide you over a wet area, which may be too soggy for passage in spring or after heavy rains. Then you cross a gravel yard in front of a maintenance building. The path reenters the woods and runs up and down along the shore to a shrubby opening. Beyond, the path ducks back into the woods, climbs over a high bank, and passes several more vantage points. After crossing a small inlet stream you emerge at the boat launch on the south shore.

This end of the pond is frequented mainly by anglers, who set up shop on the little gravel beach (no swimming allowed). "From its shining waters are taken many of the nicest kinds of trout," wrote historian J.H. Spaulding in 1855. The same might be said today, thanks to stocking by the state.

A scenic section of the paved nine-mile Franconia Notch Bike Path runs along the east shore of Echo Lake. It can be accessed from NH 18 on the north and the tramway parking lot on the south. Walking is permitted on the path, though it is not advisable when bicycle traffic is heavy. There are fine views across the water to the steep green swaths of Cannon's ski trails. Evening visitors have a fair chance of spotting a black bear feeding on the grassy slopes.

### Artist's Bluff

The cliffs of Artist's Bluff provide an easily attained pond-and-mountain panorama. The hike, 0.4 mile round-trip with 200 feet of climbing, begins on the north side of NH 18, 100 yards east of the Echo Lake Beach parking lot. (There is no parking at the trailhead.)

The red-blazed trail, maintained by the Trailwrights, climbs moderately through hardwoods, then shoots up a steep, rocky gully into scrubby birch and mountain ash. In places the footway is paved with cut granite slabs. Where the main trail bears left to continue climbing, the spur trail to the cliffs keeps straight, then makes a horseshoe bend to the south and emerges on the ledges beside a great erratic boulder.

The cliffs drop off rapidly to waving treetops below. (Keep a close eye on youngsters. The craggy face attracts many rock climbers, so please don't toss anything over the edge!) Echo Lake, broad and artistically scalloped,

*Echo Lake and Eagle Cliff*

spreads between the mountains. The barren crest of Mount Lafayette rises high above Eagle Cliff on the left. Cannon Mountain looms large on the right. The parkway winds south into the cut of the notch, with the sharp peak of Mount Liberty peering over in the distance. The eastern brink of the cliffs reveals the hooked peak of Mount Garfield rising over the long, birch-clad north ridge of Lafayette. Far to the NE are the Pilot Range and the whitish, cone-shaped Percy Peaks.

The trail continues over the wooded summit of Artist's Bluff and on to 2,340-foot Bald Mountain, with panoramic views. This complete loop is 1.6 miles, including a short road walk back to Echo Lake.

*Winter:* Walkers and skiers sometimes traverse the wind-scoured ice of Echo Lake, but the Cannon ski area pulls snowmaking water from the lake, so the ice is potentially dangerous, especially on the west side.

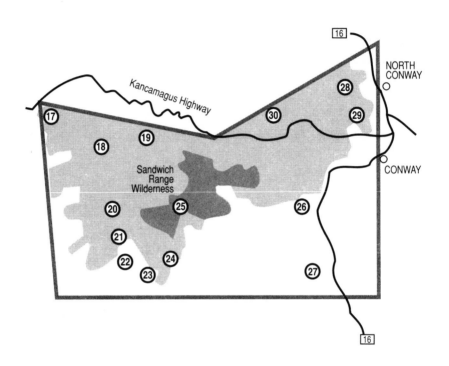

*Shoreside trail at White Lake*

# II. Southern White Mountains

THE SOUTHERN FRONTIER of the White Mountains is fortified by two chains of rugged, wooded peaks: the Scar Ridge–Mount Osceola group and the 30-mile sweep of the Sandwich Range.

The region south of the western Kancamagus Highway holds many delights for the pond explorer. The flanks of the Scar Ridge–Osceola mini-range are dotted with pretty mountain ponds: Russell, Loon, East and Little East, and the celebrated Greeleys, sequestered between the walls of Mad River Notch.

Edging the Sandwich Range on the southwest, near the ill-defined pass of Sandwich Notch, is a septet of lakelets: the three Hall Ponds, boggy Guinea Pond, roadside Kiah Pond, tiny, beaver-haunted Atwood Pond, and Black Mountain Pond, the most picturesque of the lot. To the north, within the Sandwich Range Wilderness, is the remote and elongated Flat Mountain Pond.

South of Mount Chocorua, the rocky all-star peak at the east end of the Sandwich Range, the sandy lowlands are pockmarked with glacial kettle ponds. Though outside the White Mountains proper, two of these—Heron Pond and White Lake—offer outstanding easy hikes. Near Heron Pond is the much-photographed Chocorua Lake. Northward another kettle pond, Echo Lake, lies in the shadow of White Horse Ledge near bustling North Conway. Outlying ponds in or near the SE corner of the National Forest include peaceful, conifer-fringed Falls Pond, easily accessed from the Kancamagus Highway, and swampy Red Eagle Pond, located beside the Dugway Road.

# CHAPTER 17

# RUSSELL POND

◆

**Location:** Woodstock, east of I-93
**Hiking Facts:** Roadside; optional hike, 2.5 mile round-trip,
    280-foot vertical rise
**Map:** USGS 7½' Lincoln
**Area:** 39 acres   **Elevation:** 1,653 feet
**Avg./Max. Depth:** 33/78 feet
**Activities:** Camping, swimming, canoeing, fishing (brook trout), hiking,
    picnicking

◆

Russell Pond is one of the premier get-away-from-it-all spots in the mountains. Cupped amidst gentle hardwood ridges, it's a remote and restful place, yet easily accessed by paved road from I-93. Its waters are broad, clear, and deep, ideal for a refreshing swim or a languorous paddle.

Most visitors come to stay overnight at the 87-site campground maintained near the shore by the Forest Service. Other amenities include a boat ramp, a small swimming beach, stocked brook trout, and a wheelchair-accessible fishing dock. There are no official hiking trails, but campers can fashion a pleasant exploratory stroll from a logging road and a path that has recently been widened into a snowmobile trail.

Earlier editions of the AMC *White Mountain Guide* noted that Russell Pond was a "favorite resort." For many years it could be reached only on foot, or skis. In the 1930s no less than five trails—two of them ski trails— could be followed to its shores. Trampers and anglers could stay overnight at an open-front shelter by the pond's southwestern outlet brook.

By 1960 only one trail remained—the Direct Path (later the Russell Pond Trail), a short but steep route from the Pemigewasset River valley to the west. When the Forest Service opened the Russell Pond Road and Campground in 1963, this trail was abandoned. The pond is now mostly visited by automobile (or snowmobile in winter).

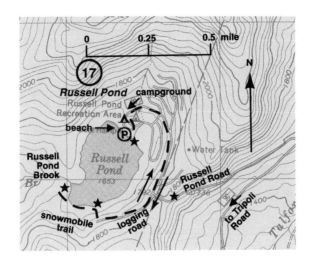

## Access

Leave I-93 at Exit 31, south of Lincoln, and drive east on Tripoli Road. In 0.3 mile you pass a gate (closed in winter) and enter the woods. At 1.8 miles turn left on the Russell Pond Road at a large sign. The side road climbs to a hairpin turn left at 3 miles from I-93. In another 0.5 mile a pull-off on the left provides a view SE toward Mount Tecumseh. In 0.2 mile, the road crests a 1,792-foot gap and turns sharp right to descend to the pond. Follow signs down a one-way loop road through the campground, past branching spurs, to a parking area by the north shore of the pond, 4.2 miles from I-93. Campers should register at a kiosk partway down the grade.

## At Russell Pond

The spruce-shaded shore opens in front of the parking lot for a broad view of the pond. You'll find the boat ramp (no motors allowed) a few yards to the right. Next to it is a paved path that descends gently to the wheelchair-accessible fishing dock.

A gravel footway leads a short distance right to the little, sunny, sandy swimming beach. A great slab of stone bridges a tiny inlet brook that splits the sand. There is no lifeguard, but near the shore the water is shallow and suitable for supervised youngsters. An informal anglers' path, obstructed in places by blow-down, leads along the west shore of the pond to several nice rock vantage points.

Russell Pond Campground, with 49 tent sites and 38 trailer sites, is arrayed on wooded slopes above the pond's NE shore. The campground was completely refurbished in the mid-1990s. A few choice sites are close to the water. It is open from May to October and generally offers a quieter camping experience than the campgrounds along the Kancamagus Highway. From late June through Labor Day free interpretive programs are offered on Saturday evenings.

## A Short Hike

The only thing lacking in recent years at Russell Pond has been trails for the hiker. The Forest Service does plan to construct a hiking/interpretive trail around the pond in the future. Meanwhile, you can still enjoy a short hike from the campground to more secluded shores.

Walk 0.5 mile (and 140 vertical feet) back up the access road to its high point, where it makes a sharp left to begin its descent to Tripoli Road. (Day hikers can park here off the road; do not block the gate.) At the corner continue straight ahead on a gated logging road and follow its gradual descent past small logged openings. In 0.2 mile the road becomes grass-grown.

Where an old skid road bears left and uphill, stay straight on a snowmobile trail. Following the route of the old Russell Pond Trail, the snowmobile trail soon bends right at a moderate downgrade through tall hemlock and yellow birch. Near the bottom the path is somewhat muddy as it hooks left to parallel the pond's south shore. As you approach a bridge over a small brook, look for a narrow but well-beaten path that angles sharply back to your right. This side path, overgrown with hobblebush, leads 150 feet to a clearing beside the ruined stone fireplace of an old camp.

A few steps left the bushes part for a peaceful vista of Russell Pond, spread wide beneath the hardwood-cloaked ridges of Russell Mountain. (Fifty years ago this 2,424-foot knob, now trailless, sported two ski trails, a shelter, and an observation tower.) This is a lovely picnic spot for two or three pond-hikers. The first to arrive can lay claim to a nice rock seat set just back from the shore. The happy shouts of swimmers carry across the water but seem far removed. On summer evenings a haze of campfire smoke hangs over the distant trees. You might see an angler drift silently by in a rowboat or canoe.

This easy hike can be extended to another picnic spot at the hidden outlet cove of the pond. Returning to the snowmobile trail, turn right, cross the bridge, and enjoy a level walk through hardwood forest. In 100 yards you curve right to follow the SW shore behind a veil of leaves. Soon the trail dips and curls right to a clearing beside the outlet at Russell Pond Brook. Once the site of a lean-to, this is now as remote a place as Russell Pond has to offer. Of the several rock seats, the best is a truncated pyramid that stands sentinel beside the outlet.

*Evening at Russell Pond*

Across the brook the snowmobile trail turns left on an old road to drop to the Pemigewasset valley. Your route, however, is to retrace your steps to the campground, with most of the 140-foot rise accomplished in one short stretch.

*Winter:* Tripoli Road and Russell Pond Road are unplowed snowmobile routes. The ski or snowshoe trek to the pond is an 8-mile round-trip with 950 feet of climbing. Park near the gate 0.3 mile from I-93. Exploring the snowy pond is a pleasure on a fine winter day, with a surprise view of Mount Moosilauke from the NE corner. Avoid the ice around the outlet by Russell Pond Brook.

# CHAPTER 18

# LITTLE EAST POND AND EAST POND

◆

**Location:** South side of Scar Ridge
**Hiking Facts:** 5-mile loop, 1,000-foot vertical rise, moderate
**Maps:** USGS 7½' Mt. Osceola and Waterville Valley

|  | Little East Pond | East Pond |
|---|---|---|
| **Area:** | 3 acres | 6.5 acres |
| **Elevation:** | 2,596 feet | 2,580 feet |
| **Avg./Max. Depth:** |  | 16/27 feet |

**Activities:** Little East, hiking; East, hiking, fishing (brook trout), swimming, picnicking

---

◆

Tucked into separate 2,600-foot pockets beneath wild Scar Ridge, the two East Ponds present contrasting types of beauty. Little East Pond is a quiet wilderness spot with shallow water, densely grown shores, and relatively few visitors. East Pond, a popular destination, is an open expanse of clear, deep water with rocky shores. Each pond has had its own trail for many years, but a recently cut path has linked them into a perfect half-day loop hike.

## Access

The trailhead is on the Forest Service's Tripoli Road, which runs 12 miles from Exit 31 off I-93 to Waterville Valley. Heading east from I-93, drive past the spur road left to Russell Pond at 1.8 miles and continue upward over gravel surface to the trailhead at 5.1 miles. Turn left and drive 200 feet up to hiker's parking.

## The Trail To Little East Pond

The East Pond Trail starts with a moderate climb up a gravel road. In 0.3 mile, where the road bears right to end at a clearing, continue ahead on a footpath through weeds and brush. The trail quickly widens into an old road

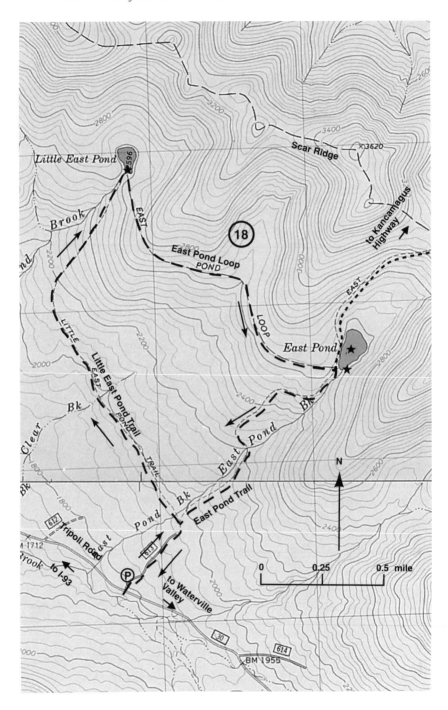

and comes to the junction with Little East Pond Trail at 0.4 mile.

In the woods to your right is the site of the former Tripoli Mill. From 1910 to 1916 a substance known as tripoli, or diatomaceous earth, was dredged from the depths of East Pond and hauled down to this mill for processing. (Tripoli is used as a polishing powder for industrial purposes.) Difficulties in separating impurities forced the Livermore Tripolite Company to close the mill after only six years of operation. Sediment cores taken in 1940 showed that the tripoli deposits are still 6–10 feet thick at the bottom of the pond.

Turn left onto the 1.7 mile-long Little East Pond Trail. (The East Pond Trail ahead will be your return route.) For the next ¾ mile you'll enjoy pleasant walking through open hardwoods on an old logging railroad bed. This was the Woodstock and Thornton Gore Railroad (1909–1914), the shortest-lived of the White Mountain logging lines. The western part of Tripoli Road also follows this railroad bed.

You hop across East Pond Brook near the start of the railroad grade stroll. At 0.7 mile from East Pond Trail you cross Clear Brook in a sharply cut little ravine. The trail bears right, leaving the railroad bed, and climbs at an easy grade, then more steeply as white birches take over the forest. Beneath the canopy is a vigorous growth of young firs that will eventually shade out the sun-loving birches. The terrain flattens as you approach the south shore of the pond, close by the trickling outlet brook. You've reached the end of Little East Pond Trail, 2.1 miles from your car. A sign points right to East Pond, 1.5 miles away via East Pond Loop.

## At Little East Pond

A few feet left of this junction the bushes part for a look at Little East Pond. Step out onto a low rock for the best view. The pond's setting satisfies with its wildness and intimacy. The wooded wall of Scar Ridge (highest summit, 3,774 feet) looms close behind the water, a patchwork of dark, pointed firs and light birch crowns rising to a triumvirate of shaggy peaks.

The pond itself is hemmed in by a dense weave of conifers and a fringe of bog shrubs. The water, dotted with lily pads, is very clear and only a foot or two deep. Local anglers say it's a fishless pond. Depending on water level, there may or may not be room to sit by the shore and enjoy the view. If the water's high, save your lunch for East Pond's open shores. (The one sitting rock at Little East Pond—a flat, sun-warmed beauty near the NE corner—can be reached only via a miserable bushwhack through blow-down and scrubby conifers.)

## East Pond Loop

From the edge of Little East Pond the East Pond Loop leads SE into the woods. Erratically blazed but easy to follow, it contours along the side of Scar Ridge, crossing two southerly spur ridges. The trail gives you an extended look at the varieties of birch-fir-spruce forest that inhabit these 2,600–2,800 foot elevations. There are many little ups and downs, but the walking is pleasant.

About 0.8 mile from Little East Pond you make a long, gradual descent to a dry brook bed. Beyond, you climb gently, then descend gradually through an open area ravaged by blow-down to the junction with East Pond Trail, 3.6 miles into your hike. Cross that trail and angle left on a side trail 100 feet to the open south shore of East Pond.

## At East Pond

The wide view of the pond, backed by a deep forested notch in the Scar Ridge–Mount Osceola ridge line, will exhilarate you after your miles in the woods. The expanse of clear, green-tinted water looks bigger than its listed 6½ acres. Though it's shallow right in front of you, it pitches down to a depth of 27 feet out in the middle. The grassy clearing offers plenty of room for a picnic. Swimming is a possibility, though there are leeches in the pond. Anglers can cast in hopes of luring one of the stocked trout from the deeper waters. If you look closely in the water near the outlet, you'll see the remains of an old rock dam from the Tripoli mining days. The outlet brook flows through a narrow ditch dug by the miners.

Beavers, present in the late 1950s, returned to East Pond in 1992. By engineering a small dam at the outlet they raised the water level and flooded the shoreline rocks that once permitted easy exploration along the east and west shores. If the south shore gets overly crowded, you can still follow East Pond Trail 150 yards north through a tunnel of conifers to short side paths dipping to rocks midway along the west shore. (Beyond, East Pond Trail climbs 500 feet to the col between Scar Ridge and Mount Osceola, then descends to the Kancamagus Highway, 3.7 miles from the pond. The north trailhead is 8.9 miles east of I-93.)

To return to your car, head south on the East Pond Trail for an easy 1.4 miles. You descend moderately on an old wagon road through white birches with thick firs beneath. After about 0.5 mile there's an abrupt transition to northern hardwood forest. The trail continues down and curves left to cross mossy East Pond Brook. After a short rocky stretch, you stroll down the old road at easy grades to the junction with Little East Pond Trail. Keep straight ahead here and you'll soon be back at the newer gravel road that leads down to the parking lot.

*Little East Pond and Scar Ridge*

*Winter:* Since Tripoli Road is not plowed, the best approach is from the Kancamagus Highway on the north. The parking area may be plowed, or there's a roadside pull-off just to the west. This is a good, long snowshoe trip if you do only East Pond (7.4 miles round-trip, 1,900 feet of climbing) or both ponds (10.8 miles, 2,300 feet). Grades are moderate. At East Pond you step into the great wide open on a sunny day. Little East is pure delight in its more accessible winter guise. Save some energy for the climb back over Scar Ridge.

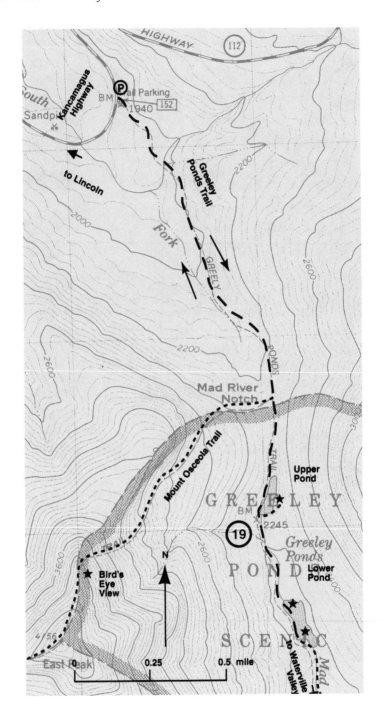

# CHAPTER 19

# GREELEY PONDS

◆

**Location:** Mad River Notch
**Hiking Facts:** 4.4 miles round-trip, 500-foot vertical rise, moderate
**Maps:** USGS 7½' Mount Osceola and Waterville Valley

|  | **Upper Pond** | **Lower Pond** |
|---|---|---|
| **Area:** | 2 acres | 3 acres |
| **Elevation:** | 2,245 feet | 2,180 feet |
| **Avg./Max. Depth:** | 19/27 feet | 3/4 feet |

**Activities:** Hiking, fishing (brook trout in both ponds), swimming (Upper Pond), picnicking

◆

Set dramatically in the glacial cleft of Mad River Notch, the two Greeley Ponds serve as dark mirrors for the steep faces of Mount Kancamagus (3,728 feet) and Mount Osceola's East Peak (4,156 feet). The deep, jewel-like Upper Pond is hemmed in by high crags and ancient conifers. The Lower Pond, shallow and boggy, bristles with the bleached skeletons of drowned trees. Both ponds offer spectacular shoreline views.

The Greeley Ponds Trail provides a gently graded route to the area from both north and south. Because the ponds are so beautiful and accessible, special care is required to protect them. Camping and fires are not allowed, summer or winter, within the 810-acre Greeley Ponds Scenic Area. A shelter once stood beside Upper Pond, but overuse and abuse prompted the Forest Service to create the scenic preserve in 1964 and to remove the shelter several years later. So, enjoy the ponds for a day trip only, and leave no trace of your visit.

## Access

The Greeley Ponds Trail connects the Kancamagus Highway (NH 112) with Waterville Valley via Mad River Notch. Before construction of "The Kanc," this trail provided trampers with a link between Waterville and the Pemigewasset Wilderness. In 1926 the Parker-Young Company of Lincoln purchased over 22,000 acres in Waterville and contemplated pushing a logging railroad through the notch. With prodding from the Society for the Protection of New Hampshire Forests, the US Forest Service acquired the land in 1928.

The northern approach to the ponds is the shorter and more popular hike. Heading east on the Kancamagus Highway from Lincoln, you'll come to a sign and paved parking area for Greeley Ponds Trail on the right, 9.6 miles from I-93.

## The Trail To Greeley Ponds

The well-worn, yellow-blazed footway leads at once into a deep mixed forest of spruce, fir, and hardwoods. Though the distance is short and the gradient slight, you soon find that this is a mountain trail, with plenty of roots, rocks, and mud. At 0.3 mile you cross two streams of the South Fork of Hancock Branch on handrailed bridges. The trail brushes by a tree-crowned boulder and climbs gradually past the Scenic Area boundary.

You cross trickling rivulets, muddy patches, and strings of bog bridges. The path twists ruggedly along the east side of a shallow ravine; then a left turn at 0.9 mile places you on an old logging road rising steadily southward. You swing right and left to the crest of Mad River Notch (elevation 2,300 feet) at 1.3 miles. The Mount Osceola Trail leaves right amidst open hardwoods, tracing a steep course to the mountain's East Peak. The actual height of land is just beyond the junction, a few yards right of the trail.

You begin a gentle descent as a cross-country ski trail joins on the right. (Bear right here on the return trip.) Just ahead an intriguing fortresslike boulder guards the trail. The cross-country ski trail swerves left as you cut right over a log bridge spanning a small brook. Meandering along a high bank through dark and wild fir woods, you catch a glimmer of water down to your left: Upper Greeley Pond. You're 1.6 miles from your car.

*Alternate Approach:* The longer south link of Greeley Ponds Trail ascends gently to the ponds from the Depot Camp trailhead in Waterville Valley (7.4 miles round-trip, 700-foot vertical rise to visit both ponds). Parts of this route date back to the 1850s, when Waterville Valley innkeeper Nathaniel Greeley developed one of the first trail systems in the mountains. After a short stint on the Livermore Road, this route shadows the dwindling Mad River up the wild valley between Mount Kancamagus and East Osceola.

## At Upper Greeley Pond

If you're coming from the north, steep side paths on your left lead down to a small gravel beach at the NW corner of Upper Pond, with a pretty view south across the water. Southward, the main trail traverses the bank above the west shore through dense evergreens. Down to the left there are glimpses of green-tinted water through the trees.

In 0.1 mile you dip to an opening at the pond's SW edge, with a view across to the cliffs on the west knob of Mount Kancamagus. Turn left on a spur trail that skirts the outlet on weathered logs, runs behind the south shore, and emerges at a grassy clearing and strip of gravel by the SE corner—the old shelter site. This is a popular picnic spot, with a striking view up to the imposing face of East Osceola, scarred by sinuous slides and overrun with tangled forest. A lower northern arm presents a palisade of gloomy cliffs. Far to the right, beyond the pond's north end, a rock-faced spur of Mount Huntington peers over the trees. A necklace of old-growth spruce and fir rims the shore. The stunted conifers don't look their age—perhaps as much as 150 years. Wind and cold and ice make for a hard life in Mad River Notch.

After you've absorbed these vistas, you might consider a dip in the clear, deep water (though there are rumors of leeches) or a cast in hopes of luring a trout. If you want a more secluded picnic spot, follow a path northward through the woods behind the east shore. Bear left at a fork to a mini-beach backed by the weathered roots of two upturned trees. You'll find wide views of water and mountain. (See photo opposite title page.)

## At Lower Greeley Pond

Return to the Greeley Ponds Trail at the SW corner of Upper Pond and turn left (south) towards Lower Pond, 0.3 mile away. The hiking and cross-country ski trails meet three times between the ponds; bear right going south to Lower Pond and left on the return trip. The trail rises slightly, then descends easily through a grove of yellow birch. The woods darken with conifers as you approach the bog north of Lower Pond.

Two short side paths lead left to a clearing of gravel and grass at the NW corner of Lower Pond, a shallow, open body of water. Skeletal snags point skyward from the swampy northern fringe. Across the notch is the misshapen dome of Mount Kancamagus's west knob, backed by a long southerly ridge. This is a nice spot to rest and watch the tree swallows and dragonflies skim over the water.

The main trail heads southward through dense conifer thickets. At 0.5 mile from Upper Pond you swing left into an open stand of white birch. Here the Greeley Ponds Trail bends right, bound for Waterville. A wide side trail left leads down to the gravelly SW shore of Lower Pond. The view north over the water places Mad River Notch into profile. This breezy little beach, with one sitting rock tucked into the trees, is yet another fine picnic spot, and the turnaround point if you've hiked in from the north.

*Bird's-Eye View:* On the way back, ambitious trampers can make a very steep and rugged side trip up the Mount Osceola Trail to a spectacular bird's-eye view of emerald Upper Greeley Pond. A ledgy slide at about 3,700 feet provides this dizzying down-look, 1.1 mile and 1,400 feet above Mad River Notch. The slide also opens distant eastern views on either side of Mount Kancamagus.

*Winter:* This is a very popular trip on snowshoes or skis from either end of the trail. The ski trail (blue diamonds) and hiking trail (yellow blazes) merge and split several times. The Kancamagus Highway end of the ski trail begins 0.2 mile west of the hiking trailhead; parking for both, as well as for Depot Camp on the south, is usually plowed. Both ponds rate high on the scenery meter in winter, with dramatic views of Mad River Notch. Be wary of weak ice around outlets and inlets, and at the boggy north end of Lower Pond. The SE corner of Lower Pond, sunny and somewhat sheltered from the notch's biting winds, makes a nice lunch stop.

◆

# SANDWICH NOTCH ROAD

The next five pond explorations are accessed by the Sandwich Notch Road, which runs 11 miles from NH 49 between Campton and Waterville Valley to NH 113 in Center Sandwich. Its west end, the most convenient approach, leaves the right (east) side of NH 49 4.1 miles from Exit 28 off I-93. The Sandwich Notch Road, mostly gravel, is very narrow, steep, and rough, with several white-knuckle pitches. Don't count on going much faster than 15 mph. The ponds along the road are described from west to east.

The road was originally built in 1803, and at one time more than 40 homes were located along its length. By the Civil War most of the houses and hill farms had been abandoned. The land has long since reverted to forest, though cellar holes, stone walls, and cemeteries can still be found. The National Forest acquired most of the land in Sandwich Notch in 1981. The road is maintained in its somewhat primitive state to discourage through traffic.

# CHAPTER 20

# ATWOOD POND

———◆———

**Location:** NW of Sandwich Notch
**Hiking Facts:** 0.3 mile round-trip, 50-foot vertical rise (outbound), easy
**Map:** USGS 7½' Waterville Valley
**Area:** 2 acres **Elevation:** 1,500 feet
**Avg./Max. Depth:** 9/15 feet
**Activities:** Hiking, fishing (brook trout), picnicking

———◆———

Atwood Pond, named for an early settler in the region, is a small but respectably deep beaver pond just off the Sandwich Notch Road. A very short walk down from the road brings you to a broad ledge beside the boggy little pond. It's a nice spot for a picnic or quiet interlude and, towards dusk, a front-row seat for observing the Atwood Pond beavers.

## Access
The unmarked path leaves at a small pull-off on the left (NE) side of Sandwich Notch Road 1.7 miles from NH 49 and 0.2 mile past the Grafton/Carroll county line, at the top of a steep grade. The rough parking slot is bordered by several boulders; other small turnouts can be found a short distance in either direction along the road.

## The Trail To Atwood Pond
The path starts as an old wood road running gently downhill through the woods. In 0.1 mile it flattens and ends at a bushy swamp. A well-worn path leads a few yards right to a clearing beneath a pair of towering white pines and lesser spruces. Several paths fan out from the opening; the middle two lead 200 feet to a glacier-scratched outcrop that slopes gently into the water.

## At Atwood Pond
From this perch you see that the dark and diminutive pond is rimmed by spruce, pine, and birch, with a shrubby meadow at its south end. It's a simple

and peaceful wooded setting, with no high mountains in sight.

With quiet and luck, you may spot a beaver cutting a V-shaped wake through the murky water. Even if none of the toothy rodents makes an appearance, there's plenty of beaver sign evident. Look for the brushy dam that holds back the outlet cove to your left, and the lodge—a muddy heap of sticks—that rises across the pond. On a red-letter day you might even spy a moose.

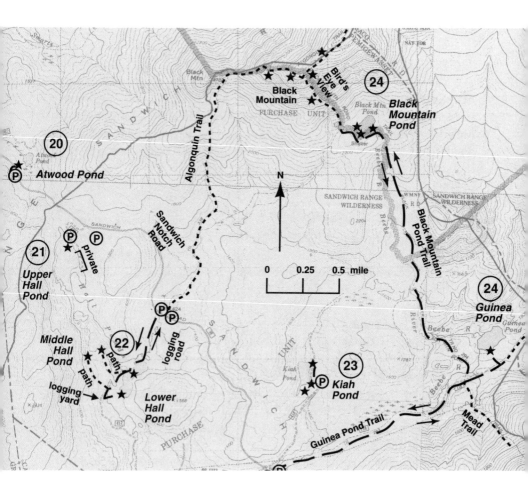

# CHAPTER 21

# UPPER HALL POND

◆

**Location:** Sandwich Notch
**Hiking Facts:** Roadside
**Map:** USGS 7½' Squam Mountains (Page118)
**Area:** 24 acres   **Elevation:** 1,580 feet
**Avg./Max. Depth:** 19/39 feet
**Activities:** Fishing (brook trout, fly-fishing only), canoeing

◆

The largest of the trio of Hall Ponds, Upper Hall shimmers beneath steep wooded slopes just SW of the height-of-land in Sandwich Notch. This deep and attractive water body is an excellent trout pond frequented primarily by fly-fishing enthusiasts. It is also known as Sandwich Pond.

## Access
Upper Hall Pond is accessed via a short, steep gravel spur road off Sandwich Notch Road. Coming from the west end of the Notch Road, the unmarked side road departs right 2.3 miles from NH 49. It makes a curving descent of 0.2 mile and 120 vertical feet to a 10-vehicle parking area at the NE corner of the pond. This side road is subject to occasional washouts.

## At Upper Hall Pond
There's a primitive boat launch with a broad view south down the pond. The massive wooded humps looming above the western shore—part of a northern spur of the low Campton Mountain–Mount Weetamoo range—lend a rugged cast to the scene.

Inveterate pond-walkers can fashion a mini-hike by parking at a pull-off on the south side of the Notch Road 0.1 mile east of the junction with the side road. The walk down to the shore is a 0.6 mile round-trip with a 120-foot climb on the way back. Though the side road continues along the pond's east shore, it soon crosses onto posted land. (The road leads to a private camp.) The swamp at the pond's north end bars access to the west

119

*Evening at Upper Hall Pond*

shore, so your exploration afoot is limited.

With a canoe or rowboat you can reach a tiny rock island near the pond's SW corner. The island's flat ledges make a terrific picnic spot and offer a unique view of Black Mountain, the humpy southern shoulder of Sandwich Mountain.

*Bird's-Eye View:* Upper Hall is one of five Sandwich Notch ponds seen in the excellent bird's-eye view along the Algonquin Trail atop ledgy Black Mountain.

*Winter:* From NH 49 Sandwich Notch Road is plowed for 1 mile to a barn, where limited parking is available through the landowner's courtesy. From here the road is a popular snowmobile route, as is the side road to Upper Hall. If you ski or walk to Upper Hall, the short side trip to Atwood Pond is worthwhile en route. Out on Upper Hall you can visit the little rock island and enjoy views of Black Mountain. If the ice is solid you can explore a rocky cove along the brook to the south.

# CHAPTER 22

# LOWER AND MIDDLE HALL PONDS

◆

**Location:** Sandwich Notch
**Hiking Facts:** 2.5 miles round-trip (est.), 150-foot vertical rise, moderate
**Map:** USGS 7½' Squam Mountains (Page 118)

|  | Lower Hall Pond | Middle Hall Pond |
|---|---|---|
| **Area:** | 15 acres | 5 acres |
| **Elevation:** | 1,380 feet | 1,460 feet |
| **Avg./Max. Depth:** | 3/5 feet | 30/56 feet |

**Activities:** Hiking, fishing (brook trout in both ponds), picnicking

◆

This pond exploration takes you along unmarked logging roads and anglers' paths to a pair of pretty ponds in the Sandwich Notch forest. Distances to the Halls are short and climbing is minimal, but there are no signs or blazes to show the way, and the routes may be obscure. This is not a trip for the casual or inexperienced hiker. The USGS Squam Mountains topo map is essential.

Lower Hall is a shallow elbow of water whose west shore provides an interesting view of Sandwich Mountain. Middle Hall, small and surprisingly deep, is a secluded pocket hemmed in by steep wooded slopes. Both ponds offer trout fishing and are visited primarily by anglers.

## Access
Take the Sandwich Notch Road east from NH 49. At 2.6 miles you reach the notch high point, elevation 1,776 feet. In another 0.7 mile the forest opens to reveal a white house on the right—the nineteenth-century homestead of the Hall family, for whom the ponds were named. Just beyond, a logging road (shown on the USGS map) leads right into the woods. This is the starting point for your hike. Park here or drive a short distance ahead over a one-lane bridge and seek a parking spot

where you can pull safely off the road. There's room for several cars at the start of the Algonquin Trail, 0.1 mile beyond the bridge.

## Lower Hall Pond

Walk back across the bridge and follow the old logging road south (left) from the Notch Road into a dark stand of conifers. You dip to cross a small brook and climb a rough, eroded stretch. The road levels, then descends to approach a recently clear-cut slope on the right. Where the road splits, take either muddy, overgrown fork for 200 feet to a grassy clearing and another fork, 0.4 mile from the Notch Road. The water of Lower Hall Pond can be seen down through the trees on your left.

For a first look at the pond, follow the left-branching path 150 feet downhill to an opening at a cove on the NE shore. Step out onto a weathered old log for a pretty view south through the crook in the pond. This is a good fishing and birding spot on this shrubby, less-visited shore.

Climb back to the clearing and turn sharp left (west) and downhill. This slash-strewn skid road drops and then runs level along the base of the clear-cut. In 0.1 mile the road bends left to cross the brook that drains from Middle to Lower Hall Pond. Beyond the brook you swing right through a hardwood grove, then a short leftward pitch through berry growth lifts you to a T-intersection with an older logging road, 0.6 mile from the Notch Road.

Turn left and follow this road into an open logging yard. Cross the clearing to its far left corner and turn 90° degrees left on a rocky spur road blocked by a bulldozed mound and a trio of boulders. (The main road continues ahead, eventually joining the Beebe River Road. This gravel road—a popular access for backwoods anglers—was reopened by the Forest Service in 1992 following logging operations. It is passable as far as the logging yard for four-wheel-drive vehicles with high clearance.)

You meander through a hemlock grove, scoot down a steep little pitch, and emerge on the shady west shore of Lower Hall for a view of Sandwich Mountain rising immensely over the water. The ledgy, lumpy mass on the left is Black Mountain, a southern shoulder; the true summit (3,993 feet) peers over on the right. Low rock seats invite you to rest awhile. The vista is especially fine in slanting evening light, a good time to spot a moose knee-deep out in the pond.

## Middle Hall Pond

This backwoods beauty, set in a forested bowl a half mile NW of Lower Hall Pond, is accessible only by a pair of dim, unmarked anglers' paths. One begins at the right fork of the T-intersection noted above, 0.6 mile from the Notch Road. The path follows this road to its end, then parallels a dry brook bed a short distance and crosses it 0.1 mile from the junction. In another 0.1 mile it runs across another brook bed with mossy ledges up on the left. Here the path turns sharply right and rises gently through dense growth to a clearing by the SW corner of Middle Hall Pond at 0.3 mile. A wet ledge offers a fishing perch and a good view across the water.

The other path leaves the aforementioned skid road between the Lower Hall Pond viewpoints where, heading in from the Notch Road, it curves left to cross the brook that connects the ponds. This obscure and overgrown path—one step removed from a bushwhack—shadows the stream for 0.3 mile to the SE corner of Middle Hall. After crossing a small brook bed near the start, the path stays on the east side of the outlet brook for 0.1 mile, then crosses and follows the west side the rest of the way. A sloping ledge tucked away in the outlet cove provides a fine view of the pond and the steep wooded humps of Mount Weetamoo looming over the west shore. Other rocks to the left offer a wider view. The shallow water here belies the amazing 56-foot depth in the center of the pond.

*Winter:* From the side road to Upper Hall Pond (see above), you can continue along the snowmobile-packed Notch Road and follow the route described above to Lower and Middle Hall. Each is a delightful winter destination. Snowmobiles sometimes follow the summer four-wheel-drive road into Lower Hall, but Middle Hall is usually free of them. A ski or snowshoe trek to all three Halls from the end of the plowed section of the Notch Road is about 7 miles round-trip with 800 feet of climbing.

# CHAPTER 23

# KIAH POND

◆

**Location:** East of Sandwich Notch
**Hiking Facts:** Roadside
**Map:** USGS 7½' Squam Mountains (Page 118)
**Area:** 6 acres **Elevation:** 1,420 feet
**Avg./Max. Depth:** 12/18 feet
**Activities:** Fishing (brook trout), canoeing, picnicking

◆

A small, rectangular sheet of water in the shadow of Sandwich Mountain, Kiah Pond is one of the more remote road-accessible ponds in the White Mountains. Kiah has limited potential for hiking, but it's a popular (if unofficial) camping area and fishing spot. If you're hiking to nearby Guinea and Black Mountain Ponds, it's worth the short drive up the side road for a look at this pretty pond before you head home.

## Access
The unmarked gravel spur road to Kiah Pond leaves the NE side of Sandwich Notch Road at a crossroads 4.9 miles east of NH 49 and 5.8 miles west of Center Sandwich. Coming from the west end of the Notch Road, the Kiah Pond spur leaves left at the bottom of a steep hill, between a powerline crossing and a bridge over Beebe River. (The trailhead for Guinea Pond Trail is just beyond.)

Peppered with potholes and protruding stones, the gently rising 0.7 mile spur road is slow going but sound and passable for conventional vehicles. It crosses the stony, trickling outlet brook just before reaching the pond. If you're uncertain about your vehicle's clearance, park on the left before the brook crossing. Otherwise, drive across to a 10-car parking area beside the pond's SE corner and a rough boat launch.

## At Kiah Pond
The spur road continues along the east shore beyond a line of boulders that

*Kiah Pond*

blocks vehicular access. (It ends 0.7 mile north at a desolate, stump-dotted beaver pond.) On summer weekends this shore becomes a miniature tent city. Kiah Pond was a busy spot in the 1800s, too, when a sawmill and several subsistence farms sprang up in the area around what was then called Currier's Pond. "Kiah" (pronounced with a long i) is merely a Yankee interpretation of "Currier," the name of an early landowner in the area.

The best views of Kiah Pond are found along the south shore. From a campsite on the south side of the outlet brook an anglers' path leads to an assemblage of boulders near the outlet. One is a perfect flat-topped picnic rock with a broad view of the pond and part of Black Mountain. Farther west along the stony shore there are striking vistas of ledgy Black Mountain and Sandwich Mountain's dark dome looming over the pond.

*Bird's-Eye View:* Kiah Pond is especially beautiful when viewed from the ledges of Black Mountain along the Algonquin Trail and the upper Black Mountain Pond Trail.

*Winter:* This is a scenic sideshow on an excursion to Guinea and Black Mountain Ponds from the east end of the Notch Road. Great views of Sandwich Mountain.

# CHAPTER 24

# GUINEA AND BLACK MOUNTAIN PONDS

◆

**Location:** East of Sandwich Notch

**Hiking Facts:** 8.8 miles round-trip, 900-foot vertical rise, moderate; add 2.4 miles, 1,100 vertical feet for Black Mountain

**Maps:** USGS 7½' Squam Mountains, Center Sandwich, Waterville Valley (Page 118)

|  | Guinea Pond | Black Mountain Pond |
|---|---|---|
| **Area:** | 10 acres | 6 acres |
| **Elevation:** | 1,450 feet | 2,220 feet |
| **Avg./Max. Depth:** | 5.5/22 feet | 9.5/32 feet |

**Activities:** Hiking, fishing (brook trout in both ponds), birding, picnicking, swimming (Black Mountain Pond)

---

◆

---

The object of this quest in the Sandwich Range wilds is Black Mountain Pond, an oval of sparkling clear water guarded by the ledgy 1,000-foot wall of Black Mountain. The fairly long but relatively easy hike to Black Mountain Pond can be broken up with a short side trip for a look at boggy Guinea Pond, with its rich bird life and interesting view of Sandwich Mountain.

If your legs are springy and your wind is sound, you can also tackle the rugged ascent to the ledges atop Black Mountain, the higher of two peaks bearing that name on the SW ridge of Sandwich Mountain. The outlooks grant wide distant views and a sensational *bird's-eye view* of Black Mountain Pond at your feet. There is a shelter near the shore of Black Mountain Pond, but it is likely to be removed by the Forest Service in the near future. Camping at this pond is discouraged because of overuse in recent years.

## Access

The hike starts at the SW end of Guinea Pond Trail, marked by a WMNF sign on the NE side of Sandwich Notch Road just south of the bridge over Beebe River. The trailhead is 4.9 miles from NH 49 and 5.8 miles from NH 113. Parking is limited and rough; an alternative is to park on the shoulder at the crossroads just north of the bridge, where the Notch Road meets the Beebe River Road (west) and the road to Kiah Pond (east).

### The Trail To Guinea Pond

From the trailhead sign, walk uphill on a rough road past a metal gate and under a power line. The trail picks up the grade of the former Beebe River logging railroad, providing easy walking through second-growth hardwoods. In 0.8 mile you emerge in an interesting area of open, brushy swampland, humming with bird and insect life. Birders will find a variety of warblers and flycatchers here in early summer. You skirt pools of water astride the trail and pass an open metal gate at 1.2 miles, with a view of Sandwich Mountain left.

At 1.3 miles a bypass splits right into the woods to circumvent a beaver-flooded section of the railroad grade. The bypass rejoins the grade at 1.6 miles, and 100 feet beyond the Mead Trail leaves right for Mount Israel at a trail sign. The Black Mountain Pond Trail leaves 20 feet farther, on the left. Note this spot and continue ahead towards Guinea Pond.

You quickly come to a pair of potentially difficult brook crossings that can be bypassed on a side path right, then a third crossing eased by step stones. Just beyond, a sign on the left announces the side trail to Guinea Pond at 1.8 miles. Mucky in spots, this 0.2 mile path winds through mixed woods and hooks right to the SE edge of the swampy pond.

### At Guinea Pond

Bear left where the path divides near the shore (the right fork leads to a campsite) and scramble over logs and step stones to a viewpoint among the bog shrubs at the water's edge. Across the pond the long, dark ridge of Sandwich Mountain fills the horizon, with the ledge-studded mass of Black Mountain on the left and the highest summit in the center. It's a pretty view, though there are no seats in front of this scenic stage.

Look for black ducks, wood ducks, or hooded mergansers out on the pond, or a belted kingfisher scouting for a finny meal. Yellowthroats, cedar waxwings, and many other songbirds call from the shrubs and woods around the pond. Beaver may be found here (look for a lodge on the south shore), and moose occasionally stroll through the area. Devoted anglers and pond-explorers can follow an obscure path leading NE behind the shore, starting at the aforementioned campsite. It meanders to another clearing near the pond's NE corner, whence a path leads to a shoreline opening and a rooty seat between a spruce and a pine. This breezy, shady perch has a wide, watery view and is perhaps the nicest spot at Guinea Pond.

## The Trail To Black Mountain Pond

Walk back to the Guinea Pond Trail and turn right to backtrack 0.2 mile to the Black Mountain Pond Trail. Turn right at the sign for this path. It dips down through hobblebush to a yellow diamond marker, then makes a creative crossing of the Beebe River on stones and logs. You climb at easy grades, following a recent relocation around a muddy section.

The trail, blazed in yellow, angles left and climbs beside the rocky, cascading brook, crossing to the right where the stream drains from an abandoned beaver swamp. You wind past a weedy meadow where I once stirred up a bear, no doubt feasting on August berries. The brook reappears on the left and leads you into the Sandwich Range Wilderness.

The trail climbs past a beaver pond on the left and crosses a mucky shelf now mostly spanned with bog bridges. Switchbacks guide you up through drier spruce woods. After traversing another muddy flat you angle left to cross the infant Beebe River, then climb over a spruce-covered knoll to a

*Black Mountain Pond*

fork in the trail near Black Mountain Pond, 2.4 miles from the Guinea Pond Trail.

## At Black Mountain Pond

The left fork leads to the shelter, but the best views of the pond and Black Mountain are found on the right-branching path, which descends 150 feet to an open, heavily camped spruce grove behind the SE shore. A few feet left a low ledgy seat opens a vista across the shimmering water to the imposing hulk of Black Mountain. The mountain wall is clothed in birches that turn to a tapestry of gold in late September. (Studies suggest that this birch forest sprang up after a fire or landslide in the 1800s or resulted from constant soil instability on the steep slope.) This shoreline opening, which basks in mid-afternoon sun, is a good picnic spot and is perhaps the best swimming locale at the pond. The water is cool and crystal-clear.

From a second point 100 feet to the right you can, water level permitting, hop across logs, rocks, and roots to an apron of ledge fringing a small, shrubby island. Rock perches on either side offer good sun exposure and wide, exhilarating views of water and mountain.

Beavers once held forth here, as evidenced by old lodges at the pond's north end. Good trout fishing is found at Black Mountain Pond, courtesy of stocking by the state. Some anglers pack in portable rafts to access the deep channel in the middle.

Climb back up to the main trail and turn right. There is a bewildering web of unblazed beaten paths between here and the lean-to; all are overgrown to some extent. Some lead to spruce groves that have been hacked and pounded by inconsiderate campers. (Because of the overuse the Forest Service will probably remove the shelter and prohibit camping in the area.)

When you find your way there, you'll see that the shelter is nicely situated above the shore at the SE corner, with a partial view of the pond. A path leads down to shoreline rocks and a wide watery view to a darkly wooded arm of Sandwich Mountain.

Black Mountain Pond was privately owned until the estate of George L. Mead donated a 2,443-acre tract to the Forest Service in 1950. The trail was opened in the early 1950s; it originally led around the east shore to an earlier shelter. In the mid-1960s the trail was relocated to the pond's west side and the present shelter was built.

Beyond the lean-to the Black Mountain Pond Trail bears right and skirts the SW shore through dense growth, then dips to the gurgling inlet brook. A few steps right a secluded rock seat offers another pretty view. A line of rocks crowds the NW shore, pressed there by expanding winter ice. Continue farther only if you're ready to take on the challenge of Black Mountain.

## Black Mountain

The fabulous views atop the Black Mountain ledges are earned with a climb of 1,100 feet in a very steep mile. The assault commences after you pass a pool on the right and a beaver meadow on the left. The trail twists and turns skyward through wild woods of birch, spruce, and fir. There are rocky scrambles and expanding views of Sandwich Notch and the Lakes Region. At about 0.8 mile there's a fine outlook on the left with your first glimpse down at the pond.

At 1.1 miles above the shelter you crest the ridge and meet the Algonquin Trail. Turn right here for a short climb to an outlook ledge with a matchless *bird's-eye view* almost straight down at Black Mountain Pond. Arrayed in a wide arc behind Black Mountain Pond are four other Sandwich Notch ponds: Guinea, Kiah (especially scenic), Lower Hall, and Upper Hall. Lake Winnipesauke and a dozen or more other water bodies can be seen in the distance, along with many mountains to east, south, and west. Walk 0.2 mile north along the scrubby ridge for views north and west from ledges on the left of the trail.

To return to your car, you can retrace your steps past Black Mountain Pond (5.1 miles) or descend the rugged but very scenic Algonquin Trail for 2.9 miles and walk 1.5 miles back on the Sandwich Notch Road.

*Winter:* Guinea Pond is more accessible in winter and offers views of Sandwich Mountain and Mount Israel. Set beneath snowy ledges, Black Mountain Pond provides dramatic scenery and a feeling of great remoteness. On the east the Notch Road is plowed to the side road to Mead Base Camp, 2.6 miles from NH 113. The Notch Road can be walked or skied 3.2 miles to the Guinea Pond Trail (used by snowmobiles), from which it is 2 miles to Guinea Pond or 4 miles to Black Mountain Pond (a long day).

# CHAPTER 25

# FLAT MOUNTAIN POND

◆

**Location:** Sandwich Range Wilderness
**Hiking Facts:** 11.2 miles round-trip, 1,200-foot vertical rise, more difficult
**Map:** USGS 7½' Mount Tripyramid
**Area:** 30 acres   **Elevation:** 2,320 feet
**Avg./Max. Depth:** 5/18 feet
**Activities:** Hiking, camping (lean-to), fishing (brook trout), picnicking

◆

In one of the least inspired episodes of White Mountain nomenclature, the name "Flat Mountain" was bestowed upon two neighboring summits in the Sandwich Range. The northern Flat Mountain (3,331 feet) is a long ridge connecting Sandwich Mountain with the Sleeper Ridge between Mounts Tripyramid and Whiteface. The southern Flat Mountain (2,940 feet) is a nondescript hump in the town of Sandwich. Their summits are only two miles apart in a less-known corner of the Sandwich Range Wilderness.

Both Flat Mountains are heavily wooded, trailless, and seldom climbed, but snuggled into the saddle between them is their namesake pond, one of the most interesting in the region. It has been accessible by trail since the 1860s. Actually, there were once two Flat Mountain Ponds (three, by some counts). A small dam built in the 1960s raised the water level and linked the pair with a narrow strait, forming a ¾-mile swath of water.

The Flat Mountain Pond Trail traces a 10½-mile horseshoe around the pond, with termini two miles apart by road. The more popular western leg (the route described here) follows the bed of the World War I–vintage Beebe River logging railroad. The eastern link penetrates deep into the Sandwich Range Wilderness up the valley of Whiteface River. Either is an attractive, leg-stretching woods walk at temperate grades. The pond is a backcountry delight, with a shelter at its south end and various views to Mount Tripyramid, Mount Whiteface, and Sandwich Mountain. The trail runs along the length of its west shore, traversing a pretty white birch forest that sprouted in the wake of a disastrous 1923 fire. Plan a full day for a visit to Flat Mountain Pond.

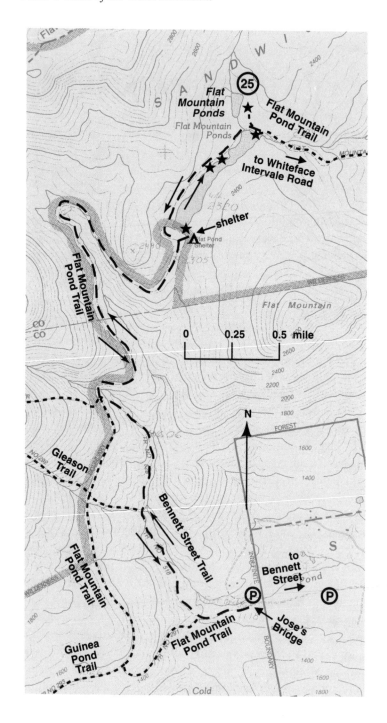

**Access**

From Center Sandwich, drive 3.6 miles north on NH 113. Keep straight (north) on NH 113A where NH 113 bears right (east). In 2.9 miles turn left on Whiteface Intervale Road and left again on Bennett Street in less than 0.1 mile. In 1.7 miles bear left at a fork, where the road becomes rougher. In another 0.5 mile there's a National Forest parking area and kiosk with Wonalancet Outdoor Club information on the left. The west leg of Flat Mountain Pond Trail begins beyond the gate.

**The Trail To Flat Mountain Pond**

From the kiosk, walk along the gravel road beyond the gate, paralleling bouldery Pond Brook. In 0.5 mile you come to a signed fork in a clearing. The Flat Mountain Pond Trail continues on the road, but here you can take a scenic shortcut on Bennett Street Trail, saving 0.5 mile each way. Bear right into the woods on the blue-blazed footpath, entering the National Forest.

The path pursues a pleasant course through hemlock groves and beech woods beside Pond Brook. You cross several small brooks, and at 1.1 miles Gleason Trail splits left. Bennett Street Trail proceeds on a rougher footway along the brook bank. At 1.6 miles you pass Great Falls, a pretty cascade and pool set in a rocky glen. After crossing a tributary, the trail bears left and climbs more steeply up a ravine, recrossing the branch brook and coming back to Flat Mountain Pond Trail at 2.1 miles.

Turn right here and hop over the brook a third time by some small cascades. From here to the pond, 2.4 miles ahead, you stride easily up the old railroad grade. The woods, adorned with many white birches, are pretty, but they're far removed from the virgin conifer forest that was cited as the "chief charm" of the area by the 1916 AMC guidebook.

Within a few years those woods would be virgin no more. As C. Francis Belcher recounts in *Logging Railroads of the White Mountains*, World War I had pushed demand and prices for lumber skyward, prompting the Woodstock Lumber and Parker-Young Companies to lay the 22-mile Beebe River line into these wilds. This logging railroad was the last of its kind in the White Mountains. (J.E. Henry's crews had already been decimating the Pemigewasset Wilderness for a quarter century.) Completed in 1918, it featured state-of-the-art engineering, including over twenty trestles and a unique hairpin turn on the approach to the ponds.

In between five-a-day lumber trains, the railroad occasionally ran excursion trips for sightseers. In 1921 a throng of 270 enjoyed a day's outing to Flat Mountain Pond aboard a specially outfitted train. Upon returning to Beebe River they let out three cheers for their gracious lumber company hosts.

There were no hurrahs two years later when 3,500 acres around the pond were scorched by fire, presumably sparked in the slash by cinders from a locomotive engine. The blaze was watched by thousands of summer visitors in the Lakes Region to the south and was widely covered in the media. It cost the life of one firefighter, who was found with this grim note pinned to his coat: "John Gray died July 13." The disastrous fire and the ensuing public outcry ended the glory days of the Beebe River railroad, though sections were in use sporadically until 1942. The white birches near and around the pond— "pioneer" trees quick to grow up after a disturbance— are a visible legacy of the 1923 fire.

After three more brook crossings, the Flat Mountain Pond Trail makes that remarkable hairpin turn by a small beaver pond, 1.4 miles from Bennett Street Trail. Beyond this disorienting bend SE, the trail curves left and northward again. Look for old rails underfoot as you amble through corridors of birches. The outlet brook appears on the right as you make the final approach to the pond.

*Alternate Approach:* The eastern link of Flat Mountain Pond Trail starts on Whiteface Intervale Road 0.3 mile beyond Bennett Street. It traverses a series of logging roads, passes a view of Mount Whiteface at 0.9 mile, follows a delightful path along Whiteface River for nearly 2 miles, and climbs to the north end of the pond at 4.2 miles. The round-trip, including a full traverse of the pond, is 10.6 miles with a 1,400-foot vertical rise.

## At Flat Mountain Pond

Approaching on the western link, 4.5 miles from your car you come to a four-way junction. Ahead, the railroad grade sinks into flooded shrubs. The path on the left is the northward continuation of Flat Mountain Pond Trail, but first turn right on a short spur path to the open-front shelter, set atop a grassy knoll overlooking the south half of the pond. The lawn in front of the lean-to is a fine picnic spot. The peaceful view includes the northern Flat Mountain on the left and the dark crest of South Tripyramid (4,100 feet) peering over a ridge far to the north. With a close look you can spot the top of Tripyramid's famous South Slide. The wooded dome to the right is West Sleeper (3,881 feet). A wider and more secluded version of this view can be enjoyed from a shoreside rock reached by a side path from the shelter clearing.

To capture the full wilderness flavor of Flat Mountain Pond, return to the crossroads and walk across the railroad grade. In 50 feet bear right where an unofficial path splits left and uphill. The Flat Mountain Pond Trail, now a narrow footpath, circles the pond's SW corner. You meander behind the irregular, bushy west shore through ethereal birch groves carpeted with lacy ferns. You look across to the southern Flat Mountain. The footway becomes rough and obscure as you traverse a bouldery slope above the pond.

A short, rocky descent to the right drops you near the water beside a giant boulder. You can scramble (carefully) to the top of this commanding, sun-struck perch to capture a fine view of the pond stretching away to the right. Hunch-shouldered Mount Whiteface (4,020 feet) rises on the left beyond the strait connecting the two parts of the pond.

Beyond a jumble of boulders, the trail tracks northward behind the shore. The way is obscure and mucky in places. You pass a sloping rock with a watery view south and skirt a finger-like cove. Then you swing left to rejoin the railroad grade, which runs close beside the northern pool of Flat Mountain Pond—a deeper and quieter 10-acre oval of water.

At the NW corner, 1.1 miles from the shelter, a rock-hop across the inlet brook places you at a T intersection where old railroad grades run left and right. The left spur was once part of a long-abandoned trail to Waterville Valley via Lost Pass, the remote cut between the northern Flat Mountain and Sleeper Ridge. In 100 yards this spur leads to an open beaver meadow with an interesting view up to Flat Mountain.

The right-hand turn is the eastern leg of Flat Mountain Pond Trail. In several hundred feet you'll come to a clearing on the right with a lovely vista SW over the water to the darkly etched ridge of Sandwich Mountain. Small rock seats invite you to linger awhile at this shady wilderness outpost before retracing your steps to your car.

*Bird's-Eye view:* Climb the steep Blueberry Ledge Trail from Wonalancet to the open smooth summit of Mount Whiteface—7.8 miles round-trip, a 2,900-foot climb. A ledge 0.2 mile below the top looks across the great south cliff to Flat Mountain Pond snaking through the forest below Sandwich Mountain. Many other lakes and ponds can be seen to the south.

*Winter:* The western link of the trail is used by hikers, cross-country skiers, and snowmobilers. Grades are generally easy, though some of the brook crossings are steep. Parking is available at the fork 0.7 mile east of Jose's Bridge. The trail's eastern leg is less often used and has limited roadside parking. The ¾-mile traverse of the pond is exhilarating, with good views of Sandwich Mountain and Mount Whiteface. Beware of soft ice at the far north end and near the dam at the southern outlet.

# CHAPTER 26

# HERON POND (LONELY LAKE)

◆

**Location:** South of Mount Chocorua
**Hiking Facts:** 2 miles round-trip, 200-foot vertical rise, easy
**Maps:** USGS 7½' Silver Lake and Mount Chocorua
**Area:** 8 acres  **Elevation:** 630 feet
**Activities:** Hiking, picnicking; swimming, canoeing, warm-water fishing at
   Chocorua Lake

◆

*A scrap of mist which trailed over the forest just at the
foot of one of the ridges of Chocorua was the spirit of a
lonely lake rising to do homage to the day-star.*
—Frank Bolles
*At the North of Bearcamp Water,* 1893

The memory of Frank Bolles, a popular regional nature writer at the turn of
the century, is preserved in a lovely nature reserve in the lowlands south of
Mount Chocorua. Donated to The Nature Conservancy by Mrs. Spencer
(Bolles) Phenix, the Frank Bolles Nature Reserve is one of eight parcels in the
700+ acres of the Chocorua Conservation Lands. These rolling forestlands
NW of Chocorua Lake have many hiking and cross-country ski trails. The
area is managed by the Chocorua Lake Conservation Foundation, formed in
1968 to conserve the Chocorua Lake Basin. Motorized vehicles, fires, and
camping are prohibited.

In the heart of the Bolles Reserve is a glacial kettle pond to which Bolles
devoted an entire chapter, "A Lonely Lake," in his natural history chronicle
of the Chocorua region. He spent many happy hours "learning the secrets
of its tenants." Here he observed bitterns, foxes, muskrats, mink, deer, porcupines, owls, hawks, ducks, schools of tadpoles and horned pout, and the
great blue heron, from which the pond takes its name.

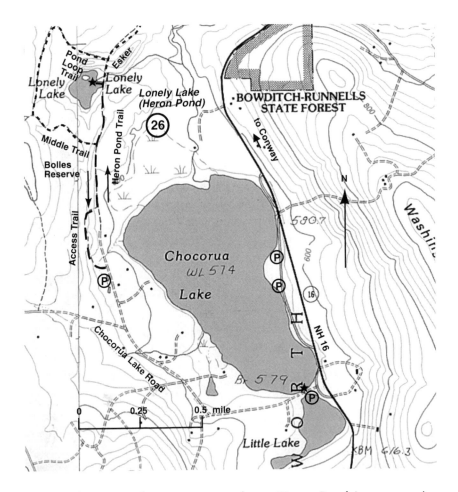

For the twentieth-century nature lover, Heron Pond is an attractive destination in any season. The walk or ski in is short and easy, and the pond, overlooked by Mount Chocorua, is a blessedly peaceful spot amidst a fine forest of oak and pine. Before or after your walk, you can picnic on the breezy south shore of Chocorua Lake and enjoy its famous view of the mountain.

## Access
Ten miles south of Conway, NH 16 runs along the east shore of Chocorua Lake. At the south end of the lake, turn west onto Chocorua Lake Road. This gravel way passes a public picnic area by the lakeshore (see below), crosses a bridge between Chocorua Lake and Little Lake, and leads past summer

homes set amidst great white pines. Bear right at a fork 0.7 mile from NH 16, and right again in another 0.3 mile. Drive 0.2 mile farther to a small parking area for the Bolles Reserve on the left, marked with a yellow sign.

## The Trail To Heron Pond

Marked by surveyor's tape and yellow plastic disks, the trail to Heron Pond crosses a wet spot on bog bridges and climbs easily to a grassy clearing at 0.2 mile. Turn right, following a sign pointing to the Bolles Reserve, descend 200 feet on an old road, and swing right again at a fork marked by an arrow. You meander through young hardwoods and a beech grove, then descend gradually for 0.1 mile to a register. Sign in here, and pick up a copy of the informative leaflet and trail map, "A Guide to the Chocorua Conservation Lands." Up to this point this "Bolles Access Trail" has been on private land, whose owners have graciously permitted access to the Bolles Reserve.

At the register the trail turns left into the Bolles Reserve and becomes the "Heron Pond Trail," following an old road shaded by big red and white pines. It shortly bends left again where a cross-country ski trail to Chocorua Lake (too wet for summer use) departs right. A climb of 0.1 mile leads you to a fork, marked by trail signs nailed to a thick white pine. Bear right onto the Heron Pond Trail.

## At Heron Pond

The right fork leads along a level corridor through young pines, then enters taller conifers rimming the steep slope of the kettle bowl that holds Heron Pond. A gentle 0.1 mile descent places you on a little saddle separating a swampy and much smaller kettle hole on the right from Heron Pond on the left. As the trail curves right to surmount a low ridge, an unmarked but well-trodden side path leaves left. Follow its meander out to a tiny rock-studded beach at the end of a wooded peninsula. A red maple shades this pretty picnic spot with a wide view of the pond. Beyond the oak-rimmed west shore rise the wooded Bickford Heights; at a modest 1,080 feet this is the highest point in the reserve. To your right is a small island crowned with tall white pines. Odd fluctuations in the water level—apparently unrelated to the water table—sometimes join this island to the mainland with a sandy spit. Look for a beaver lodge far to the left, at the south end of the pond.

Spend a quiet hour here, as Frank Bolles often did, and you may acquaint yourself with some of the wild animals that come to the shore to drink or hunt. Fishing at Heron Pond is a cast into the unknown. It is neither stocked nor surveyed by the state. Bolles noted that it was once a "famous" trout pond, but a man who begrudged the pleasures of trout-fishing released horned pout into the water. They went forth and multiplied. In Bolles's day they ranged the pond in "appalling" numbers.

Upon your return to the main trail, a 100-yard side trip left introduces you to another glacial feature of the reserve. A short, steep climb lifts you atop an esker, a sharp, narrow gravel ridge deposited by a stream of meltwater burrowing beneath the glacier. These winding ridges are popular with highway departments for their excellent sand and gravel. The south slope of this protected esker is clothed in open oak woods; the north side bears a dark cloak of hemlock and fir. From here, you can retrace your steps to your car or, using the trail leaflet as a guide, fashion a short loop hike through the woods around the pond or a longer loop over Bickford Heights (limited views).

*Heron Pond*

## Chocorua Lake

A stop at the south end of this 222-acre beauty (elevation 574 feet, maximum depth 28 feet) is a must on the drive in or out. Tall red pines shade the picnic area by the south shore, called "the Grove" on the Conservation Lands map. Swimming, picnicking, and non-motorized boating are welcome; fires and motorboats are not permitted. The view up the lake to Mount Chocorua (3,475 feet) is justly famous and graces many a postcard and calendar. But Chocorua is just one of a rugged wall of mountains that closes in the northern horizon. Left to right, and progessively nearer, you see hunch-shouldered Whiteface (4,020 feet), displaying the landslide that spawned its name; the dark dome of Passaconaway (4,060 feet); the gnarly, lumpy mass of Paugus (3,210 feet); and Chocorua with its familiar rocky pinnacle.

Access to swimming, canoeing, and picnicking along the east shore of the lake is provided by a one-way, north-to-south road off NH 16, 0.7 mile north of Chocorua Lake Road. Anglers can cast for smallmouth bass, chain pickerel, horned pout, yellow perch, and other warm-water species. This area is identified as "The Island" on the Conservation Lands map.

*Bird's-Eye View:* Many trails lead to the summit of Mount Chocorua, where the awe-inspiring panorama includes sparkling Chocorua Lake and a glimpse of Heron Pond, "green as an emerald" in the eyes of Frank Bolles.

*Winter:* This is a popular ski-touring area. Parking by the south or east shore, you can ski across Chocorua Lake, with splendid views, and follow an access cross-country trail from the NW corner to Heron Pond Trail. (Snowshoers are welcome, too, as long as they don't trash the ski tracks.) The SE corner of frozen Heron Pond offers an intimate view of Mount Chocorua's snowy cone and supporting buttresses. The whole trek is only 3–4 miles with little climbing, but note that the big lake can be inhospitable on windy days.

CHAPTER 27

# WHITE LAKE

◆

**Location:** White Lake State Park, Tamworth
**Hiking Facts:** Roadside; loop hike, 2.5 miles, minimal vertical rise, easy
**Map:** USGS 7½' Ossipee Lake
**Area:** 123 acres   **Elevation:** 441 feet
**Avg./Max. Depth:** 20/45 feet
**Activities:** Hiking, swimming, camping, canoeing, birding, fishing (brook
   trout), picnicking

◆

*...a shallow, mirror-like lake in the heart of the plain,*
*framed in snowy sand and gaunt pines.*
—Frank Bolles
*At the North of Bearcamp Water,* 1893

White Lake is not really in the White Mountains; strictly speaking, it would be considered a Lakes Region pond. But it does offer a good view of the Sandwich Range from its sandy shore, and the hiking, swimming, and other attractions at White Lake State Park are outstanding enough to justify a slightly elastic regional boundary.

Veteran New Englanders will find the environs of White Lake reminiscent of the sandy pinewoods of Cape Cod. Like the Cape's ponds, and nearby Heron Pond and Echo Lake, this is a glacial kettle pond. White Lake is set on a broad plateau known to geologists as an out-wash plain. The sandy deposits were laid down by meltwater streams flowing off the continental glacier as it receded northward 12,000 years ago.

The glacier's demise is the pond lover's delight. At White Lake you'll find a wide beach, clear water, and picturesque pine forests around the shore. An easy hiking trail circles the lake. Branch paths lead past interesting bog ponds and through an unusual grove of pitch pines. Although the beach and adjacent campground are often crowded in high summer, you'll

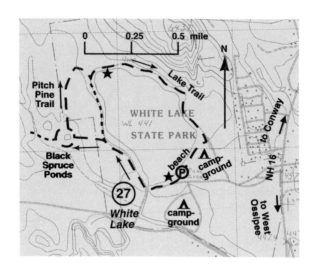

find far fewer people out on the trails. Canoeing and fishing enthusiasts will find White Lake worth a visit, too.

To get the most out of a visit to the park, pick up a copy of Ned Beecher's excellent *Outdoor Explorations in Mt. Washington Valley*. The book devotes two chapters to an interpretive exploration of the area, from which much of the following information was drawn.

## Access

The entrance to White Lake State Park is on the west side of NH 16, 1.1 mile north of its junction with NH 25 at West Ossipee. Bear left at a fork for swimming, hiking, or other day use; bear right for camping registration. Day use rates have been $2.50 per person in-season (Memorial Day to Columbus Day). The road ends in a sandy parking area behind the beach, 0.5 mile from NH 16.

The boat launch at the lake's SW corner is accessed via a side road off White Lake Road, which leaves NH 16 0.5 mile south of the state park entrance. Motors are allowed up to a six horsepower limit. A boat is the best way to enjoy the good trout fishing here.

## At White Lake

The swimming beach is a beauty, a swath of clean white sand shelving into shallow, kid-friendly water. There are picnic tables, grills, a bathhouse, a pavilion, and a playground. The park's 170 campsites are spread over three areas and are first-come-first-served; reservations are not accepted. During peak times plan to arrive early for either day use or camping.

The trail around the lake starts at the west end of the beach. Take in the watery view north to Mounts Whiteface, Passaconaway, Paugus, and sharp-peaked Chocorua, then stroll down the needle-carpeted aisle under tall pines. You'll find three species of pine at White Lake: the majestic white pine, with a feathery look and needles in clusters of five; the red pine, noted by its reddish bark and paired needles; and the pitch pine, whose twisted branches present needles in threes.

You cross the boat launch at the SW corner and wander north through mixed pines and hardwoods along the west shore. Listen for the soft trilling song of the pine warbler, coming from the treetops. The branches and bushes part for frequent views out to the water. Keep an eye out for loons in summer (take care not to disturb any nesting area) and migrating ducks in spring and fall. The steep bank to the left of the trail was the lake's shoreline many years ago, when the water level was higher.

At 0.5 mile turn left onto the white-blazed Pitch Pine Trail, marked by a sign. You step up into an enchanted forest of tall pitch pines dotted with sheep laurel, bracken, blueberry, and scrub oak. This unique plant community, fashioned by the sandy glacial soils and subsequent fires, is part of the Ossipee pine barrens. It's the northernmost such forest in New Hampshire.

In 0.3 mile you come to a T-junction at the edge of another unusual assemblage of plants. You've entered the *Black Spruce Ponds* Preserve, a conservation tract owned by the town of Tamworth. Ahead of you is one of a pair of circular bog ponds that were formed as glacial kettle holes. Each consists of a small pool of open water ringed by a spongy mat of bog vegetation. The sphagnum moss supports a ragged growth of black spruce and a dense weave of leatherleaf. The carnivorous pitcher plant thrives out on the soggy mat. This primeval environment is at once eerie and fascinating. It's also fragile; please stay on the trails.

Turn left onto an orange-blazed path and skirt the south edge of this smaller of the two ponds. The path hops up onto a pine-cloaked esker and curves west to another T-junction at the east edge of the larger bog-pond. There are good views through the trees out to the dark central pool. Bear right here on another orange-blazed trail. A short walk leads you back to a junction with the Pitch Pine Trail on the north side of the smaller pond. Swing left and gently uphill at a sign for this white-blazed path.

This section of trail meanders through the 72-acre Pitch Pine National Natural Landmark. In addition to its unique plant life, the area is an important habitat for several rare moth species. But this forest is slowly changing.

The hardy pitch pine thrives in the wake of periodic forest fires, which have flared here as recently as 1947. In the absence of fire, red and white pines and hardwoods such as red oak begin to take over. As Ned Beecher points out, this presents a Catch-22 to the managers of the pine barren. A controlled burn may be necessary to sustain its existence. Yet this option would certainly be unpopular with many park users.

About 0.4 mile from the last junction by the bog pond, the Pitch Pine Trail dips and meets the Lake Trail by the NW corner of White Lake. Turn left here, walk past a swamp on the left, and cross a stagnant inlet on a footbridge. At the far end of the bridge a side path right angles back to the north shore at a low sandy bank. From this sunny picnic spot you can survey the pond's expanse and look for waterbirds. Once I watched a loon chase off a trespassing cormorant with a skittering charge.

The Lake Trail continues its easy meander along the NE shore of the pond, mostly in deep, dark hemlock woods. Farther south you suddenly emerge in a more open forest of hardwood and white pine. Along this east shore several side paths lead right to small outlooks with views across the water to the Ossipee Range and the western peaks of the Sandwich Range. Then the main trail bears left away from the water and enters the campground area. To avoid walking through the campsites, drop down to a little shelf on the right and follow a series of well-beaten paths closer to the shore. This route eventually merges with a dirt road that leads you back to the beach.

*Winter:* The lake is a popular spot for snowmobiling and ice fishing, but the area also offers good cross-country skiing and snowshoeing. The access road is plowed to a large parking lot 0.2 mile before the beach area. A ski or hike across the lake (excellent views of the Sandwich Range) and along adjacent trails is an easy and enjoyable outing. The Pitch Pine Trail is especially pretty in a fresh cloak of snow and gets you away from the snowmobiles.

# CHAPTER 28

# ECHO LAKE
# (NORTH CONWAY)

◆━━━━━━◆━━━━━━◆

**Location:** East of White Horse Ledge
**Hiking Facts:** Short walk from parking lot; easy 1-mile loop trail around pond;
    add 2.6 miles, 1,000 vertical feet for White Horse Ledge
**Map:** USGS 7½' North Conway West
**Area:** 14 acres   **Elevation:** 470 feet
**Avg./Max. Depth:** 9/12 feet
**Activities:** Swimming, picnicking, hiking, fishing (smallmouth bass, yellow
    perch)

━━━━━━━━━━━◆━━━━━━━━━━━

*An evening spent there when the full rising moon silvers
"The Ledges," and burnishes the bosom of the lake, and
sheds its beams among its dark pine fringes, to slip slowly
down the stately columns of the larger trees, will long be
remembered as a sweet midsummer night's dream.*
—Thomas Starr King
*The White Hills,* 1859

For generations North Conway visitors have come to the sandy shores of
Echo Lake to admire its pine-rimmed water, to swim, to picnic, and to rouse
echoes off the gaunt cliffs of White Horse Ledge. This was a favored beauty
spot of purple-penned nineteenth-century writers, of whom the Reverend
Starr King was the foremost. For a fee, tourists of that era could enjoy the
reverberations of a small cannon booming off the great granite ledges.

Starr King would undoubtedly be appalled by the traffic-snarling
sprawl that has engulfed his beloved North Conway. Happily, though, the
pond and its companion cliffs are protected from the encroachments of
civilization as part of Echo Lake State Park. In 1943, when commercial
development threatened the lake, the Society for the Protection of New

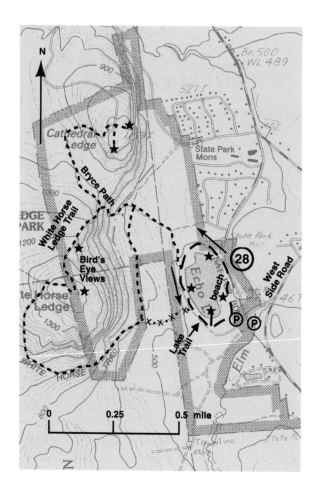

Hampshire Forests joined with the state government to raise the funds needed to acquire the parcel.

The sandy beach of this small glacial kettle pond is one of the nicest swimming and picnic spots in the valley. An easy trail circles the shore through a beautiful forest of pine and oak. Connecting paths facilitate an ascent to White Horse Ledge for a dramatic bird's-eye view of the pond.

## Access

From the stoplight by Eastern Slope Inn on US 302 in North Conway, drive west on River Road, passing under a railroad bridge and crossing the Saco River. In 0.9 mile turn left on West Side Road, and 0.5 mile beyond turn right on Old West Side Road. In 0.1 mile you'll come to the State Park entrance.

(You can avoid the infamous North Conway traffic by coming in on West Side Road from NH 16 in Conway or from US 302 between Bartlett and Glen.)

The park is officially open weekends starting Memorial Day, daily from late June to Labor Day, and weekends again in the fall. Admission has been $2.00 per person midweek, $2.50 on weekends, and free for ages under 12 and over 65. There's a large parking area behind the gate house. (During the off-season, when the gate is closed, park on a dead-end spur road left of the entrance.)

At the left (west) end of the lot a trail sign indicates hikers' access to the Lake Trail and the ledges. From the right side of the parking area a graded gravel walkway leads 100 yards down through tall pines, past bathhouses and picnic areas, to the swimming beach on the east shore of Echo Lake. Please help prevent erosion by staying off the sandy banks behind the wooden railings.

## At Echo Lake

Though apt to be crowded on a hot summer day, the east shore of Echo Lake is a compellingly scenic place. A grove of tall pines shades the sloping picnic area behind the beach. Across the green-tinted water looms the immense face of White Horse Ledge. It requires some imagination to make out the horsey pattern on the cliffs. "Newcomers at N. Conway are seldom allowed to rest until they have seen, acknowledged, and complimented the equine form of this amorphous spot," wrote a bemused Moses Sweetser in his 1876 guidebook.

You're more likely to spot brightly-clad rock climbers strung along the cliffs. White Horse and Cathedral Ledges, with their "clean" granite and varied faces, are among the most popular climbing centers in New England. Cathedral, a round-topped hulk, rears over the right (north) end of the pond. Both ledges owe their sheer eastern cliffs to the sculpting power of Ice Age glaciers.

The beach and roped-off swimming area at Echo Lake are small but delightful. The sandy bottom slopes off gently from the shore, so young-sters can safely enjoy the water. Boats propelled by oar, sail, or paddle are permitted outside the swimming area. Though not noted as an angling hot spot, the pond does hold some promise for warm-water fishing.

## The Lake Trail

The 1-mile circuit trail around the shore is a pleasant and scenic stroll. It begins as an aisle through pitch pines at the north end of the beach and leads behind the east shore through tall red and white pines and lowlier oaks. Various views of White Horse Ledge and the high, bare-topped Moat Range open through the trees. The roofline of a resort hotel (built in the 1980s on private land under the ledge) pokes above the trees.

Hemlock and spruce mix into the woods at the north end of the pond. A short path leads left to a secluded picnic table on the NE shore. At the NW corner an unsigned path splits right as the Lake Trail curves left (south) behind the west shore. You soon reach a signed trail junction where the right-branching path leads to the Bryce Path and the ledges and eventually Cathedral Ledge Road.

The Lake Trail continues straight and soon touches the shore for a view NE across the pond to the distant, tower-topped dome of Mount Kearsarge North. The trail cuts back into the woods to swing around the SW corner, passing the Red Ridge Link Trail on the right. From a piney clearing a wide path leads 100 feet left to the sandy south shore of Echo Lake and a fine view of Cathedral Ledge, with Humphrey's Ledge peering over on the right.

Returning to the main trail, turn left and in a few yards you'll come to a fork. Left returns you through picnic areas to the beach; right takes you up to the hiking trailhead in the parking lot.

## White Horse Ledge

More ambitious hikers may want to tackle the short (1.3 mile) but rugged (1,000 vertical feet) ascent to the 1,450-foot summit of White Horse Ledge. From the trail junction near the pond's NW corner, follow the route marked "To Bryce Path" NW for 0.3 mile to a crossroads. On your left is a clearing, a cabin, and an imposing view of White Horse Ledge.

Continue straight on the yellow-blazed Bryce Path, climbing very steeply with rough footing for 0.2 mile (a difficult stretch for young children). Farther up the pitch moderates, and a right turn leads on the level to a trail junction in the col between the ledges, 0.6 mile from the Lake Trail. (A right on Bryce Path will lead you to Cathedral Ledge in 0.4 mile, with a 350-foot climb; its ledgy south outlook has a fine view of Echo Lake.)

Turn left on the White Horse Ledge Trail and climb steadily through hardwoods and hemlocks. In 0.2 mile you emerge on an open ledge with a look down at Echo Lake and the neighboring hotel and across the broad valley to the Green Hills. Another 0.4 mile of ascent brings you to the summit of White Horse Ledge, where a loop path leads around the open granite slabs. You can make your way down ledges and climbers' paths to a flat shelf atop the great east cliff. There's a dazzling *bird's-eye view* of Echo Lake and a fine vista left to the Presidential Range and Carter Notch.

Keep an eye out for a soaring turkey vulture, its wings held in a tipsy V-shape. This bald-headed scavenger has recently extended its range northward into the lower valleys of the White Mountains. Peregrine falcons have nested on the ledges in some years. Heed all signs posting restricted areas during the peregrine nesting season. Also, remember that there may be rock climbers below you—do not toss anything over the edge of the cliff!

Although a longer and less steep return is possible on a southern loop of White Horse Ledge Trail, that route is not recommended due to an ill-defined relocation at the base of the cliff. Instead, retrace your steps down the steeper northern route.

*Winter:* Echo Lake is ideal for a short, easy ski or snowshoe stroll if you're sojourning in the valley. Parking is available at the park entrance. From the pond you can gawk at the ice climbers up on the ledges.

*Echo Lake*

# CHAPTER 29

# RED EAGLE POND

◆

**Location:** Albany, north of Swift River
**Hiking Facts:** Roadside
**Map:** USGS 7½' Silver Lake
**Area:** 6.5 acres   **Elevation:** 530 feet
**Avg./Max. Depth:** 4/8 feet
**Activities:** Fishing (horned pout, chain pickerel, yellow perch), picnicking

◆

This still, swampy pond spreads on a low flat beside the Dugway Road, which leads from West Side Road in Conway to the Kancamagus Highway at Albany Covered Bridge. There are no hiking opportunities here, but anglers can engage in warm-water fishing, and photographers will find a nice water-and-mountain vista featuring the bare cone of South Moat Mountain (2,749 feet). A hemlock-shaded waterfront opening could also serve as a pleasant picnic spot.

## Access

From the stoplight at the junction of NH 16 and NH 153 in Conway, drive north on Washington Street, which turns into West Side Road. Bear left at a fork, and 0.9 mile from NH 16 turn left onto Passaconaway Road, which becomes Dugway Road. Drive 1.5 miles west to a roadside sign and pull-off for Red Eagle Pond on the right. Though there are residential areas to east and west, the pond is on National Forest land. (From the Kancamagus Highway, drive 5 miles east on Dugway Road to reach the pond.)

## At Red Eagle Pond

The roadside bank overlooks the sprawling pond, speckled with pipewort, lily pads, and wild celery. The shore is fringed with hemlock, white pine, and red maple. For a good view and photo angle, follow a worn path down the slope left of the sign and walk a few steps left. Framed by hemlock boughs, South Moat rises rather majestically beyond the narrow neck of the pond.

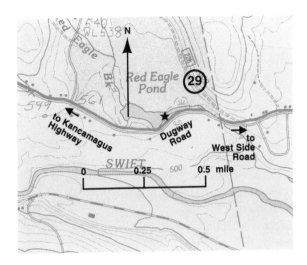

By descending a path through the hemlock grove to the right of the sign, you'll find a nice view of the pond and sharp-peaked Haystack Mountain (2,050 feet). This gravelly opening is a fairly secluded picnic spot. Anglers can follow old logging roads to the SW and north shores, but access to the water is limited by an entanglement of shrubs.

*Red Eagle Pond and South Moat Mountain*

# CHAPTER 30

# FALLS POND

◆

**Location:** Rocky Gorge Scenic Area
**Hiking Facts:** 0.2 mile round-trip, 50-foot vertical rise, easy; add 0.7 mile, 150
   vertical feet for optional loop hike
**Map:** USGS 7½' Bartlett
**Area:** 8 acres   **Elevation:** 1,115 feet
**Avg./Max. Depth:** 11.5/17 feet
**Activities:** Hiking, fishing (brook trout), picnicking

◆

The short walk to Falls Pond via Rocky Gorge gives you a two-for-one value.
Nowhere else in the mountains can you enjoy a surging waterfall and serene
mountain pond in exchange for such a minimal investment of time and
effort. Separated from the Kancamagus Highway by the Swift River and a
glacial ridge, Falls Pond has a surprisingly remote feel. A loop trail through
the spruce, pine, and hemlock forest around the pond makes it possible to
spend a leisurely hour or two exploring this pretty pocket of scenery.

## Access
There are two entrances to the WMNF Rocky Gorge Scenic Area, located on
the west (technically, the north) side of the Kancamagus Highway (NH 112).
The first, unmarked, is 3.1 miles east of the junction with Bear Notch Road
and leads directly into the parking area. The second, indicated by a prominent
sign, is 0.3 mile farther east and loops back to the parking area via a narrow
one-way road.

   A paved footway leads 100 yards north along the Swift River to the
polished granite ledges beside Rocky Gorge (also known as Upper Falls). A
footbridge spans the chasm and provides a dramatic view down to the
churning river. (See Bruce and Doreen Bolnick's *Waterfalls of the White
Mountains*.)

   From the far end of the bridge, climb a series of wooden steps amidst
deep coniferous woods. Atop this narrow little ridge—a gravel glacial de-

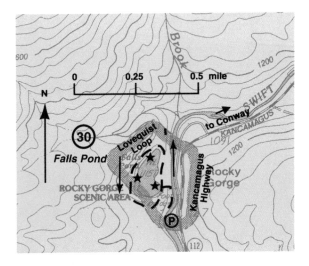

posit that separates the pond from the river—is a National Forest information sign and the junction with Lovequist Loop, the 0.7 mile trail around
the pond.

## At Falls Pond

Whether or not you plan to hike the loop, continue straight ahead down more
wooden steps to a sprinkling of boulders at the water's edge. Several rocks
provide seats suitable for viewing, fishing, or picnicking. The view of the
pond, enclosed in its dark hollow of evergreens, is intimate and lovely. A lofty
wooded spur of Bear Mountain provides a wild backdrop. This opening is on
the SE shore and captures sun in mid to late afternoon. Be prepared for plenty
of company here during summer and fall. If you seek solitude at Falls Pond,
visit in early morning or evening, when you may spot a beaver.

The undulating Lovequist Loop Trail (named in memory of a Forest
Service employee) is enjoyable in either direction. It stays back from the
shore, but there are several side paths to openings with varying perspectives
on the pond, and the woods are attractive all the way around.

Climb back to the loop junction and turn left on the wide, rolling,
needle-cushioned footway, opened in 1989 by a crew from the New Hampshire Conservation Corps. Overhead is a tall wood of red spruce and white
pine. You ascend a knoll, dip to a saddle with views of the water left through
the trees, and scale a higher knoll. Then the trail descends 100 yards along
this glacial ridge to cross the outlet brook on a footbridge.

A sign directs you left where the eastbound Lower Nanamocomuck Ski

*Falls Pond*

Trail forks right. You skirt the narrow, hidden north arm of the pond and head south behind the west shore through dark conifers. In 150 yards a well-worn path leads 60 feet left to a gorgeous vista over the water to the Three Sisters ridge of Mount Chocorua.

The main trail rises and falls to a spot where a 15-foot side path leads left to a weathered log with a broad view across the pond. At the shore you'll find labrador tea, leatherleaf, sheep laurel, sweet gale, pitcher plant, and other plants typical of boggy pond-edges. (Please don't disturb the fragile and, in some cases, rare vegetation.) On your right a tall snag leans over the water; many others have toppled in.

Near the pond's SW corner the trail briefly breaks free of the deep-shade softwoods into a bowl-like glade of hardwoods. Back among evergreens, you make a hard left to surmount a sharp little ridge that banks steeply down to the south shore. You stroll along the crest through a park-like stand of tall, straight spruce. The green-hued pond glimmers to your left, down through the trees. Look northward for glimpses of ledgy Table Mountain and a nameless nearer precipice.

Bear left and downhill as the westbound Lower Nanamocomuck Ski Trail leaves on the right. From here the Lovequist Loop descends 100 yards to the loop junction. You have an easy five-minute walk back to your car.

*Bird's-Eye View:* An interesting aerial look at Falls Pond can be enjoyed from ledges along the fire-scarred crest of 2,675-foot Table Mountain, two miles to the north. Access is provided by the Attitash Trail, which leaves the Bear Notch Road 6.7 miles north of the Kancamagus Highway. This is a rewarding half-day hike on a well-marked but little-used trail, 3.8 miles round trip with a 1,400-foot vertical rise.

*Winter:* The parking lot is plowed for cross-country skiers as an access point for the Lower Nanamocomuck Ski Trail. Rocky Gorge is impressive in its icy winter garb; use care on the ledges. Snowshoers can ramble around rolling Lovequist Loop, but keep to the edge on the section behind the east shore, where it coincides with the ski trail. Out on the pond there's a spectacular view of cliff-faced Table Mountain.

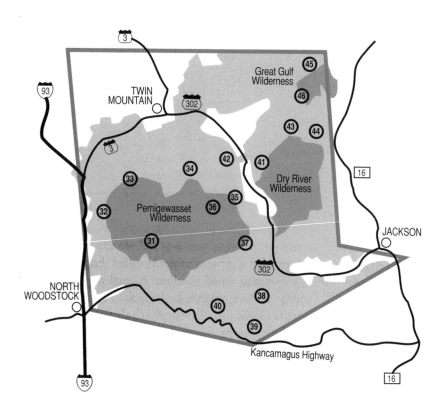

*Sawyer Pond and Owl's Cliff*

# III. CENTRAL
# WHITE MOUNTAINS

◆

COMPRISING THE HEART of the White Mountains are the "Pemi" and the Presidentials, two areas that need no introduction to most New Hampshire trampers.

Between Franconia and Crawford Notches lies the vast drainage of the Pemigewasset River's East Branch, once the backwoods empire of lumber baron J.E. Henry and his contemporaries. The deep valleys of the "Pemi" are enclosed by waves of sprawling mountains: Franconia Ridge, Owl's Head, Garfield Ridge, the Twin-Bond Range, Zealand Ridge, the Willey and Nancy Ranges, and the Carrigain-Hancock massif. The 45,000-acre core of this area is the officially designated Pemigewasset Wilderness.

Just outside the SW corner of the wilderness is Black Pond, small, dark, deep, and lovely. By the western edge, boggy little Eagle Lake nestles high on the shoulder of Mount Lafayette. Most of the central Pemi is pond-poor, but on its northern and eastern fringes sparkles an array of high, forest-rimmed lakelets. Garfield, Zeacliff, Zealand, Shoal, Ethan, Nancy, and Norcross Ponds lie alongside well-traveled trails. A half dozen more are hidden in the trailless woods, offering the most enticing pond-bushwhack possibilities in the Whites.

Amidst the lower mountains to the SE—Mount Tremont, Owl's Cliff, and Green's Cliff—are the beautifully paired Sawyer Ponds and Church Ponds. SW of these is Lily Pond, one of the highest roadside ponds in the Whites.

East of Crawford Notch and its two small lakes—Saco and Ammonoosuc, their names reflecting their watershed rivers—rise the mighty rockbound Presidentials. The Presidential Range–Dry River Wilderness is pondless, but from Mount Monroe northward the high peaks overlook the tiny alpine tarns in their craggy, windswept bowls: Lakes of the Clouds, Hermit Lake, Star Lake, and the jewel of the Great Gulf, Spaulding Lake.

# CHAPTER 31

# BLACK POND

◆

**Location:** East of Mount Flume
**Hiking Facts:** 6.8 miles round-trip, 420-foot vertical rise, moderate
**Map:** USGS 7½' Mount Osceola
**Area:** 4 acres   **Elevation:** 1,580 feet
**Avg./Max. Depth:** 15/34 feet
**Activities:** Hiking, fishing (brook trout), picnicking

◆

*At Black Pond you wonder at the isolation of the place…*
—Karl P. Harrington
*Walks and Climbs in the White Mountains,* 1926

Peaceful…tranquil…serene…. These and other soothing adjectives have often been applied to Black Pond, a dark and deep lakelet tucked into a wooded pocket by the southern fringe of the Pemigewasset Wilderness. Though only ¾ mile removed from the busy Lincoln Woods super-trail, it is, indeed, a quiet corner of the mountains. The hike into Black Pond is a longish but easy leg-stretcher along an old logging railroad grade and a gently rising spur trail. At trail's end you'll find shoreside sitting rocks with fine views of the pond and the remote Bond range in the distance.

### Access

The mall-sized Lincoln Woods parking area is on the north side of the Kancamagus Highway 5.2 miles east of Exit 32 off I-93 at Lincoln. Before setting off on your hike, stop in the Forest Service's Visitor Information Center, an attractive log cabin where free hiking literature and advice are available. Then drop down a stairway and follow signs across the suspension footbridge over the broad, rocky East Branch of the Pemigewasset River.

### The Trail To Black Pond

Turn right at the far end of the bridge onto the Lincoln Woods Trail, formerly the

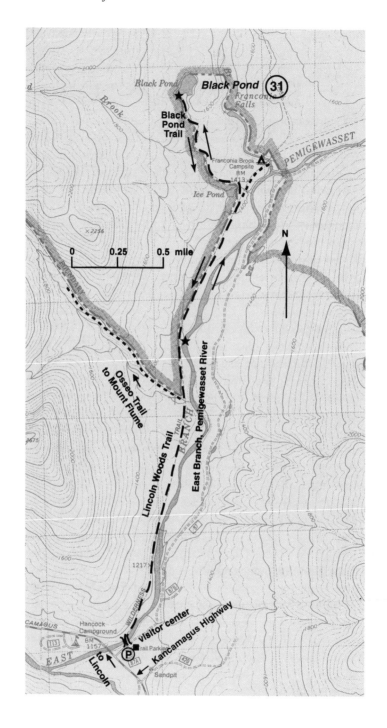

lower portion of the Wilderness Trail. (The older name now applies only to that section of the trail within the Pemigewasset Wilderness, three miles north.) You stride along the wide and nearly level grade of the former East Branch and Lincoln Railroad. This was the trunk line of the vast network of logging railroads laid into the woods by J. E. Henry, the infamous lumber baron who put the town of Lincoln on the map at the turn of the century. (The fascinating story of this line, which operated from 1893 to 1948, is delightfully told in C. Francis Belcher's *Logging Railroads of the White Mountains*.)

The walking is easy as you shadow the East Branch through second-growth forest. Old wooden ties straddle the trail in many places. You pass the Osseo Trail to Mount Flume on the left at 1.4 miles in a white birch grove. Just beyond is a clearing grown to brambles, the site of J.E. Henry's Camp 8. Where the trail flirts with the riverbank ¼ mile farther, hop out onto the rocks for a view of Bondcliff upstream (left) and rugged Mount Osceola downstream (right).

A long straightaway ensues; in places you can see ahead a half mile or more. At 2.6 miles—an hour or less from the parking lot at a brisk pace—you'll see a sign for Black Pond Trail. Turn left and walk along an old railroad spur through tall hardwoods. In 100 yards the trail leaves the railroad grade on a yellow-blazed footpath. To the left is *Ice Pond* (elevation 1,420 feet), a bushy meadow which once supplied ice for the logging camps. The stone abutment that created the pond is a few yards off the trail; there's a view of Mount Flume (4,328 feet) over the meadow.

Keep straight where an unmaintained path from Franconia Brook Campsite joins on the right. The Black Pond Trail winds along the mucky fringe of Ice Pond. Then you're briefly in the open amidst tall goldenrod and raspberry—J.E. Henry's Camp 7. Look for a gnarled apple tree left as you exit the clearing, the legacy of a logger's fruit snack decades ago.

You climb gently along a bank above Birch Island Brook, following the stream's meander through a lovely hardwood glen. At 0.5 mile from Lincoln Woods Trail you cross a gully carved by the outlet brook from Black Pond and bear right to walk beside this smaller stream. After two mucky crossings you make your final approach to the pond. A stagnant outlet pool on the right opens to an impressive view of a pyramidal wooded peak—the southern spire of Owl's Head Mountain, one of the most isolated 4,000-footers. Another minute of easy walking through darker woods brings you to the SW shore of the pond and the trail's end 0.8 mile from Lincoln Woods Trail.

## At Black Pond

A spruce-shaded granite seat is perfectly placed for a view over the dark, still pond. The shores are rimmed with red spruce mixed with white pine and hardwoods. Across the water the double-peaked ridge of Bondcliff (4,265 feet) sweeps above the treetops. Peering over on the left is the crest of West Bond (4,540 feet). The Bonds, as this mountain group is collectively known, form the high, craggy heart of the Pemigewasset Wilderness.

Other rock seats are sprinkled to the right along the water's edge. The only drawback of this south shore is that it receives virtually no direct sun. There are fine sun-warmed sitting rocks on the north and east shores (the latter with views of Owl's Head, Mount Flume, and Whaleback Mountain), but there is no continuous path around the pond. The cleared path that leads from the end of Black Pond Trail is the start of a bushwhack route used by peak-baggers to bypass the difficult crossings of Franconia and Lincoln Brooks en route to Owl's Head.

Sit quietly for a while and you'll hear a chorus of woodland birds in the summer. Sometimes a kingfisher conducts a raucous patrol around the shore. With luck you may even spot a moose. I once watched a cow and yearling forage for a half hour at Black Pond.

Though the water suits the moose, it's unlikely you'll be tempted to take a dip. Despite its surprising depth, Black Pond is as murky as its name suggests. Casting a line for trout may be a more profitable activity; the pond is stocked by the state and the fishing is reportedly good—sometimes.

One reason Black Pond is such a supremely peaceful spot is that camping is prohibited within a ¼-mile radius. "It would be overrun in a week," noted one Pemi ranger. So enjoy the pond for an hour or two, but don't plan to camp. On the return trip, be sure to bear right on Black Pond Trail where the path to Franconia Brook Campsite splits left.

*Bird's-Eye View:* The east half of Black Pond can be seen from the summit of Mount Flume, a dark pool amidst the vast leafy forest of the East Branch valley.

*Winter:* This is a relaxing half-day ski tour or hike. The spacious Lincoln Woods parking area is plowed; a parking fee is charged. The cozy Visitor Center is warmed by a woodstove. The Lincoln Woods Trail is ideal for novice cross-country skiers, though it can get icy during snow droughts. It's so popular that lanes are designated: ski tracks on the sides and a median strip for snowshoers and hikers. The Black Pond Trail is less frequented; it's an easy snowshoe trail, a bit harder for skiing. Around the fringes of the frozen pond there are good views of the Bonds, the spire of Owl's Head, Mount Flume, and the gnarled and knuckled ridges of Whaleback Mountain. Avoid the ice in the outlet cove.

# CHAPTER 32

# EAGLE LAKES

◆

**Location:** West shoulder of Mount Lafayette
**Hiking Facts:** 6 miles round-trip, 2,500-foot vertical rise, more difficult
**Map:** USGS 7½' Franconia (Page 92)
**Area:** 1.5 acres **Elevation:** 4,180 feet
**Activities:** Hiking, picnicking, AMC hut

◆

> *But these Alpine lakes always provoke a smile.*
> —Samuel Adams Drake
> *The Heart of the White Mountains,* 1882

Each summer thousands of hikers bound for Mount Lafayette pass by the tiny Eagle Lakes, a pair of boggy alpine tarns nestled near tree line in a pocket high on the west shoulder of the mountain. The smaller upper lake is well on its way to becoming a bog meadow and is little more than a pool at this point. The oblong lower pond is larger and still a legitimate water body, though it's very shallow and thickly spotted with water lilies. It's seen to best advantage from the knoll to the west, beside the AMC's Greenleaf Hut, with the barren ridge crest of Lafayette presiding majestically over the scene.

## Access

Eagle Lake and Greenleaf Hut can be accessed via the Old Bridle Path, from the east side of Franconia Notch Parkway at Lafayette Place (6 miles round-trip, 2,500-foot vertical rise); or the Greenleaf Trail from the Cannon Mountain Tramway parking lot (5.6 miles round-trip, 2,300-foot vertical rise).

## The Trail To Eagle Lake

The Old Bridle Path, originally built about 1850, is the more popular and scenic route. It ascends Lafayette's curving SW ridge, rising steadily through hardwood, birch, and fir forest. At 1.9 miles several ledgy outlooks offer spectacular views over Walker Ravine and up to the arching, slide-scarred ridge. Beyond, you climb a series of steep humps known as The Agonies, and at 2.9 miles you emerge from the scrubby firs into the hut clearing.

## At Eagle Lake

The bank beside Greenleaf Hut (open early May to mid-October) is a good place to stop for lunch and admire the view of lower Eagle Lake and the crest of Mount Lafayette (5,260 feet). The lily-choked water is fringed with a floating bog mat on its south and west edges. Dense scrub firs rim the eastern shore. Above the pond Lafayette's serrated summit ridge slants left to the knobby North Peak (5,060 feet).

Because of the fragile nature of the bogs and the surrounding alpine vegetation, you should enjoy Eagle Lake from a distance; there is no trail to the shore. Another perspective can be gained from the Greenleaf Trail as it crosses the outlet brook in the depression east of the hut. Look left for a view of the pond over the sedgy bog. A sign warns that this is a public water supply, no trespassing allowed. Beyond, the Greenleaf Trail climbs mostly in the open 1 mile and 1,000 feet to the summit of Lafayette and grand views. *Please stay on the trail above tree line.* A stroll over to the North Peak on Garfield Ridge Trail rewards you with a *bird's-eye view* of both Eagle Lakes, almost directly in line with Lonesome Lake across the notch.

An early visitor to Eagle Lake was Henry David Thoreau, who ascended Mount Lafayette in July 1858. He was fascinated by the plants in the surrounding bog and noted what appeared to be bear tracks in the mud. On the descent he boiled tea for his dinner beside the pond.

Encroaching vegetation and accumulating sediments will eventually cause the demise of this shallow glacial pond. A plaque penned by AMC naturalist Ray Welch and displayed on the wall inside Greenleaf Hut laments its passing: "...Its friends and admirers can look forward to only a few more centuries of lakehood. It will be sadly missed."

*Winter:* Eagle Lake, which freezes solid in winter, is a scenic highlight on the popular trek to Lafayette. The Old Bridle Path usually has a packed snowshoe track, making access as far as the hut relatively easy. Full winter gear is required above tree line, where conditions are often severe. Please stay on the trail and off the fragile vegetation in winter, too.

# CHAPTER 33

# GARFIELD POND

◆

**Location:** West of Mount Garfield

**Hiking Facts:** 11 miles round-trip, 3,600-foot vertical rise (3,000 in, 600 out), more difficult

**Maps:** USGS 7½' South Twin Mountain and Franconia

**Area:** 1.5 acres    **Elevation::** 3,860 feet

**Activities:** Hiking, picnicking

◆

*Messrs. Conant and Smith were so fortunate as to discover a new lake on the northwest side of Haystack Mountain, which we christened Haystack Lake.*
—Charles H. Hitchcock
*The Geology of New Hampshire*, Vol. I, 1874

In 1871 Dartmouth students C.H. Conant and Jonathan Smith happened upon a tiny pond on the high shoulder of Haystack Mountain (renamed Mount Garfield after the President's assassination in 1881). At the time they were engaged in research for Professor Hitchcock's landmark geological survey of New Hampshire. For several decades only a handful of AMC explorers and other hardy trampers fought through the tangled firs to the shore of this high, lonely tarn.

In 1915–16 a trio of AMC trailmasters—Charles W. Blood, Paul R. Jenks, and Nathaniel L. Goodrich—cut the rough-and-tumble Garfield Ridge Trail and brought "Haystack Lake" within reach of the hiking public. In 1918 the AMC approved a name change to Garfield Pond.

The pond soon became a favored wilderness camping spot. Too favored, it turned out. Campsites were hacked out of the firs and vegetation was trampled. The shelter fell into disrepair and Elizabeth Spring, the water source, dried up. The overuse prompted the Forest Service and AMC to remove the Garfield Pond Shelter and close the area to camping in 1971. A new shelter/camping area—Garfield Ridge Campsite—was constructed on

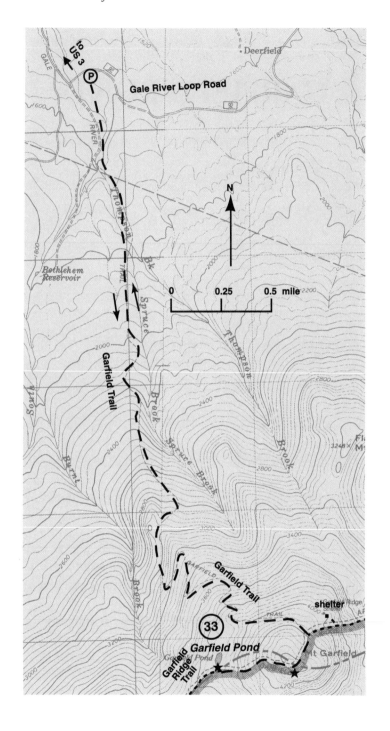

the east side of Mount Garfield. The restricted zone for camping extends for ¼ mile around the pond.

Today Garfield Pond is visited only briefly, if at all, by backpackers humping over the Garfield Ridge Trail between Mounts Lafayette and Garfield. For day hikers the pond makes a rugged but rewarding side excursion from the spectacular summit of Mount Garfield (4,500 feet). It's a remote and restful spot, with rock seats providing views of the lily-dotted water and the dense weave of boreal forest around the shore.

## Access
The Garfield Trail provides the best access to the pond. From US 3 between Franconia Notch and Twin Mountain, 0.3 mile west of Trudeau Road, drive south 1.2 miles on the west link of the Forest Service's Gale River Loop Road (FR 92). The trailhead is on the right after a sharp left turn.

## The Trail To Garfield Pond
The blue-blazed footway mostly follows the route of an old tractor road that served a fire lookout cabin atop Mount Garfield in the 1940s. Grades are easy to moderate for the 4.8 miles up to the ridge crest: northern hardwoods in the lower half, an attractive birch stand, then a painless climb up seven switchbacks through high-level firs.

There's a right turn onto Garfield Ridge Trail at 4,200 feet for a steep and rocky 0.2 mile scramble to Mount Garfield's ledgy crown, a commanding watchtower overlooking the western Pemigewasset Wilderness. The views sweep over remote birch-wooded valleys and 30 of New Hampshire's 4,000-foot summits. After gazing at these vistas, walk west on the ridge trail for a knee-jarring descent of 600 feet in 0.5 mile.

## At Garfield Pond
At the bottom of the steep grade you suddenly see the water of Garfield Pond through the trees to your right. A side path winds 200 feet down and left to a cluster of rocks on the south shore—a fine place to sit and contemplate this small, shallow, high-country pond. The thick firs give way to prickly snags around the shore. In midsummer yellow pond lilies float heart-shaped leaves on the water and poke flowered stalks above the surface. Neighborhood residents include darting dragonflies, croaking ravens, and drawling boreal chickadees. The tangled cone of Mount Garfield rises on the right. Savor the wildness of the place a while before tackling the steep pull back up to the summit.

*Garfield Pond*

For a more detailed description of the hike to Mount Garfield, see Daniel Doan's *Fifty Hikes in the White Mountains.*

*Winter:* The access road is not plowed, adding 1.2 miles at either end of the hike. Park at the junction of US 3 and Trudeau Road to the east. Mount Garfield is a spectacular winter destination, and the trail to the summit is beaten out by snowshoers fairly often. The steep pitches on either side of the cone can be challenging. Garfield Pond, enclosed by snow-crusted firs, enjoys a supremely wintry setting. The view of Mount Lafayette's icy crest from the pond's NE corner is a stunner. Experienced winter hikers can loop back to Garfield Trail via the unmarked and partly overgrown route of the old Garfield Pond Cutoff (too wet for summer use).

# CHAPTER 34

# ZEALAND AND
# ZEACLIFF PONDS

◆

**Location:** Zealand Valley and Ridge
**Hiking Facts:** 9 miles round-trip, 1,900-foot vertical rise, more difficult
**Maps:** USGS 7½' Crawford Notch and South Twin Mountain

|  | Zealand Pond | Zeacliff Pond |
|---|---|---|
| **Area:** | 4 acres | 1.5 acres |
| **Elevation:** | 2,457 feet | 3,700 feet |

**Activities:** Hiking, fishing (brook trout in Zealand Pond), birding, picnicking, AMC hut

◆

There's a special magic at work in the peaceful Zealand Valley. Perhaps it's the open forests of birch, spruce, and fir, miraculously risen from turn-of-the-century fires. Maybe it's the area's rounded, easygoing mountains, its grand, glacier-gouged notch, or the many beaver meadows that dot the lowlands. Whatever it is that weaves the spell, the Zealand region—loosely outlined by the Willey Range, Mount Hale, and Zealand Ridge—provides some of the nicest hiking in the White Mountains.

This hike leads you through the heart of Zealand country to a pair of small, boggy ponds blessed with picturesque settings. Beaver-dammed Zealand Pond reflects the birch-clad swell of Zealand Ridge and lies within sight and sound of splashing Zealand Falls. Tiny Zeacliff Pond resides in a cliff-rimmed bowl near the fir-forested crest of the ridge. Between the ponds you pass the falls, an AMC hut, and the magnificent Zeacliff outlook for a full sampling of the region's charms.

### Access

From the south side of US 302, 2.2 miles east of US 3 in Twin Mountain, drive 3.5 miles up the USFS Zealand Road, passing Zealand Campground,

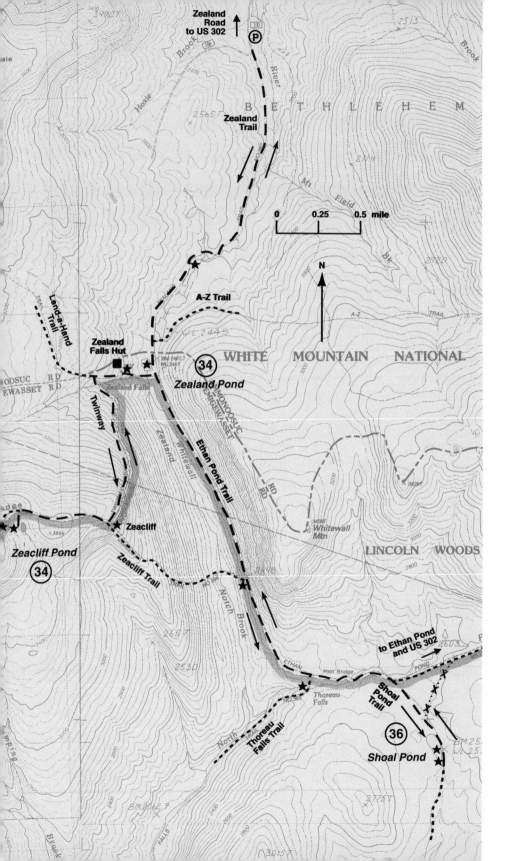

the two Sugarloaf Campgrounds, Sugarloaf Trail, and Hale Brook Trail. There's a large parking area at road's end, elevation 2,000 feet.

## The Trail To Zealand Pond

The blue-blazed Zealand Trail starts just south of the parking area. This pleasant and popular walk mostly follows the easy grade of J.E. Henry's Zealand Valley logging railroad, which shadows the Zealand River. Originally called New Zealand Valley, possibly a humorous reference to its remoteness, this area served as a training ground of sorts for Henry before he moved on to make his fortune in Lincoln and the Pemigewasset Wilderness. Starting in 1884 he pushed a railroad up the Zealand River valley, through Zealand Notch, and beyond to Shoal Pond.

In the style of the day, the loggers left behind a mess of tinder-dry slash. The great fires of 1886 (12,000 acres) and 1903 (10,000 acres) flared with such intensity that some thought life might never return to the Zealand Valley. "Death Valley," one horrified forester dubbed it. The reborn forest is a miracle worth celebrating.

At the trail's start you follow the railroad grade for 0.1 mile, then you hump through a bouldery bypass and a rooty spruce grove. You return to the grade and at 0.8 mile, with ledges in the Zealand River close by on the left, you bear right and ascend easily through deep spruce woods. At 1.3 miles a wooden plank bridge marks the first of several stream crossings in a bushy, swampy part of the valley. A half mile farther you emerge into an open beaver swamp, with your first views of Zealand Ridge ahead. A new boardwalk spans a mucky bog, and farther along beaver damming has forced a short relocation to the right. Birders can listen and look for such rarities as Lincoln's sparrow and Philadelphia vireo.

At 2.1 miles you stride down a lovely aisle of leaning birches. To the left there are views across a grassy beaver pond toward Mount Tom, a rounded 4,000-footer. Look for a huge lodge on the far shore. In its former dry state, this flat was apparently a railroad yard for the Henry logging operation. You pass the A-Z Trail to Crawford Notch on the left at 2.2 miles and shortly cross the stagnant northern outlet of Zealand Pond on a wide footbridge.

## At Zealand Pond

The trail swings around to a smooth gravel footway through the birches, shadowing the east shore of Zealand Pond. Actually, the north half of this beaver creation is part pond and part meadow. The south half is a genuine

*Zeacliff Pond and Mount Carrigain*

pond, and within 100 yards you'll come to a short side path right leading to low rocks at the water's edge, 2.5 miles from your car.

Across the murky water rises the wooded wall of Zealand Ridge, pure birch except for a line of green-black conifers along the crest. You'll attain this height with a 1,000-foot climb along the left edge. To the right the ridge rises to a spruce-capped knob that overlooks Zeacliff Pond on the south. Directly across the pond the cascades on Whitewall Brook gleam through a rift in the forest. The ledges are often sprinkled with brightly clad hikers. The roar of the brook carries across the valley. Zealand Falls Hut (built in 1932) is just to the right, out of sight in the woods.

On the opposite shore is a long, bush-grown beaver dam that controls the water level at this end of the pond. Zealand Pond is unique for its two outlets—one flowing north into the Ammonoosuc drainage, the other south into the Pemigewasset system. This oddity was noted in an 1879 story in Bethlehem's tourist newspaper, the *White Mountain Echo*, one of the earliest descriptions of what was then true wilderness.

Though it's small and shallow, Zealand Pond is reported to contain brook trout. If the fish aren't biting, you can watch the tree swallows cut graceful arcs above the water, or enjoy the exuberant birdsong rolling out of the birch woods and bushy meadows. Many hikers cruise right by this restful spot, anxious to reach the falls and hut. Unless you have reason to hurry, a stop here is well worthwhile.

## The Trail To Zeacliff Pond

The Zealand Trail ends at a junction 100 yards south of the side path to the pond. The Ethan Pond Trail continues ahead into Zealand Notch; turn right here onto the Twinway. Bog bridges and step stones lead you to a crossing of the pond's boggy southern outlet brook amidst a tangle of alder. A rock staircase lifts you a steep 0.2 mile to the hut, passing a side trail left to Zealand Falls. Hikers lounging on the front porch offer friendly greetings. The hut clearing commands a stunning view of Mount Carrigain through Zealand Notch. Step out onto the ledges of Whitewall Brook for a down-look at Zealand Pond—a chocolate-colored pool amidst the birches—with the dark crown of Mount Tom rising beyond.

Follow the Twinway up behind the hut, past the Lend-a-Hand Trail on the right, and hop across two branches of Whitewall Brook. Now comes the crux of the hike—a grinding mile's climb to Zealand Ridge over a rocky footway. The effort is lightened by the fern-filled birch forest that has re-claimed this slope in the wake of the fires.

The forest darkens with softwoods along the upper part of the climb. The trail bears right at a sign, 1.2 miles from the hut, as a short loop path leads ahead to the Zeacliff ledges. Don't miss this spectacular 3,600-foot perch overlooking the rolling forests of the eastern Pemigewasset Wilderness, with the distinctive humps of Mount Carrigain dominating the southern skyline. See if you can spot the glimmers of Shoal Pond and Norcross Pond. Eastward you look across Zealand Notch to the tumble of rocks on Whitewall Mountain and beyond to the Presidentials.

Back on the Twinway, you follow a swath of ledge westward along the shrubby ridge, with occasional views. You dip to the Zeacliff Trail junction on the left, climb easily over a scrubby swell, and enter an open, mossy ridgecrest fir forest. These fine woods are home to the boreal chickadee, the absurdly tame spruce grouse, and other interesting birds of the higher elevations. At 1.7 miles from the hut (4.4 miles from your car) you reach a sign for the spur trail to Zeacliff Pond. Turn left and descend 0.1 mile through the firs.

## At Zeacliff Pond

The side trail makes a rocky descent to the north shore of this boggy but beautiful little pond, site of an AMC shelter until the 1950s. The best views are along short side paths that leave the spur left and right just before it reaches the pond's mucky fringe.

Taken 75 feet, the left path leads to a sunny opening with a view right and up to the cliffs that overlook the pond, and across the water through snags drowned when beavers raised the waterline years ago. The best spot at Zeacliff Pond is gained by following the right-hand path, which winds a few yards through the woods and then makes a fairly difficult scramble over boulders and ledges along the shore. (Walk on the rocks and roots; avoid stepping on any vegetation.) In 200 feet you come to a sloping spine of rock that reveals the entire pond, with the solid bulk of Mount Carrigain rising in picturesque fashion on the horizon. The sun-sparkled water is fringed with sedgy, snag-dotted meadows and an old beaver lodge on the right. Sunny through early afternoon, this ledge is a good place for a high mountain picnic.

For the return trip, retrace your steps up the spur path and back along the Twinway and Zealand Trail. If you have energy to burn, you can continue westward on the Twinway, climbing steeply to a ledge outlook in 0.3 mile. This spot provides a unique perspective on Ethan, Shoal, and Norcross Ponds and a glimpse of Zeacliff Pond down through the firs.

*Winter:* The unplowed Zealand Road adds 3.5 miles each way, so this is a long trek. The hut, 6.2 miles from US 302, is open on a caretaker basis. Skiers and snowshoers often traverse Zealand Pond. Zeacliff Pond, sunny and sheltered, is a gorgeous little place in winter. Combined with the Zeacliff outlook, it makes an excellent snowshoe trip from the hut.

# CHAPTER 35

# ETHAN POND (WILLEY POND)

◆

**Location:** West of Crawford Notch
**Hiking Facts:** 5.5 miles round-trip, 1,600-foot vertical rise, moderate
**Map:** USGS 7½' Crawford Notch
**Area:** 5 acres   **Elevation:** 2,820 feet
**Avg./Max. Depth:** 2/4 feet
**Activities:** Hiking, camping (lean-to), fishing (brook trout), picnicking

---

◆

*While engaged in this hunt, we discovered a beautiful*
*little pond about two miles back of the Notch House, one*
*of the sources of the Merrimac. The appearance of this*
*pond and its situation pleased me much, as I thought it*
*would afford abundance of amusement for our visitors*
*such as were fishermen.*
—*Lucy Crawford's History of the White Mountains*, 1846
edited by Stearns Morse, 1978

Ethan Allen Crawford was to the White Mountains what Babe Ruth was to baseball—a compelling figure who dominated his era and captured the public imagination. The Crawford name and legend, more than any other, is woven into early White Mountain history, and Ethan was the giant of that fabled clan.

He was an explorer, path-maker, guide, bear-wrestler, moose-slayer, road-builder, trapper, trout fisherman, and woodsman extraordinaire. He was also one of the first White Mountain innkeepers, serving as host and raconteur to guests such as Nathaniel Hawthorne, Ralph Waldo Emerson, and Daniel Webster. (Some historians note that the Crawford legend also has a darker side that has never been fully explored. Read the fascinating history written by Ethan's wife, Lucy, and see for yourself.)

Over the years thousands of hikers have come to appreciate Ethan's 1829 discovery of a pretty lakelet beneath the frowning western cliffs of Mount Willey. Ethan Pond, sometimes referred to as Willey Pond, is an appealing destination for a leisurely day's hike from US 302 in Crawford Notch. The walk in is a good but not overly strenuous climb through varied forests. The wild spruce-woods setting of the pond is enhanced by a distant view of the Twin Range and the looming presence of Mount Willey. A nearby lean-to is a busy way station for backpackers trekking along the Ethan Pond Trail, a link in the Appalachian Trail.

## Access
The trailhead for Ethan Pond Trail is found on a paved side road on the west

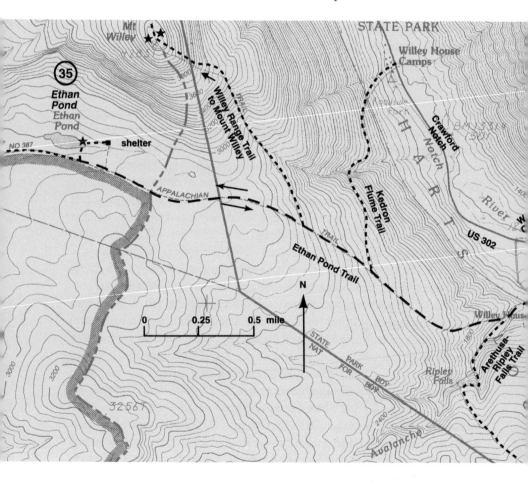

side of US 302, 1 mile south of the Willey House site in Crawford Notch State Park. In season, the road bears a sign for Ripley Falls; off-season, look for the sign for Webster Cliff Trail across the highway. Drive steeply uphill for 0.3 mile to a parking area at road's end.

## The Trail To Ethan Pond

The white-blazed trail climbs up a bank to the Maine Central Railroad, an engineering marvel when it was pushed through the Notch in the 1870s. After a long hiatus, passenger service was reinstated in 1995 with the opening of the Crawford Notch Scenic Railway.

Beyond, the trail traverses a bank and climbs to a junction with the yellow-blazed Ripley Falls Trail, which leads 0.3 mile to that spectacular cascade. (See Bruce and Doreen Bolnick's *Waterfalls of the White Mountains*.) Bear right on the Ethan Pond Trail for a sharp 0.3 mile ascent on an old logging road lined with white birches.

The grade eases as you traverse an open hardwood slope, rich in hobblebush and hermit thrushes and laced with seeps and small brooks. At 1.3 miles a double white blaze foretells the junction with Kedron Flume Trail, a steep alternate route from the Willey House site. The forest darkens with spruce as you climb moderately to another junction at 1.6 miles. Ahead, the Willey Range Trail shoots up one of the steeper pitches in the mountains—1,600 vertical feet in 1.1 miles—to the 4,285-foot summit of Mount Willey.

The Ethan Pond Trail makes a hard left here and proceeds steadily uphill with rocky footing. In 0.3 mile the trail levels out on the broad height-of-land (2,900 feet) that joins Mount Willey with the trailless ridge to the south. The woods—spruce, fir, a scattering of white birch and mountain ash—are wild and attractive. Wood sorrel and shining club moss grace the forest floor. Keep an eye out for moose sign.

Bog bridges lead you through a wet sag ravaged by blow-down. You cross a small brook, hump over a darkly wooded knoll, and soon begin a very gradual descent along an interesting plateau carpeted in a boggy, shrubby forest of spruce and fir. More bog bridges, placed by the trail crew of the AMC's New Hampshire Chapter, ease your passage over soggy ground. At 2.6 miles a sign on the right marks the side trail to Ethan Pond.

## At Ethan Pond

The rocky, rooty side trail winds downward for 0.1 mile through mossy spruce woods, passing a view up over the trees to the cliffs on Mount Willey's west face. You emerge at the narrow eastern end of the pond, next to the small inlet brook. Pick a boulder-seat—there are several good ones sprinkled across this little shore—and enjoy the marvelous view westward across the water. On a nice day this prime picnic spot is awash in sunshine from late morning through sundown.

The pond, shaped like a spearhead pointing east, is rimmed with spruce, fir, and tamarack. The latter tree puts on a display of golden foliage in October. At its west end the pond gives rise to the North Fork of the Pemigewasset River's East Branch, which has led some to assert that Ethan Pond is the ultimate headwater of the Merrimack River.

On the western horizon is the Twin Range; left to right, you can spot Bond, Guyot, Zealand Ridge, and South Twin. Close by on the right (north), Ethan Pond is hemmed in by a cliffy western arm of Mount Willey, an abode for croaking ravens. By rock-hopping a few yards left (SW), you can gain a better view back up to brooding Mount Willey and its slash of dark cliffs. The whole place has a wild, wonderfully remote feel to it, especially when a fresh breeze from the west brings waves to lap against the rocks.

Across the boulders, a short path leads 100 yards up to the eight-person lean-to hidden away from the pond amidst dark conifers. Several tent platforms are tucked back into the woods. This is a busy area on summer weekends. (A large bear was terrorizing campers here in August 1992, perhaps seeking retribution for the indignities perpetrated on its ancestors by Ethan Allen Crawford. You might want to check with the Forest Service or AMC for an update if you're planning an overnight.)

Though it's quite shallow, Ethan Pond has long had a reputation for good trout fishing. In 1830, the year after he found the pond, Ethan Allen Crawford guided several fishing parties here. The first trip was especially bountiful: "...we caught in a short time about seventy nice salmon trout...On the bank of the Pond we struck up a fire, and after dressing a sufficient number of them, we cooked them in real hunter style...." (Catch-and-release was not a common practice in Crawford's day.) Today's legal trout limit at Ethan Pond is five fish or five pounds, and fires should be built, if at all, only in designated places at the shelter/tent platform area.

For a full day's trek you can extend your hike 2.8 miles westward to remote Shoal Pond, or tackle the climb up the Willey Range Trail to Mount Willey for grand views of Crawford Notch, the Presidentials, and the eastern Pemigewasset Wilderness, plus a dramatic *bird's-eye view* of Ethan Pond gleaming amidst the evergreens 1,500 feet below.

*Winter:* Ethan Pond is a superb outing for snowshoers or strong

*Ethan Pond and the Twin Range*

backcountry skiers. The immense hulk of Mount Willey, fronted by ice-draped cliffs, dominates the scene; the view of that gaunt peak from the frozen pond is unforgettable. The side road to the trailhead is not plowed, adding 0.3 mile each way and 200 feet of climbing to the hike. A parking area is usually plowed at the road entrance off US 302.

# CHAPTER 36

# SHOAL POND

◆

**Location:** Pemigewasset Wilderness, west of Crawford Notch
**Hiking Facts:** 11.8 mile round-trip, 500-foot vertical rise, more difficult
**Map:** USGS 7½' Crawford Notch (page 170)
**Area:** 5 acres   **Elevation:** 2,538 feet
**Avg./Max. Depth:** 2/4 feet
**Activities:** Hiking, fishing (brook trout)

◆

A century or more ago, before logging railroads and hiking trails had invaded the Pemigewasset Wilderness, adventurous fishermen told of a fabled trout pond hidden deep in the spruce forest west of Crawford Notch. "...Its location baffled the search of many an anxious disciple of Izaak Walton," wrote AMC trailman Karl P. Harrington in his 1926 classic, *Walks and Climbs in the White Mountains.* The elusive sheet of water was often referred to as "unknown pond." Early maps used the name, "Howe's Pond."

The secret of what is now known as Shoal Pond was soon unveiled by J.E. Henry's Zealand Valley logging railroad. Before the turn of the century Henry's crews had skinned the spruce woods around this oval of shallow water. Subsequent fires completed the devastation, leaving a phalanx of bleached poles lining the shore.

Like other gems of the Zealand-Eastern Pemi region, Shoal Pond has made a heartening recovery from the torment inflicted by the "wood-butchers." Today it sparkles inside a dark forest rim of spruce, fir, and tamarack on a high, boggy plateau SE of Zealand Notch. Aside from its own quiet beauty and the brook trout that might lurk within, this remote wilderness pond is worth a visit for its outstanding shoreline views of Mount Carrigain and the mountains around Zealand Notch.

## Access

The easiest of three trail approaches to Shoal Pond comes in from the north via Zealand Notch. Though it's a longish hike, almost all of the walking is on nearly level railroad grades, with several scenic diversions along the way. The hike starts at the end of the Forest Service's Zealand Road (see *Zealand Pond*).

## The Trail To Shoal Pond

The first 2.5 miles of the hike are on the Zealand Trail. At the junction just beyond the viewpoint at Zealand Pond, keep straight ahead on the Ethan Pond Trail, part of the Appalachian Trail. (The Twinway leaves right for the short ascent to the AMC Zealand Falls Hut.) For the next 2 miles you walk south along the gravelly grade of the Zealand Valley railroad through spectacular Zealand Notch. The first mile is a pleasant stroll through a white birch forest that sprouted in the wake of the great Zealand fires of 1886 and 1903. The footway becomes rougher where rock slides and washouts have cut across the trail.

As you approach the junction with Zeacliff Trail, 3.8 miles from your car, you emerge from gnarled birches into an open area of talus on the side of Whitewall Mountain. For the next ¼ mile the views are magnificent. Midway along this open stretch a flat-topped granite boulder provides a fine viewing perch. The vista includes Mounts Carrigain and Hancock to the south, Mount Hale to the north, and the birch-clad slope and high crags of Zeacliff westward across the Notch.

Back in the woods, now mixed birch, spruce, and fir, a 0.7 mile jaunt leads you to an eastward curve and the junction with Thoreau Falls Trail. (The Thoreau Falls Trail leads 0.1 mile right and downhill to broad, sun-washed ledges atop the twisting cascade. This prime picnic spot commands a wild view up to the high ridges of Mounts Bond, Guyot, and Zealand. See Bruce and Doreen Bolnick's *Waterfalls of the White Mountains*.) In another 0.2 mile you cross the North Fork of the Pemigewasset River's east branch on a sturdy footbridge, and 0.3 mile beyond you reach the junction with Shoal Pond Trail. You're now 5.1 miles into your hike, amidst the bushy and boggy country typical of the upper North Fork region.

Bear right (south) into the Pemigewasset Wilderness on the blue-blazed Shoal Pond Trail. You enjoy 0.8 mile more of easy railroad-grade walking, at first beside shrubby bogs, then through damp spruce forest carpeted with bright green sphagnum moss.

*Alternate Approaches:* An eastern approach, shorter but more strenuous, can be made from the east end of Ethan Pond Trail off US 302. From the side trail to *Ethan Pond*, 2.6 miles from the road, the Ethan Pond Trail makes a gradual 2-mile descent to Shoal Pond Trail through spruce woods and bushy bogs, keeping just south of the North Fork. The round-trip to see these two quintessential wilderness ponds is 11 miles with 1,900 feet of climbing—1,500 in, 400 out. Backpackers can approach from the south end of Shoal Pond Trail at Stillwater Junction; see Daniel Doan's *Fifty Hikes in the White Mountains.*

## At Shoal Pond

Water glimmers to the right through the trees as you approach the pond, and soon the trail dips slightly to parallel the east shore. Walk past a very muddy side path near the pond's NE corner. In another 50 yards a better path dips 15 feet right to the shore and a view of Zeacliff and Zealand Ridge over the conifer-rimmed water.

From here you can sometimes make your way southward along the water's edge on rocks, sticks, and the bony roots of standing snags. Little rock-and-gravel beaches provide views south to the imposing hulk of Mount Carrigain (4,680 feet) and north towards Zealand Ridge and ledgy Whitewall Mountain (3,405 feet) framing Zealand Notch. This sunny shore is wilderness bliss on a breezy summer day.

If beaver damming or abundant rainfall submerges the beaches, don't trample the sweet gale and leatherleaf that fringe the shore. Instead, return to the main trail and walk 80 yards south to a small clearing. Just beyond, a second side path winds 50 feet to the shore near the pond's south end, offering a nice watery view to Zealand Notch.

The north woods feel of Shoal Pond is reflected in its bird life. You might encounter Canada jay, boreal chickadee, spruce grouse, and rusty blackbird. I've seen a great blue heron here, and once a double-crested cormorant was sunning itself on a rock out on the pond, a strange sight so deep in the forest.

The return to your car is by the same route.

*Bird's-Eye View:* Sweeping views of the eastern "Pemi," including glimpses of Shoal Pond, are found atop Zeacliff to the north and Mount Carrigain to the south.

*Winter:* The Ethan Pond approach is the only practicable day trip in winter, and it is a wonderful outing for the experienced winter traveler. Overnighting skiers often come in from Zealand Falls Hut, though the open stretch through Zealand Notch can present a treacherous sidehill in crusty conditions. Frozen Shoal Pond exhilarates with its great views of Mount Carrigain, Zealand Notch, and the Willey Range. A protruding rock seat near the pond's NE corner faces south to the sun and the lordly spread of Carrigain.

# CHAPTER 37

# NANCY AND NORCROSS PONDS

◆

**Location:** Nancy Range
**Hiking Facts:** 8.6 miles round-trip, 2,200-foot vertical rise, more difficult
**Maps:** USGS 7½' Bartlett and Mount Carrigain

|  | Nancy Pond | Norcross Pond |
|---|---|---|
| **Area:** | 4 acres | 7 acres |
| **Elevation:** | 3,100 feet | 3,120 feet |

**Activities:** Hiking, birding, picnicking

◆

Nancy and Norcross Ponds grace a remote conifer-clad plateau in the wildlands between Crawford Notch and Carrigain Notch. The shallow tarns are centered amidst a cluster of four peaks—Mounts Bemis, Nancy, Anderson, and Lowell, all over 3,700 feet—known as the Nancy Range. None of these summits is accessible by trail, but the Nancy Pond Trail provides a marvelous introduction to this interesting region.

The area was partially logged in the early 1900s but for many years was seldom visited by hikers. The Nancy Pond Trail was first opened from Crawford Notch to the ponds in 1938. It was immediately obliterated by the great hurricane that swept through New England that fall. Not until 1960 was the footway reopened.

The strenuous hike to the ponds offers a cornucopia of mountain delights: fine hardwood forests, lofty cascades, a primeval stand of spruce and fir, and a wide view west to the Pemigewasset Wilderness. The tableland that holds the ponds is a good place to find unusual birds of the northern boreal forest. Nancy Pond, dark and mysterious, is surrounded by somber spruce forest. Exhilarating Norcross Pond opens wide to the sky and distant views of the Twin-Bond Range. The ledges at the west end of the pond are a premier picnic spot to cap off your hike.

## Access

The Nancy Pond Trail, marked by a WMNF sign, leaves the west side of US 302, 1.2 miles north of Sawyer River Road and 1 mile south of the Davis Path trailhead by Notchland Inn. There is limited roadside parking at the trailhead and a larger parking area across the highway.

## The Trail To The Ponds

The yellow-blazed trail angles to the right through nice hardwood forest, passing an information kiosk at 0.1 mile. Following a succession of logging roads and connecting paths (all well marked), you climb gently NW, crossing a dry streambed and then Halfway Brook. Just past the brook there's an important left turn onto another logging road (bear right here on the descent). You shadow the red-blazed National Forest boundary on your right and begin an easy climb along a bank high above Nancy Brook.

At 1.6 miles you bear right to cross the boulder-strewn brook, then left to follow it into a deep ravine. Here an abandoned trail to the toppled fire tower atop Mount Bemis departs up-slope on the right. At 1.8 miles you pass the remains of a mill used by the Lucy family of Conway for timber salvage after the 1938 hurricane. A crumbling brick furnace on the left is the most obvious sign of the operation.

The trail climbs over a rougher footway into white birch forest, passing two gravel slides that have slipped off the steep slope to the right. At 2.4 miles you cross the brook to its left (south) side and come to the foot of the spectacular lower drop of Nancy Cascades. (Be sure to make a left turn here

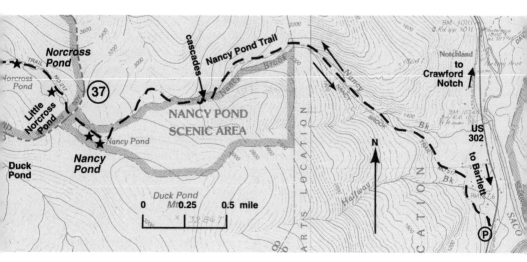

on the descent, where a false path leads ahead.) A pool and surrounding rock seats make this a nice resting spot. (See Bruce and Doreen Bolnick's *Waterfalls of the White Mountains*. As the Bolnicks relate, the many Nancy names in this area recall a tragic tale of the 1770s, in which a young woman perished in a blizzard whilst pursuing a heartless lover who had made off with her life's savings.)

Steep switchbacks lead you skyward through a wild spruce-fir forest that somehow flourishes on this precipitous slope. There's a view of a middle cascade at the top of the first zigzag and a glimpse of Giant's Stairs and Mount Resolution from the third. At the top (2.8 miles) the trail abruptly levels as Nancy Brook changes to a gentler stream.

From here to Nancy Pond you ascend gradually through a spellbinding stand of virgin conifers. The rooty trail winds amidst tall red spruce, living and dead, their long trunks shingled in scaly gray bark. In summer the spiraling carols of the Swainson's thrush lend a mystical quality to this dense moss-grown forest. You follow the dwindling brook, crossing it three times, and climb several small rises. Amidst flat, boggy terrain you arrive at the NE shore of Nancy Pond, 3.4 miles into your hike.

## At Nancy Pond

Walk a few yards left on an overgrown side path for a look at this dark, wild pond, the ultimate source of Nancy Brook. The shallow waters are lined with bog shrubs and dismal spruces. In summer white-throated sparrows lift their sad whistles along the shore. To the west the wooded dome of Mount Anderson (3,740 feet) looks over the trees. There are no rock seats on this marshy shore; it's a "stand-up" view, but a lovely one. This remote sanctuary was invaded by logging roads during the 1910s, when the Saunders family of Livermore (noted for their relatively conservative cutting tactics) pushed their operations from the Sawyer River valley up the basin of Whiteface Brook. In 1964 the WMNF established the 460-acre Nancy Brook Scenic Area. Today Nancy Pond appears pristine once more.

The trail skirts the north shore through dense bushy growth, with occasional glimpses of the water. A path leads 10 feet left to a clearing with a vista across the pond to the massed ranks of conifers on the south shore. You might spot a family of black ducks, or hear the squeaky song of the rusty blackbird. This is the closest you'll find to a picnic spot at Nancy Pond. Anglers take note: neither pond is stocked by the state, so fishing here is questionable.

The main trail continues over bog bridges past the west end of the

*Norcross Pond*

pond, with good views over the shrubs, and slices into the woods. These firs are home to the tame spruce grouse and the quiet black-backed three-toed woodpecker, which often feeds on the stubs of dead conifers. Climbing over a small rise, you leave the Saco drainage and enter the Pemigewasset watershed. You pass Little Norcross Pond on the left, well on its way to boghood. Its sedgy meadow is dotted with pitcher plants. (Please refrain from walking out on this fragile vegetation.)

## At Norcross Pond

The trail climbs over another wooded swell, enters the Pemigewasset Wilderness, and dips to the east end of Norcross Pond, named for an early logger. The pond debuts dramatically, presenting an open expanse of water with the summits of the Twin Range—Bond, Guyot, South Twin, and North Twin—arrayed on the horizon. The north (right) shore is dotted with rocks; spiky snags line the south shore. Mount Anderson, its dense fir cover broken by a slash of dark cliffs, presides above. A gravelly spot at the corner provides the best view. On a sunny day it's one of the sweetest spots in the mountains.

The trail tracks through the fir woods along the north edge of Norcross Pond, opening to occasional watery vistas. By the narrow, mucky west end you circle through dense conifer growth, then cut across a fir grove to a campsite clearing. Bear left here to the outlet brook, 4.3 miles from your car, where ledges offer a memorable view west down the valley of Norcross Brook and out over the rolling Pemigewasset Wilderness. The bare ridge crest of the Franconias peers over the nearer Bond-Twin Range. Behind you is the natural ledge dam that rims the west end of the pond. It's strewn with the remains of an old beaver dam, which once raised the water level and drowned many shoreline trees.

The Nancy Pond Trail continues westward down the valley of Norcross Brook, linking with Carrigain Notch Trail in 2.8 miles. Unless you're out for an extended backpack, retrace your steps after enjoying the view. Be sure to bear right (east) at the campsite back in the fir woods.

For more natural history on the Nancy Pond area, see chapter 14 in Ned Beecher's *Outdoor Explorations in Mt. Washington Valley.*

*Winter:* The ponds are magnificent in winter, especially Norcross, where you can snowshoe/ski down the middle with Mount Anderson on your left, Mount Nancy on your right, and the Twin Range on the horizon. Nancy Pond is more accessible in winter and offers an imposing view up to Mount Nancy from its frozen surface. The steep switchbacks beside the cascades make for vigorous snowshoeing and can be treacherous in crust or ice, when crampons may be desirable. There's usually enough room to park on the highway shoulder at the trailhead. Adventurous sorts can ski up from a base camp in the Pemigewasset Wilderness to the west.

# CHAPTER 38

# SAWYER PONDS

◆

**Location:** Livermore, west of Mount Tremont
**Hiking Facts:** 3.4 miles round-trip, 350-foot vertical rise, easy; add 0.2 mile, 100 feet for Little Sawyer Pond
**Map:** USGS 7½' Mount Carrigain

| | Sawyer Pond | Little Sawyer Pond |
|---|---|---|
| **Area:** | 47 acres | 11 acres |
| **Elevation:** | 1,936 feet | 2,060 feet |
| **Avg./Max. Depth:** | 44/100 feet | 14/28 feet |

**Activities:** Hiking, camping (lean-to), picnicking, fishing (brook trout in both ponds, horned pout in Sawyer), swimming

◆

*By daylight Sawyer Pond was more beautiful—*
*although, like all small mountain ponds, a little*
*lonely, pitiful, and* triste.
—J. Brooks Atkinson
*Skyline Promenades: A Potpourri,* 1925

Sawyer Pond is a backcountry beauty—broad, clear, and a hundred feet deep. Its shores open to impressive views of Mount Tremont and Owl's Cliff, steep-sided mountains that embrace the pond's remote, wooded bowl. The 1½ mile hike in from Sawyer River Road is an easy forest ramble, ideal for families and novice hikers.

With a lean-to and five tent platforms by its shore, Sawyer Pond is a favorite camping spot. If you're after solitude at Sawyer, your best bet is visiting midweek or off-season. Even at peak times, though, the shores are expansive enough for a private picnic.

For the inveterate angler or pond-explorer, the short side trip to secluded Little Sawyer Pond is an attractive option. This beautiful tarn is cupped in spruce forest above the big pond and is reached by an unmarked path. The area around both ponds is part of the 1,130-acre Sawyer Ponds

Scenic Area. Camping at the ponds is prohibited except at the tent platforms and lean-to.

## Access

The Sawyer Pond Trail makes a six-mile traverse between the Sawyer River Road (FR 34) on the north and the Kancamagus Highway on the south. The pond is just 1.5 miles from the northern trailhead, the far more popular approach. The gravel Sawyer River Road leaves the west side of US 302 3.9 miles west of Bear Notch Road in Bartlett and 2.1 miles south of the Davis Path trailhead. It ascends 3.7 miles SW up the narrow valley, passing the logging ghost town of Livermore, to a large parking area at its gated terminus. Sadly, this isolated trailhead has been the site of several break-ins, so leave nothing valuable in your car.

## The Trail To Sawyer Pond

Walk up the road past an information kiosk and gate and in 100 yards turn left at a sign to cross the rocky Sawyer River on a sturdy footbridge. (The Sawyer River Trail continues straight ahead on the road.) The river and pond are named for Benjamin Sawyer, an early settler who in 1772 helped Timothy Nash—the reputed discoverer of Crawford Notch—coax a horse through that rugged pass and prove that it was a feasible route between coast and mountains. For some time the pond was known as Bemis Pond, after Samuel Bemis, a Boston dentist and tireless explorer who took up residence in the Notch in the mid-1800s.

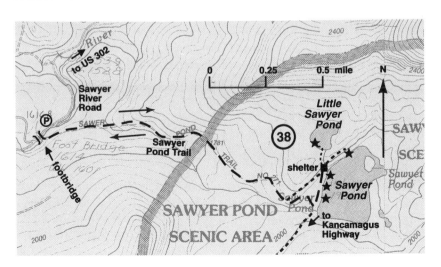

On the south bank you pass a register, climb a short steep pitch, and bear left (east) into the woods. The grade quickly eases as you meander through the deep mixed forest typical of the Sawyer River valley. The dark underlying theme is tall red spruce, mixed with scattered pine, fir, and hemlock. Yellow birch, sugar maple, and other hardwoods provide lighter accents. These woods were never clear-cut or burned, thanks to the foresighted logging practices of the Saunders family, the region's resident lumber barons.

In 0.3 mile you dip to cross the pond's nameless outlet brook on a plank bridge, then pick up an old logging road that rises gently on the north bank. In 0.1 mile look left for a regal yellow birch perched on a high boulder-throne, its roots twisted tenaciously around the rock. Soon the trail pulls away from the brook and climbs gradually, in places wet and rocky. The muddiest areas are expertly bridged with log-and-rock cribbing. Near the top of the grade a map and sign delineate the ¼-mile Restricted Use Area around Sawyer Pond.

The trail splits briefly and rejoins, then quickly divides again at the 1.4 mile mark. At this second junction the left branch (straight) leads past the tent platforms and reaches the shoreside shelter in 0.2 mile. Bear right on the main trail and approach the SW corner of Sawyer Pond through thick spruce. At 1.5 miles the main trail swings right to cross the outlet brook and head south to the Kancamagus Highway. Turn left here on a path that plunges into dense softwoods behind the shore.

*Alternate Approach:* Some hikers opt for the long southern way in on Sawyer Pond Trail, starting from a parking area on the north side of "the Kanc" 1.4 miles west of Bear Notch Road (9.4 miles round-trip, 800-foot vertical rise). An immediate challenge is the ford of the Swift River. The quick-moving water is often pocket-deep on an adult; old sneakers and a walking stick are invaluable for this crossing, which should not be attempted in high water. The rest of the trail is a long, easy woods walk—through white pines at the start, then amidst birch, beech, and other hardwoods, where bear sign is common. There are gentle climbs up the slope of Birch Hill and over a low 2,000-foot divide just south of the pond.

## At Sawyer Pond

The shoreline path leads you northward into open, beaten-out spruce woods near the tent platforms. Passing by the Group Fireplace area, you can choose from several shoreline openings with expansive views of the pond. These pretty picnic spots are shaded by spruce, hemlock, and pine. Across the drifting water looms a great mountain wall. On the left is the rolling, cliff-shod crest of Mount Tremont (3,371 feet). In the middle the ridge drops from Tremont's highest summit to a deep col, then rises abruptly to the rounded summit of Owl's Cliff (2,940 feet). A set of ledges juts from the center of this wooded knob like a rocky Cyclopean eye. These waterside resting spots are also good places to push off for a swim. The water is clear and the bottom is gravelly near the shore, though mucky farther out.

Beyond the viewpoints the shore path crosses a muddy spot and emerges on a bank beside Sawyer Pond Shelter, a busy place that commands an open view of the pond and its mountainous backdrop. By continuing northward on the shore path you can access several secluded picnic spots. The well-beaten footway crosses a small brook—the outlet of Little Sawyer Pond—and winds through sloping spruce woods where thoughtless campers have hacked down trees for firewood. In the next hundred yards there are several nice waterside vantage points.

About 0.15 mile beyond the shelter is a square-topped granite boulder reached by a short but easily overlooked side path. This rock, with room for two hikers and packs, catches sun until mid-afternoon. The pond stretches away to the south, with the hulk of Green's Cliff (2,926 feet) to the right, over the trees. Mount Tremont and Owl's Cliff tower close by on the left. It's a fine place to loaf on a hot summer day.

Nearby across the water is what appears to be a small, steep-sided knoll topped with tall white pines. It's actually an island—one of the few you'll find in a White Mountain pond. This islet figured prominently in *Skyline Promenades*, a delightful account of a backpacking journey across the White Mountains published in 1925 by young J. Brooks Atkinson. (The author went on to become a Pulitzer-Prize-winning journalist and longtime drama critic for the *New York Times*.)

In the midst of their trek, Atkinson and his cohort Pierre arrived at the south shore of Sawyer Pond near dusk. Finding the shoreline shrubs intolerably tangled, they took to the water, floating their packs on an improvised raft, and made for a knoll that promised a dry campsite. After setting up camp in the dark they settled in for a good night's sleep. In the morning, however, "there were difficulties as yet unknown and unconsidered... Looking towards Mount Tremont, Pierre suddenly let out a savage howl: 'Good God! we're on an island!' And so we were!" The pair concluded their misadventure by wading shoulder-deep through muddy water to the NE shore.

Beyond the granite perch the shore path is rougher and little-used. Retrace your steps south to the shelter and the main trail, with the option of a side jaunt to Little Sawyer Pond.

## Little Sawyer Pond

To visit this hidden gem, follow a path up the slope behind the shelter and past the toilet. The woods are honeycombed with herd paths; the correct one slabs right and upward across the slope to a Restricted Use Area sign and map. Just before the outlet brook, an overgrown side path leaves sharp left and twists through scrub and blow-down along the SW shore of Little Sawyer Pond. It passes openings with limited views and ends at a shoreside clearing (no camping allowed). Here the trees part for a superb view of Little Sawyer, its bushy shores darkly fringed with spruce and pine. The dark mass of Mount Tremont forms a rugged backdrop. This pond has a lovely, remote feel, quite different from the open expanse of Big Sawyer.

*Bird's-Eye View:* Pick a clear day and climb to the ledgy summit of Mount Tremont. The hike from US 302 via the Mount Tremont Trail— 5.6 miles round-trip, 2,600-foot vertical rise—is described in Daniel Doan's *Fifty More Hikes in New Hampshire.* The view of Sawyer Ponds sparkling in the forest, backed by waves of mountains, is one of the finest anywhere.

*Winter:* Although considerably longer, this trip is worth the trouble. The Sawyer River Road is an unplowed snowmobile route, adding 3.7 easy miles each way from US 302. Limited parking is available off the highway. An equidistant approach is the Sawyer River Trail from "The Kanc," provided the rocky Swift River crossing near the start is negotiable. The Sawyer Pond Trail from the Kanc involves a potentially dangerous crossing of the Swift.

The north section of Sawyer Pond Trail is an easy snowshoe or moderate ski route. The white expanse of Sawyer Pond is a delight to explore on a sunny day, and you can poke around the island-knoll by the NE corner. There are glimpses of Mounts Hancock and Carrigain from the far shore. Winter is a good time to circumnavigate Little Sawyer Pond, a difficult task in summer. The whitened ledges of Mount Tremont dominate the view from both ponds.

# CHURCH POND
# (BIG CHURCH POND,
# BIG DEER POND)

◆

**Location:** Livermore/Albany, north of Kancamagus Highway
**Hiking Facts:** 2.8 mile loop, minimal vertical rise, easy; river crossing at start
**Maps:** USGS 7½' Mount Carrigain, Bartlett, Mount Tripyramid, Mount Chocorua
**Area:** 16 acres   **Elevation:** 1,260 feet
**Avg./Max. Depth:** 10/24 feet
**Activities:** Hiking, birding, fishing (brook trout, horned pout, chain pickerel), picnicking

◆

*Church Pond is a natural beauty spot. With artistically
curved outlines, dotted with gray rocks and fringed with
dark firs, this little sheet of water is a veritable gem set in
the dark recesses of the wilderness.*
—Charles Edward Beals, Jr.
*Passaconaway in the White Mountains,* 1916

Church Pond and its trailless companion, Little Church Pond, sparkle in splendid isolation amidst the spruce and pine forests and moose-haunted bogs of Albany Intervale. This expansive basin—ringed by mountains and threaded by the Swift River and Kancamagus Highway—is thought to be the bed of an ancient glacial lake. It was prized by settlers for its abundant game, and in the early 1900s it yielded a rich harvest of timber to the Conway Lumber Company. Since then the forest has regenerated handsomely.

Once past the Swift River crossing at the start, the easy hike around the Church Pond Loop Trail will surprise you and delight you. In 2.8 mellow miles you'll see somber spruce forests, towering pines, and intriguing bogs.

Where the trail touches beautiful Church Pond, you'll find mountain views, a secluded picnic rock, and a knoll of red pines that is perfectly magical when it captures the sighing summer breeze off the water. The hike is best saved for mid- to late summer or early fall, when the river is low, the trail is at its driest, and the aggressive hordes of mosquitoes have pretty much disappeared.

The area around Church Pond is a treat for birders and wildlife buffs. In his minor classic about the Passaconaway region, Charles Edward Beals, Jr., recounted tales of chance meetings with bear and Canada lynx; the human protagonist often beat a hasty retreat to civilization. Deer were so common that these were often referred to as the Deer Ponds. Today you're more likely to see a moose, or signs thereof.

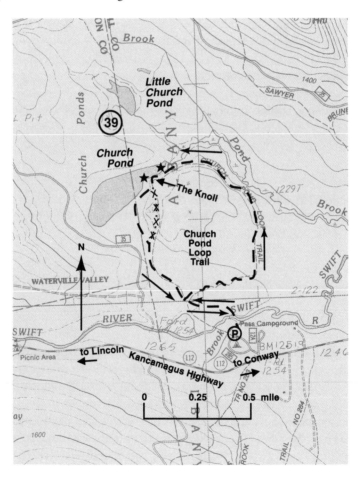

Beals also noted that the pond was named for Charles Church, a settler who ran a lumber business in the area in the mid-1800s. Robert and Mary Hixon, in their *Place Names of the White Mountains,* bestow the honor upon nineteenth-century landscape artist Frederick E. Church.

## Access
You'll find the trailhead for Church Pond Loop Trail in the Passaconaway Campground on the north side of the Kancamagus Highway (NH 112), 2 miles west of Bear Notch Road and 20 miles east of Lincoln. From the campground entrance bear left on a road that leads to Campsites 12-33. The one-way loop leads to a small parking area at the trail sign between sites 18 and 19. If space is tight, park across the highway in the lot for the UNH/ Mount Potash Trails.

## The Trail To Church Pond
Within 100 feet the trail drops you at the south bank of the Swift River. (Avoid a side path to the right.) The water is normally one-and-a-half to two feet deep with a fairly quick current. A pair of flip-flops or old sneakers and a walking stick are useful aids for traversing the stony river bottom. Do not attempt this crossing in high water! True to its name, the Swift moves rapidly after a heavy rain. For safety's sake, and to protect the fragile trail through the bogs, explore elsewhere in wet weather.

From the river's north bank the trail follows a dry, cobbled brook bed for a few yards, then cuts right into the woods—an obscure turn marked by a wooden arrow. Soon a detour loops right to cross a shallow stream. The trail angles left through a brushy tangle, then curves right into hardwood forest. About 0.3 mile from your car you enter a white pine grove and reach the loop junction. The somewhat drier left branch, your return route, leads to the pond in 0.8 mile. If the weather has been dry, bear right on the 1.4-mile eastern half of the loop.

You walk a narrow, needle-carpeted path under tall pine and spruce. The footway is edged with bunchberry, Canada mayflower, and feathery beds of haircap moss. In 0.2 mile from the loop junction the eastbound Upper Nanamocomuck Ski Trail, marked with blue diamonds, branches right. Stay straight on the yellow-blazed hiking path. You swing left into a deep forest of red spruce. You'll be walking through these lovely coniferous woods most of the way to the pond.

The next stretch may be wet in rainy seasons. Then you're back on drier ground. Put your head down and slog through any mud sections; skirting to

*Church Pond from the Knoll*

the side only widens the footway and worsens the problem. Wearing sneakers or light boots helps lessen the impact.

After passing a grassy, bushy bog on the right, the trail jogs left to skirt a large open bog of heath shrubs, tamarack, and black spruce. In summer you may hear unusual birds such as the ruby-crowned kinglet, white-winged crossbill, and the rare Lincoln's sparrow. You meander through a cathedral-like grove of spruce and pine, then bear left at an arrow and descend to low ground. For 200 yards you root-hop through a black spruce bog where the footing can vary from reasonably dry in late summer to squishy during wetter seasons. Bog bridges are probably in the cards someday for this stretch of trail. Beyond this sogginess the trail makes a sharp left turn only a few yards from the east end of Church Pond, 1.7 miles from your car.

## At Church Pond
You climb onto a low ridge that parallels the narrow eastern arm of the pond. Red pines and boulders dot this swell of dry ground. Large sawed trunks testify to a former blow-down. Beyond the short rise a side path angles 75 feet right and down to a big flat-topped boulder projecting into the murky water. This hidden perch is a premier picnic rock. There's a long view left to the broader western reach of the pond below hardwood-cloaked Sugar Hill. To the right Owl's Cliff and Mount Tremont rise past the boggy eastern shore.

In summer the rock picks up afternoon sun and mosquito-repelling breezes. Singing birds, twanging frogs, and patrolling dragonflies enliven the scene. A nap may be in order.

The main trail winds through red pines, red spruce, gray birch, and clumps of sheep laurel. A short ascent brings you to a gravelly clearing amidst a lovely stand of red pines. Known simply as "the Knoll," this restful spot overlooks the sparkling western spread of Church Pond. To the north there's a glimpse of Green's Cliff through the trees.

Steep spur paths lead down the graveled slope to shoreline views. The bottom of the right-hand path offers a rooty seat and a broad, peaceful vista over the pond to the ridges of Mount Tripyramid. Standing, you can look left of "the Trips" and peer up the valley of Sabbaday Brook into the heart of the Sandwich Range Wilderness. The dark haystack of Mount Potash looms on the far left. For the angler, the glimmering water offers varied fishing possibilities. It's not, however, recommended for swimming.

Your return route from the shore of Church Pond is the western branch of the loop trail. Head south a few yards along the top of the Knoll, then turn right (west) and descend to the black spruce bog that borders the pond. (Avoid an abandoned path that leads south into an open bog.) A long chain of topped-log bog bridges provides easy passage over the mucky terrain. In 0.1 mile the walkway bears left. There's a short unbridged passage through an opening in the bog, then the footway alternates between more bog bridges and stretches of damp but negotiable ground.

About 0.4 mile from the Knoll you reach a junction with the westbound Upper Nanamocomuck Ski Trail. The hiking trail leads south through mixed woods with occasional mud holes. Then you stroll beneath a canopy of towering white pines. A leftward curve brings you back to the loop junction, with the two stream crossings between you and your car.

*Bird's-Eye View:* Views of Church Pond are found at northerly outlooks on Mount Hedgehog (2,532 feet), Mount Potash (2,670 feet), and Mount Passaconaway (4,043 feet); a southern viewpoint on Owl's Cliff; and the ledgy summit of Mount Tremont.

*Winter:* Church Pond can be included in a 10-mile ski tour of the Upper Nanamocomuck Ski Trail from Bear Notch Road or Lily Pond. The summer loop trail may be used only if you can find a safe crossing of Swift River, perhaps by bushwhacking upstream. Use great caution, for the Swift River rarely freezes well. Park in the plowed trailhead lot across the highway. The frozen pond offers great views of Green's Cliff, Mount Tremont, Bear Mountain, and the Sandwich Range from Chocorua to Tripyramid; Passaconaway and Potash are especially impressive.

# CHAPTER 40

# LILY POND

◆

**Location:** Kancamagus Highway
**Hiking Facts:** Roadside
**Map:** USGS 7½' Mount Carrigain
**Area:** 4 acres   **Elevation:** 2,060 feet
**Avg./Max. Depth:** 4/5 feet
**Activities:** Roadside viewing, fishing (brook trout)

◆

Before the construction of the Kancamagus Highway in the 1950s, Lily Pond was a wild and lonely little water body. Few visitors disturbed its boggy repose in the high-country forests below the headwaters of the Swift River.

Now most of the thousands of visitors who drive by each year give Lily Pond scarcely more than a passing glance. If you're "doing the Kanc," allow a few minutes to stop and absorb the quiet beauty of this shallow, somber pond. It offers the non-hiker a rare look at a high mountain pond, usually obtainable only after several miles of trail walking.

## Access
The Lily Pond pull-off, with room for several cars, is on the north side of the highway 2.6 miles east of Kancamagus Pass and 7 miles west of Bear Notch Road. The pond is located on a sloping curve in the road just west of the trailhead for Livermore Trail. Drivers must be alert to make the stop in time.

## At Lily Pond
At the pull-off you have an elevated view over the squarish, murky pond, rimmed with pine and spruce. In midsummer an abundance of sedges gives the pond a grassy look. An elongated eastern spur of Mount Huntington provides a darkly wooded backdrop. Walk to the upper (west) end of the pull-off for a unique view of Mount Carrigain (identified by its observation tower) rising in the distance over the pond.

For a closer look, descend a gravelly path down the bank to the muddy

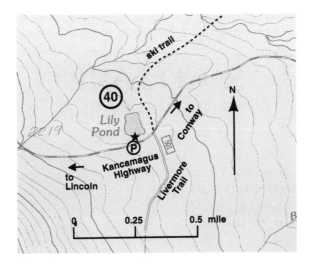

shore. Look and listen for birds, such as black-throated blue, yellow-rumped, and Nashville warblers, ovenbird, red-winged blackbird, and maybe a pair of mallards "tipping up" to feed on the bottom. Perhaps you could catch a trout; though small and shallow, Lily is a stocked trout pond.

If the water's low, you may be able to hop across the numerous whitish rocks along the eastern shore. That's about the only hiking opportunity at Lily Pond, which is better suited to perambulation by moose. But it's worth a stop to sample the spirit of this wind-ruffled lakelet, wild still despite the intrusion of the highway along its flank.

*Winter:* Lily Pond is at the western terminus of the Upper Nanamocomuck Ski Trail. There's room for several cars to park along the roadside. By skiing out on the pond you'll find views of Mount Carrigain, Mount Kancamagus, and North Tripyramid.

CHAPTER 41

# SACO LAKE

◆

**Location:** Crawford Notch, north of Gateway
**Hiking Facts:** Roadside; 0.5 mile loop hike, easy
**Map:** USGS 7½' Crawford Notch
**Area:** 6 acres **Elevation:** 1,887 feet
**Avg./Max. Depth:** 5/6 feet
**Activities:** Hiking, fly-fishing (brook trout), picnicking, canoeing

◆

*...the gem of the Notch.*
—Julius H. Ward
*The White Mountains,* 1890

Sparkling Saco Lake, the source of the Saco River, is a pretty roadside sight along US 302 just north of the Gateway of Crawford Notch. For many years it was a natural amenity for the Crawford House, a famed hotel set just across the road from 1852 until it burned in 1977. The pond was enlarged and deepened for the pleasure of the hotel's guests—who included five US presidents—and was outfitted with a flotilla of boats so they could "float on its crystal tide."

Today the pond is a popular spot for fly-fishing enthusiasts, picnickers, and guests at the AMC's Crawford Notch Hostel, located on the old hotel site. (The AMC purchased the property in 1979.) A short trail-and-road-side loop hike rewards with varied views of the pond and surrounding mountains. It's one of several attractive easy walks around "Crawford's."

## Access
There's a spacious gravel pull-off on the east side of US 302 by the outlet of Saco Lake, 0.1 mile north of the Gateway's rocky cleft. This spot, with a wide view of the pond, is at the south end of the loop trail. Here you can picnic, put in a canoe, or roam along the shore for some fly-fishing. Additional parking is available at the AMC hostel, across the road from the north end of the loop trail.

### The Saco Lake Trail

Maintained by the AMC, this 0.3 mile pleasure path traces a semicircle around the east shore of the pond. A leisurely traverse makes this a very rewarding outing. Kids will enjoy balancing on the log bridges and scrambling up the trailside ledges.

From the parking spot at the south end, cross a bridge over the outlet culvert and enter thick fir woods at the trail sign. By the SE corner a three-log bridge spans an inlet brook. Bear left, then right as the trail curves with the shoreline, passing a large sloping ledge on the right. You walk through a cut in a large fallen birch and cross a cove on a double-log bridge.

Look left across the water to the old Crawford House railroad depot, where once the Astors and Vanderbilts arrived in their private railroad cars.

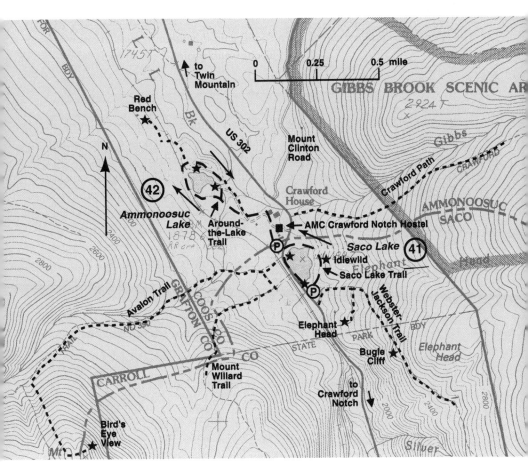

The building was beautifully restored in the 1980s and now serves as an AMC information center. The gentle Rosebrook Range rises in the distance. Beyond, dark shoreline firs part for views west to rounded, wooded Mount Tom (4,051 feet) and craggy Mount Avalon (3,442 feet), two peaks of the Willey Range.

Midway along the east shore you approach darkly wooded crags and ledges on the right. This is Idlewild, once a favorite sylvan haunt for guests of the Crawford House. The woods here were "combed and brushed and perfumed, and otherwise adorned for a summer pleasance," according to Chisholm's 1902 guidebook. Visitors could choose from many "rustic seats" to enjoy the view westward across the pond. Sturdy wooden ladders led up to ledgy outlooks. Today a steep, stone-step path climbs up the two-tiered ledge. Use caution, especially when the rocks are wet. The two levels offer different perspectives on the pond and mountains behind the security of iron railings.

Beyond the Idlewild path, the Saco Lake Trail passes a flattened beaver lodge near some jagged rocks thrust above the water. A small ledge seat gives a view that includes Mounts Tom, Avalon, Field (4,340 feet), and Willard (2,865 feet). You skirt the small, sheer cliff of Idlewild, cross another log bridge, and take in views from the NE corner of the pond.

The trail leaves the shore, rises slightly, and swings left through a tunnel of firs and past a garden of lacy ferns. As you enter a fine hardwood grove, a side path right climbs 50 feet to a small canine graveyard of unknown origin. Here lie Puck (1912), Betty (1916), and Munchen (n.d.). The main trail crosses a streambed and soon leads to US 302.

Turn left on the highway shoulder to complete your loop. A grassy flat by the pond's NW corner looks across the water to the great mass of Mount Webster (3,910 feet) looming over the Gateway. A nearer spruce-clad ridge carries Elephant Head and Bugle Cliff, two ledgy viewpoints.

Before completing the road-walk to your car, consider a visit to the AMC information center across the way. Excellent displays outline the colorful history of the notch.

*Bird's-Eye View:* You can look down on Saco Lake from the crest of Mount Avalon, a 3.8 mile round-trip with 1,500 feet of climbing via the Avalon Trail. A more accessible down-look is offered by Elephant Head, an open crag overlooking the notch and reached by an easy 0.6 mile round-trip hike (150 vertical feet) on the Webster-Jackson Trail and a spur path.

*Winter:* A pleasant stroll or ski across Saco Lake can be incorporated into a winter exploration of Ammonoosuc Lake, Elephant Head, and other

*Saco Lake*

interesting spots on the Crawford's plateau. The AMC hostel is open in the winter, and there is ample parking.

In earlier days the ice of Saco Lake was cut for the use of the Crawford House and other area hotels. Ray Evans, longtime area resident and hiker and maintainer of Saco Lake Trail, helped cut the ice in the 1930s. Each year 2,000 cakes would be hauled by horse teams to the Crawford House icehouse, to be stored for the pleasure of the next summer's guests.

CHAPTER 42

# AMMONOOSUC LAKE

◆

**Location:** North of Crawford Notch
**Hiking Facts:** 1 mile round-trip, 75-foot vertical rise outbound, easy; add 1
    mile, 100 feet for Red Bench
**Map:** USGS 7½' Crawford Notch (page 201)
**Area:** 4 acres   **Elevation:** 1,820 feet
**Activities:** Hiking, fishing (brook trout), picnicking, swimming

◆

*Half an hour alone on this bit of water, with a wild
forest around its entire shore, is one of my choicest
memories of the Crawford Notch.*
—Julius H. Ward
*The White Mountains*, 1890

Spruce-shadowed Ammonoosuc Lake is the inner sanctum of "Crawford's," the interesting plateau north of the Gateway of the Notch. Once a private preserve for well-heeled guests of the Crawford House, this dark little pond is now enclosed by National Forest land. An easy trail leading from the AMC's Crawford Notch Hostel loops around the shore, offering views of neighboring peaks and access to a pair of shoreside picnic spots. This short, pleasant hike can be extended with a side trip to Red Bench, a forest opening with a unique view of the Presidential Range.

## Access
The hostel and trailhead are on the west side of US 302, 0.3 mile north of the Gateway and 0.2 mile south of the junction with Mount Clinton Road. Ample parking is available in a hikers' lot beside the hostel entrance road.

    Walk north on the driveway, passing a cluster of cabins and the gray Shapleigh Studio, where Frank H. Shapleigh painted landscapes for Crawford House guests from 1877 to 1894. The building was restored in 1989 and now serves as the primary lodging for the AMC hostel. To the left a fine view of the Willey Range unfolds across the open grounds. As you draw even with the old carriage barn on the right, a signpost marks the Around-the-Lake Trail on the left.

## The Around-The-Lake Trail

Turn left onto an old road that once provided vehicular access to Ammonoosuc Lake. It soon enters the woods, curving right and downhill to a marked junction. Here the Around-the-Lake Trail splits left off the road and descends gently through open hardwoods to the loop junction.

Bear left on the loop's western link, which dips to cross a brook on a plank bridge. You swing left through hardwoods, then right into a gloomy stand of conifers. The footway twists along a bank through spruce and fir, then plunges and makes a hard right to Merrill Spring, a trickle of water seeping down a mossy bank into the SW corner of Ammonoosuc Lake. Here you get your first tree-screened glimpse of the pond, its surface as somber as the pointed evergreens crowding the shores.

During the heyday of the Crawford House, Merrill Spring (named for one of the hoteliers who managed the property) was famed for its purity. In 1886 Dr. Edwin J. Bartlett of Dartmouth College analyzed the water and concluded that "the Merrill Spring is undoubtedly one of the purest waters in the world." His opinion was proudly displayed in the hotel's promotional literature. The water was reported to maintain a 40-degree temperature year-round. Twin Mountain resident and local hiking legend Ray Evans recalled that during his days as a bellhop and doorman at Crawford House in the 1920s and 1930s, guests could sample the water of Merrill Spring from a pump-fed fountain in the hotel lobby. Today the little well at the spring has fallen into disrepair, but the water is presumably as pure as ever.

Beyond Merrill Spring step stones guide you across a boggy spot. The trail hugs a steep bank along the pond's west shore. A curtain of fir boughs frames several vistas over the water. To the east, beyond the pond, ridges clad in old-growth spruce part to reveal the boreal crest of Mount Clinton, a 4,310-foot peak of the Southern Presidentials. Up-slope to your left are the tracks of the recently re-opened Crawford Notch Scenic Railway.

A short pitch by the pond's NW corner lifts you to a junction with the spur to Red Bench. This left-branching path rolls through hardwood forest and across the railroad tracks. The trail crosses a bridge by a small gorge and reaches the scarlet wooden seat in 0.5 mile. The woods open eastward to an unusual close-up of the Presidentials, including Mounts Jefferson, Clay,

Washington, Monroe, and Eisenhower. The view is especially fine in evening light. The exuberant Julius Ward opined that if one could choose a final outlook on the world before saying farewell, Red Bench at sunset might well top the list.

From the Red Bench junction, the moss-bordered Around-the-Lake Trail hooks right through spindly spruces above the north shore. Shortly you come to another junction, signed: Down to the Lake. This side path angles right and down to a sunny, grassy opening with the finest view of Ammonoosuc Lake. You gaze southward over the placid water and spearlike spruces to the mountains framing Crawford Notch: Jackson and Webster on the left, Willard's low dome on the right, its gentle north slope giving no hint of the great cliffs facing south to the pass. On a still day the pond mirrors this mountain profile in picturesque fashion. With luck you might spot a beaver, a great blue heron, or a foraging moose.

The main trail crosses a dry brook bed and swerves right through a tunnel of conifers behind the NE shore. The steep glacial ridge on your left is littered with scrawny blow-downs, like a giant's game of pick-up sticks. You pass a plank seat with a restricted view over the water and emerge from the woods at the narrow east end of the pond. Look up to the right for a view of craggy 3,442-foot Mount Avalon. Here the outlet flows through a small rock-and-concrete dam en route to the Ammonoosuc River. (The name "Ammonoosuc" has its origins in an Abenaki word meaning "fish-place.") Step across a wooden footway to a weedy meadow with a nice view back down the pond to the Rosebrook Range beyond. Once the site of a beach house for the use of Crawford House guests, this clearing is a fine picnic and swimming spot.

To make the slightly uphill return to your car, follow the old road southward across a brook to a trail sign. From this junction you can 1) keep straight on the road, a slightly shorter route, or 2) bear right on the Around-the-Lake Trail, reaching the loop junction in 100 yards. Bear left here and you'll come back to the road at the edge of the Crawford House grounds.

*Winter:* This is a nifty little ski or snowshoe trip. Out on Ammonoosuc Lake you'll find views of Mounts Avalon, Willard, Webster, Jackson, and Clinton. Watch for soft ice and a bit of open water along the south shore, where springs seep into the pond. The Presidential Range view from Red Bench is even better with the leaves off the trees.

CHAPTER 43

# LAKES OF THE CLOUDS

◆

**Location:** Mount Monroe/Mount Washington col
**Hiking Facts:** 6.6 miles round-trip, 2,550-foot vertical rise, more difficult; add
    0.8 mile and 350 feet for Mount Monroe
**Map:** USGS 7½' X 15' Mount Washington; AMC/Washburn Mount Washing-
    ton and Presidential Range

|  | Upper Lake | Lower Lake |
|---|---|---|
| **Area:** | 0.4 acre | 1.2 acres |
| **Elevation:** | 5,050 feet | 5,025 feet |
| **Avg./Max. Depth:** | 6.5 feet | 8.5 feet |

**Activities:** Hiking, picnicking, AMC hut

◆

*...set like glittering diamonds in rough granite frames...*
—John H. Spaulding
*Historical Relics of the White Mountains*, 1855

What White Mountain hiker has not seen or heard of Lakes of the Clouds? New Hampshire's premier alpine ponds are photogenically set in the rocky, windswept saddle between Mount Washington (6,288 feet) and Mount Monroe (5,384 feet). Thousands of trampers pass by the tarns on the Crawford Path each year, bound for the summit of The Big One. The lakes and their namesake AMC hut are familiar landmarks in the southerly view from Mount Washington.

The lakes are worthy of a visit in their own right, apart from the peaks. Nowhere else in the Whites will you find such a grand landscape of tarn, crag, and tundra. The naturalist can study some of the 110 species of plant life found in the surrounding alpine zone. The sharp-eyed geology buff will spot many examples of glacial action, starting with the lakes themselves, which lie in basins scooped out by the continental ice sheet. (See Bibliography for good natural history guides to the alpine zone.)

The pleasures of the lakes are not easily won, for the hike up the

Ammonoosuc Ravine Trail from the Cog Railway Base Road is steep and arduous. An alternative is to drive or ride to the summit of Mount Washington and trek down the Crawford Path, but even this involves tiring rock-hopping on the descent and a 1,200-foot slog on the return. Hikers staying over at the hut can approach via other trails from north, south, and east.

The lakes area is above the trees, completely exposed to wind and weather, and likely to be 10° to 15° colder than the trailhead. Wear suitable footgear and bring warm and waterproof clothing, map, compass, water, food, and other necessities of above tree-line travel.

If you go on a fine weekend day in summer, you'll see why these are often dubbed "Lakes of the Crowds." *It is extremely important to stay on the trail in this fragile, heavily used area.*

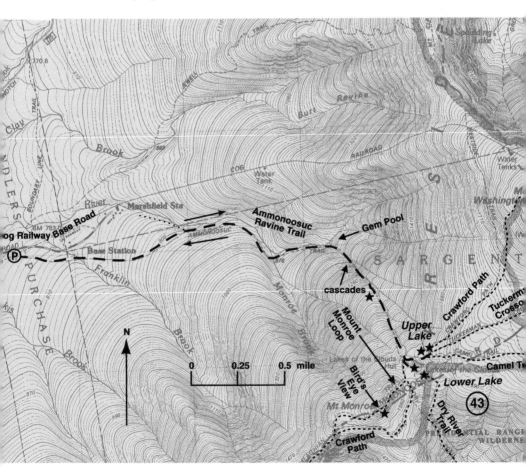

## Access

From US 302 at Fabyan (near Bretton Woods), turn east on the Cog Railway Base Road. In 4.3 miles you cross the Mount Clinton Road (an alternate access from US 302). In another 1 mile look for the hikers' parking sign on the right. The large paved lot is equipped with toilets and an information kiosk. At 2,500 feet, it's one of the loftiest trailheads.

## The Trail To The Lakes

The blue-blazed Ammonoosuc Ravine Trail starts at the east end of the parking lot. For the first mile you follow a new link, cut in 1986 when the trailhead was moved away from the privately owned Cog Railway Base Station. It rises easily with soft footing through open, parklike woods of fir and birch. At 0.3 mile you dip to cross Franklin Brook, and at 0.4 you step over a double pipeline.

At 1 mile the trail descends to meet the older route from the Base Station beside the rocky Ammonoosuc River. Bear right and ascend gradually along the stream on a rougher footway. Amidst the firs you pass a memorial to Herbert J. Young, a Dartmouth student who died here in December 1928. Higher up the woods get scrubbier; across the river you see strips of trees flattened by landslides. You cross Monroe Brook at 1.7 miles, and at 2.1 miles you emerge beside Gem Pool, a basin of crystal-clear water fed by a moss-fringed cascade.

Cross the brook and turn right to begin a steep and relentless pitch up hundreds of stone steps. If you find the climb grueling, think of the trail crew who grunted the rocks into place. In 0.2 mile a small sign marks a side trail right to the Gorge, where you can view a pair of spectacular waterslides from an airy perch. (See Bruce and Doreen Bolnick's *Waterfalls of the White Mountains.*)

The staircase soars upward another 0.2 mile to a minor brook crossing and the first outlook west over the valley. The Mount Washington Hotel gleams white in the distance. Ledgy scrambles lift you past a series of cascades as you cross and recross the brook. The ascent continues through scrub and over inclined ledges of quartzite and schist. Views open within the ravine and out to the NW. On the left great scree slopes sweep up to the summit of Mount Washington, with antennae peering eerily over the crest. Though the grade is still moderately steep, the climb seems easier amidst the openness of scrub and ledges.

Near the top the hut and the bouldery heap of Mount Monroe appear abruptly. Follow cairns and blazes up to the Crawford Path by the SW corner of the hut, 3.1 miles from the trailhead. When the hut is open (mid-June to mid-September), you can stop in for a glass of lemonade and a candy bar and peruse the interesting displays about alpine zone ecology. The stone wall in front is a popular resting spot.

### At The Lakes

The two lakes are only a couple hundred feet apart, but have differing elevations, drainages, and characters. From a trail junction at the NE corner of the hut, you can visit each pond in turn.

For the Upper Lake, follow the cairns of the Crawford Path eastward. The Lower Lake soon opens on the right, beyond its two narrow north arms. Step over a hose that supplies the hut with drinking water (take care to protect its purity) and hop rocks across the outlet brook, the birthplace of the Ammonoosuc River. After an easy climb through krummholz (dwarfed fir and spruce) you dip to the south end of Upper Lake, a narrow oval of shallow, crystal-clear water. The cone of Mount Washington rises massively behind and right of the pond. A sheared-off crag on the left (west) shore shows the contorted folds typical of the Presidentials' metamorphic rocks. At the far (north) end you see a small meadow but no visible outlet. The pond, fed by springs and runoff, drains underground through the rocks.

There's a trailside rock seat on the left a few yards up from the low point. It's worth your while to climb another 200 feet to the junction with the Tuckerman Crossover and Camel Trail. By the signpost there's a striking view over Upper Lake, with the hut and distant mountains beyond.

To visit the larger and deeper Lower Lake, retrace your steps 0.1 mile to the hut and turn left on the Dry River Trail. This path, much less used than Crawford Path, rises slightly and dips left towards Lower Lake, providing a good look at the pond and its rocky basin. The trail runs above the west shore and drops nearly to water level to circle the SW corner on broken rock. Look left across the water for a good view of Mount Washington.

The footway skirts the south shore through thick scrub and angles up and left through a tumble of rough boulders. Scramble up to the first of several cairns on this slope, where a rock seat provides the nicest—and quietest—picnic spot at the lakes. A beautiful view opens NW across the pond and its enclosing bowl, with Burke Mountain and other Vermont peaks on the horizon. Here, away from the bustle of the hut, you can look and listen for the summer birds of the alpine zone—the white-throated sparrow, yellow-rumped and blackpoll warblers, and dark-eyed junco.

Life in the lakes themselves is limited by the bitter climate. Both ponds freeze solid early in the winter, and ice-out is normally not complete until early to mid-June. Fish life is nonexistent. (The state made several fruitless attempts at trout-stocking in the 1950s and 1960s.) Even during the few months when the ponds are ice-free, rapid fluctuations in temperature and water level make for a difficult life. Nevertheless, a study by Claire Buchanan (see Bibliography) recorded over 15 species of aquatic insect present in the lakes. Most survive the winter by burrowing into bottom mud. Remarkably, spring peepers and American toads are summer breeders at the lakes, migrating over dry land from lower elevations.

From your viewing perch, retrace your steps on Dry River Trail back to the hut.

## Mount Monroe

No trip to the lakes is complete without a side jaunt to the craggy summit of Mount Monroe. This adds 0.8 mile (round-trip) and 350 feet of climbing to your day. Follow the Crawford Path south 0.1 mile from the hut and turn right on the Mount Monroe Loop. Stone steps and a ledgy scramble hoist you to the level ridge crest and the summit rocks beyond. From the top, look NE along the ridge for a terrific *bird's-eye view* of the lakes sparkling at the base of Mount Washington's summit cone. Equally magnificent is the vista SW down the range. All told, the summits of 32 New Hampshire 4,000-footers can be spotted.

To return to your car, retrace your steps to the hut for a knee-jarring descent of the Ammonoosuc Ravine Trail. Use care on the ledges, which can be slippery when wet.

*Winter:* This wild, wooly, near-polar landscape is accessible *only* to fully-equipped winter hikers with plenty of above tree-line experience. The weather can be brutal, and fatal to the unprepared tramper. The hut is closed, so there is no shelter. The steep Ammonoosuc Ravine Trail is not a good winter approach, and it may be impossible to drive to that trailhead. The usual approach to the Lakes-Monroe area is from Pinkham Notch via Lion Head and connecting trails. The terrain between the lakes and Bigelow Lawn can be bewildering in winter. Don't even think of trying this trek on anything but a clear, calm, and relatively warm day. *Please stay on the trail at all times above treeline.* Snow cover is thin, and the alpine plants are just as fragile in winter, if not more so. Above tree-line camping is permitted only where snow depth is two feet or more and is prohibited on the pond surfaces.

## The Lakes: Past and Future

Their beauty and key location have made these tiny lakes among the most visited and celebrated places in the White Mountains. If you come to the lakes, you can take pleasure in their storied past, and take care to preserve this fragile environment for future generations to enjoy.

According to Laura and Guy Waterman's *Forest and Crag*, the ponds were noted in two accounts of Darby Field's landmark 1642 climb of Mount Washington. This was a key clue in the attempt to unravel the mystery of Field's route to the summit, for which a definitive answer may never be known.

The lakes were formally opened to the hiking world when the legendary Crawfords blazed their Crawford Path to Mount Washington via the Southern Presidentials in 1819. The Crawfords knew the larger lake as Blue Pond, a name inspired by an 1820 trek in which Ethan Allen Crawford guided several notables from nearby Lancaster to the summit of Mount Washington. The party, bolstered by liberal portions of a drink called "O-be-joyful," bestowed names upon several Presidential peaks. Descending, they took a long break at the ice-cold pond, "partaking of its waters, until some of us became quite blue, and from this circumstance we agreed to give it the name of Blue Pond..." (*Lucy Crawford's History of the White Mountains*). Another early name for the lakes was "Washington's Punch Bowl." Over the years the Crawfords guided many famous visitors along the way by the lakes.

The Crawford Path has since led thousands of self-guided hikers past the lakes' shores. The exposed walk is delightful on a fine day but potentially deadly when the weather goes bad. In the early summer of 1900, two hardy trampers—William B. Curtis and Allan Ormsbee—died from exposure when they pressed on past Mount Monroe in a fierce storm of rain and sleet. In response, the AMC built a refuge hut somewhat beyond the lakes. In 1915 this was replaced by a stone building near the ponds—still standing as part of today's Lakes of the Clouds Hut. In that same year, the steep and spectacular Ammonoosuc Ravine Trail was cleared and opened by AMC trailmeisters Charles Blood, Nathaniel Goodrich, and helpers.

The new hut (since expanded to a 90-person capacity) and trail made the lakes one of the most popular tramping locales in the mountains. The exponential growth of hiking in the 1970s endangered peace and solitude and the vulnerable alpine vegetation. From the twisted, dwarfed krummholz of black spruce and balsam fir to the delicate June blooms of diapensia and Lapland rosebay, these low-lying plants—islands of Arctic vegetation

*Upper Lake of the Clouds and AMC hut*

left in the wake of the retreating glaciers—thrive in a climate of relentless wind, cold, and ice. But they can't handle the crunching of Vibram-soled boots. One careless step can destroy years of hard-won growth. Of special concern is the endangered *Potentilla Robbinsiana*, a species of cinquefoil found only in this area.

In the past two decades the AMC and Forest Service have gone to great lengths to educate hikers about the need for stewardship and thoughtful hiking in the alpine zone. Less subtle but necessary techniques include the defining of trails with low rock walls and the closing of the flat area east of Mount Monroe to protect the endangered plant. Much progress has been made, and you can contribute by walking only on the marked trails and encouraging others to do the same. If you must leave the trail, take care to walk only on exposed rocks. Needless to say, no camping is allowed in the alpine zone through the warm months and only on two or more feet of snow in winter. If we all follow these simple guidelines, the lakes and the alpine zone will continue to enchant and delight for many years to come.

# CHAPTER 44

# HERMIT LAKE

◆

**Location:** Tuckerman Ravine
**Hiking Facts:** 4.8 miles round-trip, 1,850-foot vertical rise, moderate
**Maps:** USGS 7½' x 15' Mount Washington; AMC/Washburn Mount Washington and Presidential Range
**Area:** 0.3 acre   **Elevation:** 3,857 feet
**Avg./Max. Depth:** 3/4 feet
**Activities:** Hiking, camping (lean-tos), picnicking

◆

*The lake is, indeed, a hermit, dwelling always apart in
its hollow among the spiring spruces, a tiny level of water,
strangely beautiful for its placidity amid all the turmoil
and grandeur about it.*
—Winthrop Packard
*White Mountain Trails*, 1917

The Tuckerman Ravine Trail, the #1 hiking trade route to Mount Washington, is traversed by thousands upon thousands of hikers each year, and with good reason. The grandeur of the bowl-like cirque and its encircling crags rivals any mountain spectacle in the East.

But even on the busiest summer weekends, relatively few trampers pause to see delightful little Hermit Lake. This dark tarn is as petite as they come—about the size of the Frog Pond on Boston Common, wrote nineteenth-century prose-poet Julius Ward—but adds a sweet finishing touch to this magnificent mountainscape. The lake's name, coined in 1853 by S.B. Beckett, a guidebook publisher from Maine, has been applied in a general sense to the complex of shelters in the vicinity. The pond itself nestles in a small fir-bound scoop just north of the main trail. Whether you're intent on reaching the summit or just up to see the ravine, the short detour to Hermit Lake is time well spent. The loop path to the shelters shows you both sides of the tarn and leads to a picnic table that presents one of the grandest lunch views in New England.

## Access

The access to Hermit Lake is, of course, the Tuckerman Ravine Trail, the I-93 of White Mountain footpaths. It starts behind the Visitor Center at the AMC's Pinkham Notch Camp, located on the high point of NH 16 between Glen (11 miles south) and Gorham (11 miles north). There is ample parking that spills out to the shoulder of the highway on the busiest days. The Visitor Center offers maps, books, free literature, refreshments, advice, and interpretive displays.

## The Trail To Hermit Lake

The Tuckerman Ravine Trail starts behind the Visitor Center, bearing left as Old Jackson Road splits right. The footway up to the floor of the ravine is a wide, rocky tractor road that rises at a moderate but steady grade. Hardwood

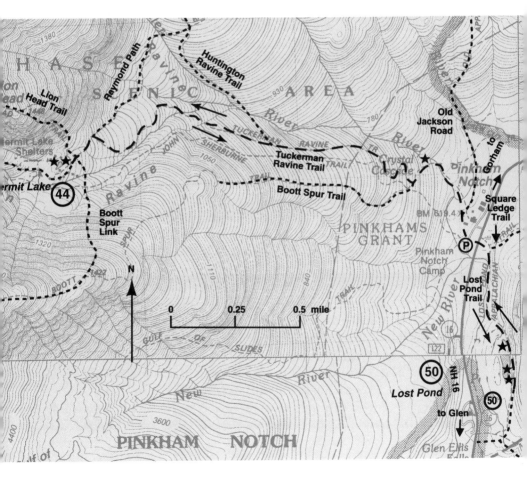

forests at the floor of the notch give way to spruce and fir partway up. Landmarks along the way include Crystal Cascade at 0.3 mile, Huntington Ravine Trail at 1.3 miles, and Raymond Path at 2.1 miles. At 2.3 miles you reach a junction where Lion Head Trail leaves right. About 100 yards beyond, the east end of the shelter loop departs on the right.

## At Hermit Lake

Follow the side path past a lean-to and a wooden railing to the top of a little bluff above the east shore of the pond. Here you'll find a clearing with a grand view of the ravine mirrored in the dark water. The upper bowl and its headwall—famed for white-knuckle spring skiing—occupy center stage. During the last Ice Age, centuries' worth of snowfall packed down to form an alpine glacier. Over time the ice plucked rocks from the sides of the basin to form this vast amphitheater, called a "Mountain Coliseum" by early White Mountain writers. The glacier also dammed up the little basin of Hermit Lake by dumping a low ridge of debris known as a terminal moraine.

The high, jagged ridge on the left is Boott Spur, fronted by the impressive Hanging Cliffs. Close by on the right loom the rough crags of Lion Head. Julius Ward wrote that Hermit Lake "is the only place from which you can see the ravine at full advantage." (Please stay off the eroded paths that lead down the steep bank to the shore; the view is better where you are.)

One notable visitor to this viewpoint was Henry David Thoreau, who explored, camped, and botanized in the ravine in 1858. One of his companions cast vainly for trout in Hermit Lake. (Although the pond is listed in the state's freshwater fishing guide, biologists believe it's too shallow and hard-frozen in winter to support fish life.) Thoreau's sojourn was actually somewhat of a misadventure, as his guide accidentally set fire to the scrub farther up the ravine, laying several acres to waste. Thoreau himself sprained his ankle so badly that he was laid up in camp for several days.

Because overuse threatened to destroy this beautiful but fragile environment, camping is prohibited in the ravine except at the eight lean-tos. (Ten tent sites are available December 1—April 1, when deep snow cushions their impact.) Five of the wooden shelters are hidden in the fir woods surrounding Hermit Lake. Tickets must be purchased at the Pinkham Notch Visitor Center; first-come-first-served, maximum stay seven nights. Fires are not permitted; you must cook with a camp stove. Please carry out all of your own garbage and any other litter you find. Stay on the established trails, and keep out of the marked Revegetation Areas. Rules such as these may chafe at the independent-minded camper, but the alternative would be to close the area to overnight use entirely.

For a more intimate view of Hermit Lake, return to Tuckerman Ravine Trail and continue another 200 feet SW to the clearing and complex of buildings once known as "HoJo's," a reference to the days when burgers and coffee were served up to hungry spring skiers. (Food service was discontinued in the early 1970s.)

From the upper right (NW) corner of the clearing, pick up the west link of the loop path to the shelters. The rocky footway descends, passes a side trail left to the winter tent sites, and continues to the SW corner of Hermit Lake. From here the little oval of water, bound by a tangle of stunted fir and birch, looks dark and mysterious, a hermit indeed. The path runs a few yards along the shore to a tall boulder that provides a fine view of the pond. (Beyond, the path climbs left into the woods and loops around to the shelters.) After communing with the hermit's spirit, retrace your steps to the clearing on Tuckerman Ravine Trail.

Turn right to head to the upper ravine and the summit of Mount Washington (but only if the weather is fair). Even if you're not up for much more climbing, you can make a short, rewarding jaunt in this direction. Just beyond the HoJo's clearing, you'll come to a railing on the left where you look over a meadow and a tiny, shallow pondlet. (Keep to the trail at this fragile spot.) The view here includes a cascade on the ravine's Little Headwall, with the upper bowl beyond.

A rocky 0.2 mile climb will lift you to a jumble of great boulders on the right of the trail. With careful rock-hopping you can gain access to wonderful picnic perches with views around the ravine and east to the Carter Range and Wildcat Range.

To return to your car from HoJo's, retrace your steps down the relentlessly rocky Tuckerman Ravine Trail.

*Bird's-Eye View:* Grand views of Hermit Lake and the ravine are found along the Lion Head Trail to the north and Boott Spur Trail to the south.

*Winter:* The hike into Hermit Lake (in the general sense) is a moderate and popular winter trip. The trail is packed out by Sno-Cats and boots up to the shelter area. The Tuckerman landscape is spectacular in winter, and Hermit Lake—frozen solid—is a wild little spot from which to take it in. (The upper ravine is hazardous in winter due to avalanche danger.)

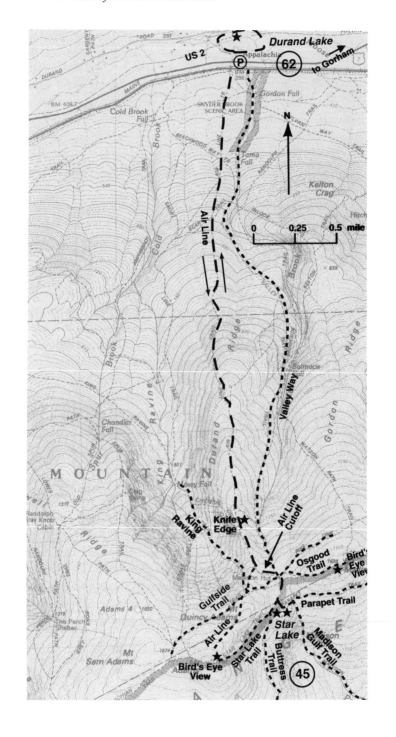

# CHAPTER 45

# STAR LAKE

◆

**Location:** Mount Adams–Mount Madison col
**Hiking Facts:** 8.0 miles round-trip, 3,600-foot vertical rise, more difficult
**Maps:** USGS 7½' X 15' Mount Washington; AMC/Washburn Mount Washington and Presidential Range
**Area:** 0.5 acre   **Elevation:** 4,896 feet
**Activities:** Hiking, picnicking, AMC hut

◆

> *In the saddle between Madison and Adams there is a tiny lakelet, filled with clear, sweet water. To this the temporary name of Star Lake has been applied, on account of its extreme height and because it mirrors so perfectly the constellations above.*
>
> —Moses F. Sweetser
> *The White Mountains: A Handbook for Travellers,* 1881

In the Highlands of Scotland, a small alpine pool such as Star Lake would be one of a thousand nameless lochans ("small lakes") sprinkled across the hills. In the White Mountains, where nature has not been so lavish with her disbursement of water bodies, Star Lake is worthy of a title, and a visit.

The pond itself is a simple affair—a half-acre circle of shallow water sprinkled with lichen-dotted rocks. Its position in the craggy arena of the Adams-Madison col, nearly a mile above sea level, is what sets Star Lake apart. The stark rock pyramids of these Northern Presidential peaks tower on either side—Mount Madison (5,366 feet) on the NE and Mount Adams (5,799 feet) on the SW. Overhanging the pond are the corrugated crags of Mount John Quincy Adams, an Adams sub-peak. On the south is the Parapet, a low rocky battlement atop the headwall of Madison Gulf. It's a rare pleasure to see a placid pool amidst such rugged rock scenery.

## Access

The imaginative hiker can fashion a half-dozen hiking routes to Star Lake from the intricate web of Northern Presidential trails. The simplest and dullest is to plod up Valley Way from US 2 at Appalachia to the AMC's Madison Hut, which is open from June through mid-September. A more scenic route from Appalachia takes the Air Line up Durand Ridge, with spectacular views from the Knife Edge, then follows Air Line Cutoff to the hut. Either route is 8 miles round-trip with a 3,600-foot vertical rise. The most dramatic and challenging approach is up the headwall of Madison Gulf via the Great Gulf and Madison Gulf Trails (11.2 miles round-trip, 3,500 feet from the Great Gulf parking area on NH 16).

## At Star Lake

From the hut the Star Lake Trail rises gently for 0.2 mile to the west shore of the lake. In midsummer look for the showy yellow blooms of mountain avens beside the trail. A sloping lichen-glazed ledge, located trailside midway along the shore, offers a seat overlooking the rocky pool and the cone of Mount Madison.

For the even more dramatic view from the other side, go back a short distance towards the hut and turn right on the Parapet Trail. Off to the left is a sheep-back ledge of white quartz, a landmark easily spotted from the neighboring ridges. A trailside ledge provides a perch overlooking Star Lake, the great rock stack of Adams, and the gaunt cliffs of John Quincy Adams. In 50 yards the Parapet Trail makes a sharp left; a spur leads 50 feet ahead to the Parapet, a ledge with an outstanding view of Madison Gulf, Mount Washington, and the Carter-Moriah Range.

*Bird's-Eye View:* The rocky watchtowers of Madison and Adams offer spectacular views of Star Lake, each with the other peak as a backdrop. The top of Madison is reached from the hut with a steady climb up the Osgood Trail; 1 mile round-trip, 560-foot vertical rise. Adams is a bit tougher: 1.6 miles round trip, 900-foot vertical rise from the shore of the lake via Star Lake Trail. The climb up the steep east face of the mountain is brutal, with a good deal of strenuous rock-hopping. From the summit you can also espy Storm Lake, perhaps the smallest and highest (5,200 feet) named pool in the mountains. This rock-strewn pondlet, fringed with clumps of deer's hair, an alpine sedge, is found beside the junction of the Gulfside and Israel Ridge Trails on the gently sloping SW ridge of Adams.

When visiting these alpine pools, please remember to stay on the trail or walk only on bare rocks if you leave the trail.

*Winter:* The Adams-Madison col is one of the more accessible alpine areas in winter, and the scenery is dazzling. Valley Way has moderate grades, is sheltered nearly to the hut (closed in winter), and is often packed out by peak-baggers. Full winter regalia is needed above tree line. Again, remember to stay on the trails and off the alpine plant life.

*Star Lake and Mount Madison from Mount Adams*

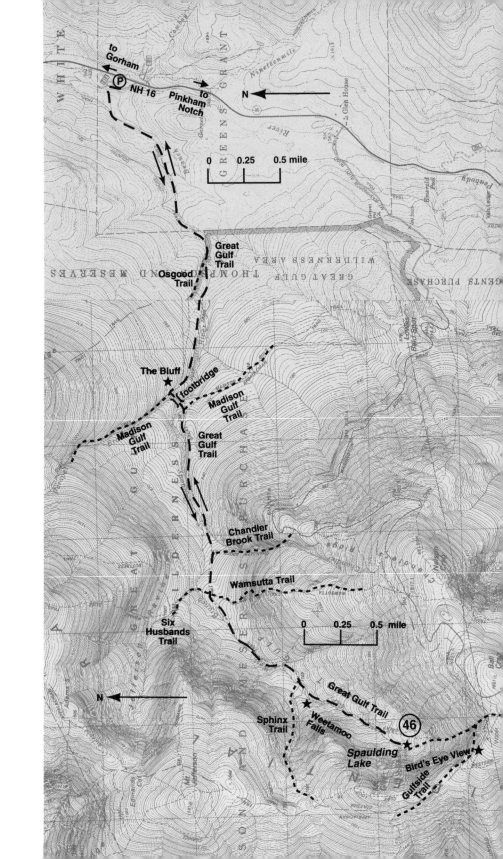

# CHAPTER 46

# SPAULDING LAKE

◆

**Location:** Great Gulf Wilderness
**Hiking Facts:** 13 miles round-trip, 2,900-foot vertical rise, more difficult
**Maps:** USGS 7½' X 15' Mount Washington and 7½' Carter Dome; AMC/
 Washburn Mount Washington and Presidential Range
**Area:** 0.5 acre  **Elevation:** 4,228 feet
**Activities:** Hiking, picnicking

◆

*"The Gulf of Mexico" and "Spaulding's Lake"*
*are at least worth a trip from the Atlantic,*
*from all who would look with proud satisfac-*
*tion upon nature in her sublimest mood.*
 —John H. Spaulding
 *Historical Relics of the White Mountains,* 1855

The Great Gulf has long been an inspiration for hikers. Bulldozed by an ancient alpine glacier, this huge cirque sprawls for four majestic miles between Mount Washington and the Northern Presidentials. Its wild, tangled forests are threaded by the West Branch of the Peabody River, a brawling stream strewn with immense boulders and graced with tumbling cascades. Bold ridges and slide-scarred walls sweep upward to the barren crests of the Northeast's highest peaks. The gulf's imposing 1,600-foot headwall is twice as high as that of the more notorious Tuckerman Ravine.

Hidden within its deepest recess, 6½ miles from the road, is the jewel of the gulf: tiny Spaulding Lake. Its setting might be the most spectacular of any White Mountain pond. Save a special day for this long but rewarding trek.

The gulf first came to notice when Darby Field and his two Native American companions made the premier ascent of Mount Washington in 1642. The cirque was originally dubbed the "Gulf of Mexico." In 1823 a party led by Ethan Allen Crawford became lost in a cloud and "wandered about until we came near the edge of a great gulf...." Crawford's remark gave the valley its present name.

An early explorer was botanist James W. Robbins, who poked around the gulf for several years starting in 1829. John H. Spaulding, historian and manager of the Tip-Top House on Mount Washington, visited the gulf in 1853 and applied his family name to the tiny tarn nestled therein. He engraved his initials on a rock slide beside the pond, "as an apology for the name given this solitary sheet."

The first trail into the basin was blazed by guide Benjamin F. Osgood in 1881. In an explosive burst of path-making from 1908 to 1910, AMC trailman Warren Hart and an enthusiastic band of volunteers built a network of trails in the gulf that rank with the boldest and most spectacular in New England. (See Laura and Guy Waterman's *Forest and Crag*.)

The Great Gulf's special qualities were recognized by the US Forest Service in 1959, when 5,400 acres were designated as a "Wild Area." In 1964 the gulf achieved official Wilderness status when Congress passed the Wilderness Act.

## Access
The Great Gulf Trail begins at a large parking area for the Great Gulf Wilderness on the west side of NH 16, 6 miles south of US 2 in Gorham and 5 miles north of the AMC's Pinkham Notch Camp.

## The Trail To Spaulding Lake
From the north end of the parking lot walk 100 yards down an old paved road and bear left to cross the Peabody River on an impressive suspension footbridge. The blue-blazed trail swings left and rises to a junction with the Great Gulf Link Trail from Dolly Copp Campground. Turn left here and parallel the river's West Branch through cool hemlock woods.

At 0.7 mile, just beyond the first of several ski trail junctions, the trail curves away from the river and ascends gently through hardwood forest. At 1.6 miles you enter the Wilderness. The Osgood Trail to Mount Madison branches right at 1.8 miles.

At 2.7 miles, after a short, steep climb, you emerge from the woods at a gravelly opening known as the Bluff. A wooden marker identifies the first of several designated campsites you'll pass along the trail. (Low-impact camping is essential to retain the wilderness character of the gulf. Except at designated sites, you must camp at least 200 feet from trails and streams. No camping is allowed beyond the Sphinx Trail junction. Please stay out of all areas marked by "Revegetation" signs.) A boulder on the right offers a superb view of the craggy mountains around the gulf. A high ridge off Mount Washington across the valley is capped by a 4,072-foot nubble called the Horn—which is 150 feet lower (!) than Spaulding Lake.

Beyond the Bluff the Great Gulf Trail drops steeply left as Osgood Cutoff continues straight. You hop across Parapet Brook, hump over a hogback ridge where upper Madison Gulf Trail departs right, and cross the West Branch on a swinging footbridge. Here the lower Madison Gulf Trail forks left, while the Great Gulf Trail swings right on the south bank of the rocky river. You walk through the moss-grown coniferous forest typical of the inner gulf. The gradient is easy to moderate, but the footing is rough. At 3.1 miles you pass Clam Rock, an overhanging bivalve-shaped boulder. At 3.9 miles you dip to cross Chandler Brook; on the far bank the Chandler Brook Trail leaves left for the Auto Road.

Moderate climbing continues through fir glades to a four-way junction with Six Husbands and Wamsutta Trails at 4.5 miles. The Great Gulf Trail cuts through blow-down areas and passes the site of a former shelter. Openings provide views up to the "Knees" of Jefferson, craggy ridges of stupendous steepness.

Brookside climbing leads to a series of surging cascades and picturesque pools, commencing at 5.2 miles. Soon you cross the West Branch and a tributary. At 5.6 miles, amidst a flat of wild fir forest, the Sphinx Trail departs right. Follow the sparsely blazed Great Gulf Trail carefully as you recross the West Branch and undertake a short climb to the pool at the base of pretty Weetamoo Falls. (See *Waterfalls of the White Mountains*, by Bruce and Doreen Bolnick.)

The trail shoots upward on a bouldery footway, penetrating the upper gulf. The West Branch shrinks to a small mountain brook. You obtain tantalizing glimpses of the rocky headwall. One last pitch amidst scrubby firs and gnarled birches lifts you to the north end of Spaulding Lake at 6.5 miles.

## At Spaulding Lake

The outlet rocks provide your first view of the pond. It's a stunner, the more so because you've trekked so far to see it. The craggy, curving headwall of the gulf seems about to overpower the diminutive pond. Stunted conifers and gaunt rocks crowd the shores. A huge boulder rises from the scrub at the far end of the pond. The whole scene is surpassingly wild, even awesome, a term seldom applicable to our modest Eastern mountains.

*View over Spaulding Lake to Mounts Adams and Madison*

The trail traverses the east shore over an assortment of boulders deposited by slides and frost action. Looking down into the pellucid water you see slow-decaying tree trunks on the gravel-streaked bottom. Because of its shallowness and high elevation, Spaulding Lake supports no natural fish life, though hardy conservation officers once packed fingerling brook trout down the headwall for stocking each June. Ray Evans, a Fish and Game employee for 37 years, recalls that 2,000 fish would be hauled in annually to stock the pond and the West Branch. Each man carried 500 of the two-inch trout in a can specially fitted with canvas shoulder straps. (The pond is no longer stocked.)

A tumble of rocks that spills down to the shore by the pond's SE corner is a good spot for a lunch break. Energetic trampers can continue a short distance past the pond to a short, rough side path that leads right across the inlet brook and twists through the scrub to the aforementioned giant boulder. A scramble to the rock's peaked ridge line rewards with a striking vista north over Spaulding Lake and down the gulf to the rocky cones of Mount Adams and Mount Madison. Behind you is the headwall, where you might spot a silhouetted hiker on the rim, a puff of Cog Railway smoke, or the gleam of a car along the Auto Road.

*Bird's-Eye View:* Beyond Spaulding Lake the Great Gulf Trail scales the headwall with a climb of 1,600 feet in a rather strenuous half mile. To the right, crags along the rim-top Gulfside Trail open memorable views of the yawning cirque, the Northern Presidentials, and Spaulding Lake glimmering amidst the dark forest below. (Stay on the trail, or walk only on bare rocks.)

*Winter:* The Great Gulf is even more awesome in winter. Strong parties can experience its grandeur on a long day trip to Spaulding Lake. The Great Gulf Trail is good for snowshoeing, save for an occasional devilish sidehill. The upper Gulf is less-visited in winter; expect tons of snow and some heavy breaking. In places it may be easier to follow the frozen brook than the snowbound trail. You'll find the little pond buried in wind-carved snowdrifts. The views up to the snow-and-ice-draped headwall are unrivaled in the winter Whites. Keep away from the steep walls of the Gulf unless you're experienced in assessing avalanche danger.

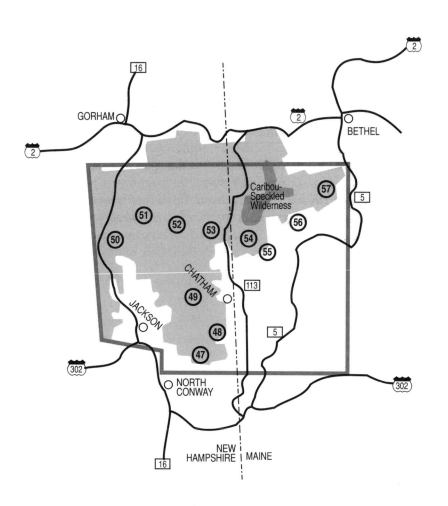

*Beach at Virginia Lake*

# IV. Eastern
# White Mountains

EAST OF THE PRESIDENTIALS the White Mountains align themselves in a series of successively lower ranges, spilling over into the hill and lake country of western Maine. The ponds of this region are relatively few but offer a variety of attractions.

The south-central part of the eastern Whites, mainly the town of Chatham, is dominated by the dome of 3,268-foot Mount Kearsarge North (formerly Mount Pequawket) and its lower northward extension, the Gemini–Mount Shaw range. Arrayed around these mountains are two small, boggy ponds—Shingle and Province—and magnificent Mountain Pond, the largest road-free water body in the Whites. The twin peaks of Doublehead overlook Mountain Pond on the west.

Across Pinkham Notch from Mount Washington the Wildcat Ridge and Carter-Moriah Range march northward in a flurry of 4,000-foot peaks. At the western base of Wildcat is tranquil Lost Pond, with spectacular shoreline views of Mount Washington's eastern ridges and ravines. The diminutive Carter Ponds are tucked into Carter Notch, the high rocky cleft between Wildcat and Carter Dome.

The only water bodies found in the broad Wild River valley (between the Carter-Moriah Range on the west and the Baldface-Royce Range to the east) are the boggy channel known as No-Ketchum Pond and a series of trailless beaver ponds. In a glacial cirque on the east side of the Royce Range is Basin Pond, man-made but exceptionally beautiful.

East of scenic Evans Notch is a jumble of lower mountains in western Maine, topped by 2,906-foot Speckled Mountain. On the southern fringe of these ridges are swampy Shell Pond, a ringer known as Horseshoe Pond, and the broad sheet of Virginia Lake, recently added to the National Forest.

At the eastern base of 1,930-foot Albany Mountain lies a peaceful chain of small, easily accessible ponds: Broken Bridge, Crocker, and Round.

# CHAPTER 47

# SHINGLE POND

◆

**Location:** Chatham, SE of Mount Kearsarge North
**Hiking Facts:** 5.6 miles round-trip, 1,200-foot vertical rise, moderate
**Map:** USGS 7 ½' North Conway East
**Area:** 2 acres   **Elevation:** 1,710 feet
**Activities:** Hiking

◆

This boggy little oval rests at the base of Mount Kearsarge North and provides an interesting view of that tower-topped peak. Encircled by a ring of leatherleaf and drowned trees, Shingle Pond is located beside the Weeks Brook Trail, a long and little-used back-door route up the mountain from South Chatham. The pond's name was applied by George P. Bond, whose 1853 map was one of the earliest of the White Mountains.

## Access

Drive north on ME/NH 113 from Fryeburg ME. At 2 miles from US 302, bear left (straight) on Green Hill Road where ME/NH 113 goes right. You'll pass Hurricane Mountain Road on the left in another 3.3 miles. At 0.4 mile beyond this junction, turn left onto a gravel road (FR 317) marked by a brown hiker symbol. A kiosk and gate mark the trailhead and parking (relocated here in 1993) 100 yards in.

## The Trail To Shingle Pond

Walk up the gravel road beyond the gate through a logged area, bearing left just past a bridge at 0.3 mile. At 0.5 mile bear right and uphill on a branching road, then quickly left on a trail into the woods. This new section of trail bypasses a timber harvest area, then rejoins the old trail. You rise gradually, then moderately on old logging roads through nice hardwoods. Near the top the woods become sprucey and wilder. The final approach to the pond leads you through a fine grove of spruce and hemlock.

## At Shingle Pond

The trail veers right just before reaching the pond, 2.8 miles from your car. A side path leads 60 feet left to a clearing and beyond to the brushy edge of the woods for a better view. From here a string of strategically placed poles enables you—with careful balancing—to traverse the band of thickly-grown leatherleaf and squishy sphagnum that rims the pond, reaching the water's edge with boots dry and bog untrampled.

Your reward is the best view of lily-dotted Shingle Pond, with the broad, spruce-clad hulk of Kearsarge North spread to the NW. The mountain is nicely reflected in the water; indeed, the pond was once known as Mirror Lake and early AMC guidebooks made special mention of the "remarkable" view. Dragonflies and birds are plentiful—I once saw chimney

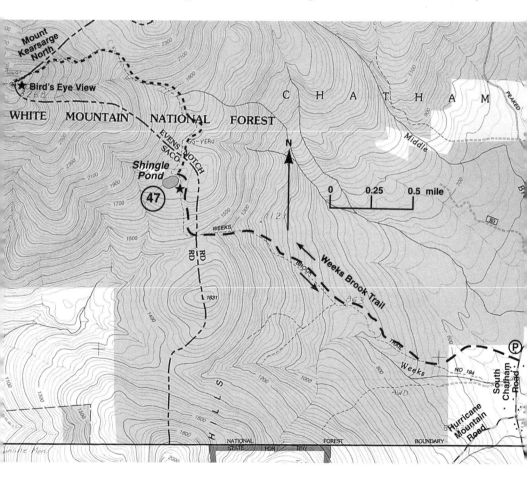

*Shingle Pond and Kearsarge North*

swifts dip into the water for drinks on the wing. To find a picnic spot, you must retreat to a log seat in the woods with a more restricted view.

Beyond the side path the Weeks Brook Trail circles the east shore, providing different perspectives on the pond across the bog, but there's no other place to get down to the water.

*Bird's-Eye View:* Ambitious hikers will opt to continue 2.1 miles and 1,550 vertical feet to the ledgy crown of Kearsarge North. The summit fire tower, the last of its kind in the White Mountains, was completed in 1951 and is listed on the National Historic Lookout Registry. The tower is no longer staffed, but it is in good condition and is open to hikers. In addition to its famous horizon-stretching vistas, the summit offers a fine bird's-eye view of Shingle Pond, a dark oval nestled on a forested plateau. The round-trip to pond and peak is 9.8 miles with a 2,750-foot vertical rise.

*Winter:* Typical of bog-rimmed ponds, Shingle Pond is more accessible in winter. And it's worth visiting for its imposing close-up of Kearsarge North. Roadside parking is usually available by the trailhead. The Weeks Brook Trail is used by snowmobiles, sometimes all the way to the pond.

# CHAPTER 48

# PROVINCE POND

◆

**Location:** Chatham, east of Mount Shaw
**Hiking Facts:** 3.2 miles round-trip, 400-foot vertical rise, easy
**Maps:** USGS 7 ½' North Conway East and Chatham
**Area:** 12 acres **Elevation:** 1,326 feet
**Avg./Max. Depth:** 6/11 feet
**Activities:** Hiking, fishing (brook trout), camping (lean-to), picnicking

◆

Province Pond is nestled in one of those peaceful nooks of the mountains seldom visited by hikers intent on the Presidentials or other more glamorous objectives. It's a boggy hourglass of water overlooked by the low but intriguing peaks of Mount Shaw (2,585 feet) and the Gemini or Twins (North Peak, 2,519 feet; South Peak, 2,490 feet).

Fifty years ago this mini-range extending northward from Mount Kearsarge North boasted a ridge-crest trail and several connecting paths. Today the Province Brook Trail into the pond is the only remaining trail in the area. The hike is an easy ramble up old logging roads, ending at a sun-drenched lean-to on the north shore.

## Access

Heading north from Fryeburg on ME/NH 113, bear left on Green Hill Road (towards South Chatham) at a fork 2 miles from US 302. In another 3.3 miles you pass Hurricane Mountain Road left, followed by a series of branching gravel roads, also on the left. The third of these is Peaked Hill Road, or FR 450. Turn left here, 0.8 mile north of Hurricane Mountain Road and just past a National Forest "Healthy Environment" sign. (Coming south on South Chatham Road, this junction is 4.4 miles from ME/NH 113.) Drive 2.4 miles up the gravel road to its end.

## The Trail To Province Pond

The Province Brook Trail leaves left from the parking area at a sign. You stride

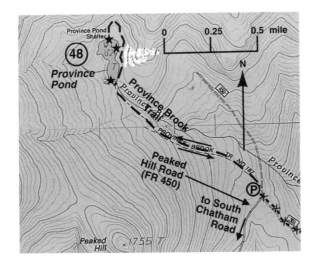

up a wide old logging road at a mellow grade through hardwoods and hemlocks. Logged areas open on the right for the first ⅓ mile; then you cross a small brook and enter deeper woods. At about 0.7 mile the trail guides you into a shady hemlock grove. The grade slackens as the footing becomes wet and rocky. Log corduroy and bog bridges ease you over the soggiest spots. Partway through this damp section a Forest Service arrow directs you right at a fork.

At 0.9 mile you rock-hop across a brook and bear left through another dark stand of hemlocks. After a short, wet descent you cross a tiny stream and approach Province Brook amidst towering hemlock and spruce. Great boulders are crowned with moss and polypody ferns. You see evidence of selective logging across the brook. The trail curves left around a cabin-sized boulder supporting its own patch of forest, including one spruce at least 50 feet tall. You continue on 100 feet, cross a snowmobile bridge over Province Brook, and arrive at the south end of Province Pond.

## At Province Pond

A grassy, gravelly clearing on the left overlooks the shallow, boggy south arm of the pond, dotted with the blunt stubs of drowned trees. The water here was raised by the old beaver dam beside you and a small man-made dike beyond, concealed by grass and bushes. The double wooded summit of Mount Shaw rises above a tangle of snags on the west shore. Northward up the length of the pond you see the shelter on the distant shore, ¼ mile away by trail.

The Province Brook Trail plunges into thick growth behind the east

*Province Pond and Mount Shaw*

shore and quickly issues into a deep, dark grove of hemlocks. The trail splits for 200 feet—a wide snowmobile trail down to the left, the narrow yellow-blazed hiking path up on the right. The two trails rejoin, only to branch again 100 yards beyond. This time you go left on the hiking trail, while the broad snowmobile trail runs right, uphill and away from the pond.

In 200 feet you pass a large yellow-blazed boulder beside the trail. Descend gently for another 50 yards and look left for a huge, peaked boulder on the shore. A short side path leads through the open woods to this remarkable chunk of granite. It's sculpted as a tapered A-frame, like a Goliath-sized Sierra Designs tent. The "door" faces out to the north half of Province Pond, a deeper saucer of water.

By scrambling out to the right side of the boulder you'll find a passable seat and the best views at Province Pond. Across the dark water the rounded summits of the Gemini rise on the left. The wooded wall of Mount Shaw looms directly across. The green-roofed shelter stands out on the right.

Beyond the boulder the Province Brook Trail crosses an inlet spring by the pond's NE corner and bears left well north of the shore. You step through a cut in a giant fallen hemlock into a bright, leafy stand of beeches. Curving left again, you come back to the pond beside the sawed-log shelter.

The south-facing lean-to has a great sun exposure and a wide view of the pond. A fringe of sedge, brush, and muck gives the pond a decidedly boggier look from this perspective. The A-frame boulder is prominent to the left. A dark waterline on its face, two or three feet above the current level, hints at former beaver activity in the pond. An old beaver lodge is visible on the opposite shore.

If the bugs are tolerable, the shelter makes a sunny lunch spot. Anglers may want to poke around the shore for a better casting spot. Province is reputed to be a good trout pond (Sweetser's nineteenth-century guidebook noted it as such); one local sportsman I met there reported that the fish tend to congregate around a boiling spring along the west shore.

The walk out from Province Pond is a quick and easy exit-hike—a half hour or so from shelter to trailhead at a brisk pace.

*Winter:* Peaked Hill Road is not plowed, adding 2.4 miles each way. Both the road and the Province Brook Trail are snowmobile routes. The 8-mile round-trip to the pond is a rather easy ski tour or winter hike. There are good views of Mount Shaw and the Gemini from the frozen pond. The shelter is a sunny picnic spot.

# CHAPTER 49

# MOUNTAIN POND

———————◆———————

**Location:** Chatham, east of Mount Doublehead
**Hiking Facts:** 2.7 mile loop, minimal vertical rise, easy
**Maps:** USGS 7 ½' Chatham
**Area:** 124 acres **Elevation:** 1,509 feet
**Avg./Max. Depth:** 12/15 feet
**Activities:** Hiking, fishing (brook trout), camping (lean-to), picnicking, swimming, canoeing

———————————————◆———————————————

Picturesque Mountain Pond is the largest undeveloped water body in the White Mountains. Along with its sparkling expanse of blue water (¾ mile long and, at its widest, ¼ mile across), Mountain Pond's charms include photogenic mountain views, varied and beautiful forests, resident loons, and an easy hiking trail around the shore. A circuit of the pond makes for a relaxing half-day walk, or you can pack in to the lean-to on the north shore for a leisurely overnight.

## Access

Mountain Pond is tucked away in the remote basin drained by the East Branch of the Saco River and its tributary, Slippery Brook. Follow NH 16/ US 302 north for 3.7 miles from the stoplight in downtown North Conway and turn right (east) onto Town Hall Road, marked by a green sign. (This is 1.5 miles south of the 16/302 junction in Glen.) In 0.2 mile the road crosses NH 16A, swings northward, and winds upward through residential areas. Bear left at a fork at 2.5 miles, where the pavement ends. You enter the National Forest at 3.3 miles; the road is now called Slippery Brook Road. Bear right at an unmarked fork at 5.8 miles, and at 6.5 miles you'll see the sign for Mountain Pond Loop Trail on the right. There's ample parking in a clearing off the road.

## The Mountain Pond Loop Trail

The trail starts as a level logging road leading east through second-growth woods. In 0.1 mile there's a boggy area where beavers sometimes flood the trail. A gentle climb through tall spruce and birch brings you to the loop junction at 0.3 mile. A sign points left to the Mountain Pond Shelter. I recommend doing the loop in this clockwise direction, for it gives an immediate reward and saves the best views for last.

## The North Shore Loop

Walking left, you quickly come to a wide side path to the right leading 200 feet to rocks sprinkled at the narrow west end of Mountain Pond. The water stretches away to the east, enclosed by wooded shores. The broad NE corner is hidden from view, but this first look shows you that the pond is a big one. This is the put-in point for canoeists making the short portage from the parking area.

The main trail winds away from the shore through deep forest. The footway is rocky, as it is along several stretches around the loop. There's a wealth of tree species here: yellow birch, white ash, red spruce, and sugar maple, to name a few. It's a grand forest, but it was grander still in its virgin state. The 1916 AMC *Guide* made special note of the "great hemlocks," large maples and birches, and "scattered white pines" near Mountain Pond.

Over the next five years, however, the Conway Lumber Company felled these majestic giants and hauled them back on the (Saco) East Branch Railroad to the hungry mills. As C. Francis Belcher describes it, this was one

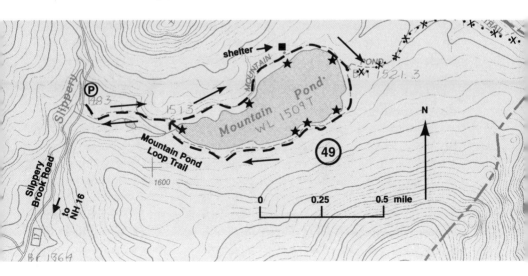

of the great cut-and-run operations in the annals of White Mountain logging. The Conway Lumber Company had two good reasons to hurry: World War I had driven lumber prices to unimaginable heights, and the US government was eyeing the East Branch region for inclusion in the new White Mountain National Forest. By 1920 the cutting was complete, and the forest quickly began its regeneration. The area has recovered so well that a second generation of trees is under harvest in the valley, though on a much more controlled scale.

You soon enter woods where spruce predominates. About 0.4 mile from the loop junction, as the trail bears slightly left through a grove of softwoods, walk 100 feet right through a heavily camped area to a rocky opening on the shore. A low rock seat and morning sun exposure invite you to rest awhile and enjoy the broad view over the pond.

Keep your eye out for loons—they've often been spotted here in recent years. One may suddenly pop up nearby for a close look, then dive and vanish for a long 45 seconds, only to reappear far out on the pond. Or maybe you'll hear a wild yodel carrying across the water. Be extra careful not to disturb these magnificent swimmers during the summer nesting season.

Beyond this shoreside stop, the trail leads through a bushy area where the woods were devastated by a windstorm in December 1980. This blow temporarily closed a number of trails in the Chatham region during the early 1980s. Some paths were never reopened. You'll see evidence of the storm in several other places as you make your way around the pond.

At 0.6 mile from the loop junction you come to the WMNF Mountain Pond Shelter on the left, a tidy eight-person lean-to with a tree-framed vista across the pond. The main trail jogs right to the shore. If you're not deterred by the rocky bottom and reports of leeches, a pair of shoreline openings may tempt you into a cooling dip. Or you might cast a line here in hope of luring a trout. Back in the 1880s Sweetser's guidebook tantalized anglers with this statement about Mountain Pond: "It is claimed that the largest speckled trout ever caught in New England have been taken here."

Beyond the shelter, the trail runs briefly in the open along the shore, passing a spring, then ducks back behind shrubs and conifers. As you curve around the pond's NE corner, a narrow side path leads 50 feet right through the bushes for a view down the pond to the twin rounded peaks of the Doubleheads.

In another 100 yards you reach a former trail junction. The abandoned and overgrown east link of Mountain Pond Trail, which once provided access from the Cold River valley in Chatham, comes in from the left through an area grown thick with saplings since the windstorm. A sign nailed to a spruce informs you that the WMNF Mountain Pond Cabin, once located by the south shore, was removed in 1982 due to overuse and vandalism.

## The South Shore Loop

Bear right on the south half of the loop trail, once known as the Mountain Pond High Country Cabin Trail. Angling back towards the pond, the path touches the shore beside a white birch for a fine view of the Doubleheads. Soon you swing around the SE corner through spruce and hemlock woods with dense undergrowth. A bushy opening beside an upturned spruce reveals a watery view towards the bare white cone of South Baldface (3,569 feet), flanked on the left by the birch-clad summits of Mounts Sable (3,519 feet) and Chandler (3,335 feet).

Farther on, at the end of a rocky tunnel of firs, is a clearing on the right, grown to small birch and pin cherry. At the far (west) side of the opening, a side path on the right leads 150 feet over boulders and through a light screen of bushes to a tumble of rocks at the shore. Here you'll find the premier view of Mountain Pond. To your left, beyond a long reach of water, the Doubleheads are artistically positioned at the pond's west end: North Peak (3,050 feet) on the right, South Peak (2,938 feet) on the left.

*Mountain Pond and the Doubleheads*

Northward the Baldfaces rise above the water, with the darker north summit (3,610 feet) peering out behind the bleached south peak. On a clear day this is one of the most captivating spots in the mountains.

Back on the rocky loop trail, you wind through mossy spruce woods. In about 0.2 mile you pass two outlook rocks with good views of the pond but lacking the mountain vistas you've just enjoyed. The trail now cuts well back into the woods. You cross a small inlet brook amidst big yellow birches, then wind through stands of tall, stately spruce. A rock-hop over the outlet brook leads you to the end of the loop, with an easy 0.3 mile stroll back to your car.

*Bird's-Eye View:* Climb North Doublehead from the Dundee Road in Jackson (4-mile loop, 1,800-foot vertical rise, including both North and South Peaks; see Daniel Doan's *50 More Hikes in New Hampshire*). A ledge just east of the summit cabin provides a fine view of the pond and the East Branch valley. Mountain Pond can also be viewed from the bare summit of South Baldface, a spectacular perch accessed via the rugged Baldface Circle Trail from NH 113 in North Chatham (7.4 miles round-trip, a 3,050-foot vertical rise; or 9.8 miles, 3,550 feet for the loop over South and North Baldfaces).

*Winter:* This is a good winter destination if you like the exhilaration of wide open spaces. The Town Hall/Slippery Brook Road is plowed for 3.3 miles from NH 16/US 302; park at a turnaround just before a WMNF gate. Walk or ski up the road (used by snowmobiles and sometimes by logging trucks) to the trailhead at 3.2 miles. If the pond is well-frozen you'll find splendid views of the Doubleheads and Baldfaces from its windswept expanse. Keep an eye out for soft ice near the inlet, outlet, and occasional springs. The round-trip is 7 to 8 miles, depending on how far you traverse the pond or its shore.

# CHAPTER 50

# LOST POND

◆

**Location:** Pinkham Notch
**Hiking Facts:** 1.4 miles round-trip, 75-foot vertical rise, easy
**Maps:** USGS 7 ½' X 15' Mount Washington; USGS 7 ½' Stairs Mountain;
   AMC/Washburn Mount Washington and Presidential Range (Page 215)
**Area:** 4 acres   **Elevation:** 2,060 feet
**Avg./Max. Depth:** 2.5/3 feet
**Activities:** Hiking, picnicking

◆

If you're looking for a pond hike that's small on effort and large on reward, Lost Pond is for you. The walk in is decidedly non-stressful, the shoreline views of Mount Washington are magnificent, and the waterside rocks are ideal for picnicking or loafing. Though the traffic on nearby NH 16 is never fully out of earshot, Lost Pond is a tranquil place and a good choice even on a gray day when the high peaks are muffled in cloud. Cameras are a must on a clear day!

This shallow four-acre sliver of water is set in the lower east side of Pinkham Notch. Originally formed by a post-glacial rock slide from Wildcat Ridge, it's been dammed and raised by beavers in more recent times. Lost Pond is visited year-round by hikers of all ages from the nearby Pinkham Notch Camp, North Country headquarters for the AMC. After admiring the pond you can extend your hike to Glen Ellis Falls or Square Ledge, or visit the AMC's Visitor Center and learn more about the Mount Washington/Pinkham Notch environment.

### Access
Parking for Lost Pond Trail is found at Pinkham Notch Camp on the west side of NH 16, 11 miles north of US 302 in Glen and 11 miles south of US 2 in Gorham. The trail starts at a sign diagonally (SE) across the highway from the entrance to the Pinkham Notch complex.

## The Trail To Lost Pond

Leaving the east side of NH 16, the Lost Pond Trail quickly bridges a sluggish stream—the infant Ellis River—draining from a moose-haunted beaver pond on your left. Beyond the bridge you swing right and up into the woods, immediately passing Square Ledge Trail on the left. (This trail leads 0.5 mile and 400 vertical feet to a crag with a good view of Pinkham Notch and Mount Washington.)

The white-blazed Lost Pond Trail, a short link in the Appalachian Trail, rises and falls over a wide, hard-packed relocation. Then you rejoin the original path for a pretty stretch through fir and birch along the east bank of the Ellis River, now swelled by the larger Cutler River draining from Tuckerman Ravine. At one especially lovely spot a gently sloping ledge slips into a deep pool shaded by leaning yellow birches. At 0.3 mile the trail veers left away from the river, bridges a small tributary, and climbs moderately up a rocky footway amidst white and yellow birch. The grade soon eases and at 0.5 mile you catch a nice view south down the pond across a bog meadow on the right.

## At Lost Pond

The trail proceeds to the pond's NE corner and the first in a succession of gorgeous vistas along the east shore. As you enter a glade of gnarled yellow birches, shoreline openings offer a big-screen panorama of 6,288-foot Mount Washington, the northeast's highest. The mountain's east face, gouged by ancient glaciers, displays its famous broad-spreading ridges and bowl-like ravines. Left to right, you see the Glen Boulder ridge, the Gulf of Slides, Boott Spur, Lion's Head (Tuckerman Ravine, enclosed by the two preceding ridges, is hidden from this angle), the summit cone with its antennae, the ravine of Raymond Cataract, Huntington Ravine, and Nelson Crag.

The boulder-strewn trail meanders past more vistas of Mount Washington, with the left portion of the view sliding out of sight and craggy Huntington Ravine taking center stage. About midway along the east shore you'll come to a great flat rock overlooking the north half of the pond and part of the Mount Washington panorama. If that perch is occupied, a lower rock nearby offers another picnic site.

Beyond these seats the thickly wooded knoll across the pond obstructs the views of "Big George," but the rugged trail leads past more rocks with nice waterfront vistas. Near the beaver dam at the pond's south end is a huge split boulder featuring a mini-Matterhorn peak. Reached by a careful scramble, this craggy throne lifts you five feet above the brown-tinted water.

*Lost Pond and Mount Washington*

It offers good sun exposure and a photogenic view north down the pond to a convergence of distant ridges.

The Lost Pond Trail continues its rocky way for 0.3 mile beyond the pond, descending slightly to join the Wildcat Ridge Trail near Glen Ellis Falls. To visit the falls, follow this trail right for 0.1 mile, stepping over the outlet brook from Lost Pond and then rock-hopping across the Ellis River (difficult in high water). Scramble up a gravel bank, cross the highway, and follow the path to the falls back under the road from the south end of the parking lot. You'll reach the spectacular falls in 0.2 mile. (See Bruce and Doreen Bolnick's *Waterfalls of the White Mountains*.) Otherwise, enjoy a leisurely stroll back from the pond along the route you came in, with the option of a side excursion up to Square Ledge.

*Winter:* This is a deservedly popular ski or snowshoe jaunt for Pinkham Notch visitors, easy and rewarding. The views of Mount Washington's snow-clad cirques and ridges are dazzling in the sun. It's also a good choice for a moonlight tour or hike.

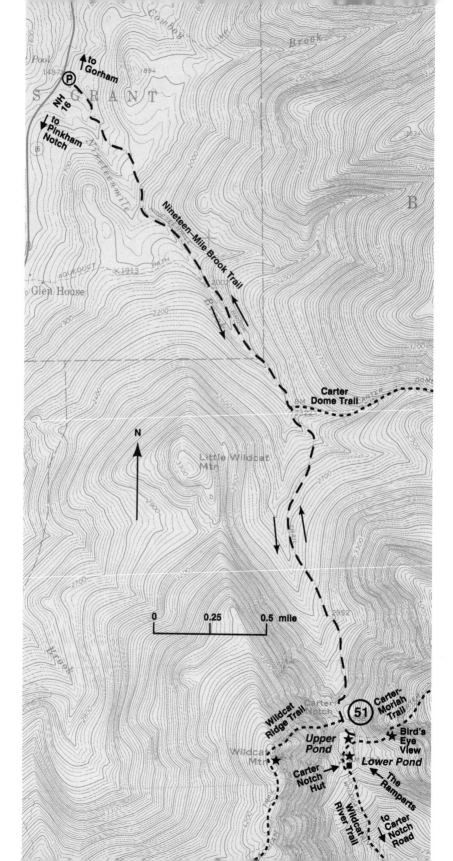

to Gorham

P
NH 16

to Pinkham
Notch

S GRANT

Pool

Glen House

AQUEDUCT     PATH

Nineteen-Mile Brook Trail

Carter
Dome Trail

N

Little Wildcat
Mtn

0     0.25     0.5 mile

B

Wildcat
Mtn

Wildcat
Ridge Trail

Carter
Notch

51

Carter-
Moriah
Trail

Upper Pond

Bird's
Eye
View

Carter
Notch Hut

Lower Pond

The
Ramparts

Wildcat
River Trail

to
Carter
Notch
Road

# CHAPTER 51

# CARTER PONDS

◆

**Location:** Carter Notch
**Hiking Facts:** 7.6 miles round-trip, 2,000-foot vertical rise, more difficult
**Map:** USGS 7½' Carter Dome

|  | **Upper Carter Pond** | **Lower Carter Pond** |
|---|---|---|
| **Area:** | 1.1 acres | 0.6 acre |
| **Elevation:** | 3,290 feet | 3,280 feet |
| **Avg./Max. Depth:** | 5.5/15 feet | 7/10 feet |

**Activities:** Hiking, fishing (brook trout), swimming, picnicking, AMC hut

◆

*I wonder if every pilgrim does not at this point laugh
with pure joy and caper a bit on road-weary legs, for here
in the gruesome depths of the great Notch, at the climax
point of its wildness, is a little clear mountain lake where
surely no lake could be, set in thousand-ton fragments of
mighty broken ledges.*

—Winthrop Packard
*White Mountain Trails,* 1917

Carter Notch, the striking cleft between Carter Dome and Wildcat Mountain,
is a masterwork of glacial artistry. Seen from afar, it presents the classic U-
shaped profile of an ice-scoured gap. Within the notch, where high mountain
walls shadow a wild jumble of boulders, the scenery is simply overpowering.
The unexpected finishing touch to this monumental work is a pair of tiny
rock-rimmed ponds in the very heart of the pass. They soften this grim
landscape and add a delightful sparkle when the midday sun floods the notch.

Originally called "Lakes of the Winds" by an exploring party in 1853,
the ponds received their present name in tribute to Dr. Ezra Carter, a nineteenth-century New Hampshire physician who poked around the mountains in search of medicinal herbs and roots. Carter Notch and Ponds have
been popular with trampers since the late 1800s, when the first crude shel-

ter was raised beside the northern and larger lakelet. In 1904 the AMC built a small log cabin on the site, to be replaced in 1914 by a stone hut just south of the smaller pond that is still in use today. Carter Notch Hut, capacity 40 persons, is open with full service from early June to early September and on a caretaker basis the rest of the year.

The fairly long but pleasant valley paths into the notch from north (Nineteen-Mile Brook Trail) and south (Wildcat River Trail) have been in use for many years. The ponds offer surprisingly good swimming and trout fishing. To cap off your day, you can make a short but very steep climb to a craggy overlook.

## Access

The Nineteen-Mile Brook Trail provides the shortest and most popular route into Carter Notch. The trail begins at a parking area on the east side of NH 16, 2.3 miles south of Dolly Copp Campground and 1 mile north of the Mount Washington Auto Road.

## The Trail To Carter Ponds

Moderate grades, attractive forests, and pretty stream scenery make this walk up the valley of boulder-choked Nineteen-Mile Brook very fine indeed. The first 0.7 mile is wide and well-graded through shady hemlocks. You traverse two ledgy spots on the brook bank; then at 1.2 miles you pass a small concrete dam holding a pool of crystal-clear water. The footway becomes rockier as you pursue a rolling streamside course through gleaming yellow birches.

The Carter Dome Trail on the left marks the halfway point at 1.9 miles. You cross two tributaries on log bridges; at the second a ledge left of the trail offers a nice resting spot. Beyond, the way leads through lovely glades of white and yellow birch. An understory of hobblebush seems to float above the forest floor.

Higher up the trail becomes wet and rough in places. A thick growth of mountain maple and young conifers crowds the edges. Level stretches alternate with short, steeper pitches; then a sustained rocky climb of 0.4 mile lifts you to the height-of-land amidst a ridge-top fir forest. At 3.6 miles you plant your boots on the crest of Carter Notch, elevation 3,388 feet. The Wildcat Ridge Trail departs right for the 1,000-foot climb to the summit of Wildcat Mountain. The Nineteen-Mile Brook Trail descends steeply southward through thick fir growth, angling left and down to the north shore of Upper Carter Pond.

*Alternate Approach:* Take the Wildcat River Trail, from the end of

Carter Notch Road in Jackson; 8.8 miles round-trip, 1,600-foot vertical rise. This is a splendid walk up the forested valley of Wildcat River. The grades are easy to moderate with a steep rise to the notch. (See Daniel Doan's *Fifty More Hikes in New Hampshire*.)

## Upper Carter Pond

This beautiful pond, ringed by rough boulders and bristly firs, opens dramatically when you emerge by the icy little inlet stream. The great wall of Wildcat Mountain (4,422 feet) dominates the scene, rising 1,000 feet almost directly above the west shore. Birch and fir cloak the steep slopes, except where a gaunt cliff breaks the forest cover on a northern buttress. As it circles the east shore—a distance of no more than 100 yards—the trail passes several superb sitting rocks. My favorites are a low, table-flat ledge at the NE corner and a tall, sloping boulder a few steps before the junction with the Carter-Moriah Trail. (This trail leads 1.2 miles to the summit of Carter Dome and onward over the range to Gorham.) The latter perch looks directly down into the green-brown water, where small trout lurk above the algae-covered bottom.

In high summer, these east-shore rocks enjoy sun through a good part of the afternoon. When the sunshine beams down, the pond sparkles and the notch is a bright and exhilarating place. The curtain is drawn in late

*Upper Carter Pond*

afternoon (about 5:00 P.M. in late July), when the sun dips behind Wildcat Mountain. As the shadows draw across the pond, the mood changes to the gloomy desolation so beloved of nineteenth-century White Mountain scribes.

Beyond the junction the Nineteen-Mile Brook Trail crosses the small outlet stream that flows between the ponds. Off to the right are more fine boulder-seats and one outlying rock from which anglers cast for trout in deeper water. In his *Smoke From a Thousand Campfires*, longtime Conservation Officer Paul Doherty notes that the Upper Pond was stocked with trout as early as 1914 by anglers from nearby Jackson. Doherty himself initiated state stocking in 1950. Each spring for 23 years he made the trek into the notch, hauling fingerling trout in metal pack cans. Many remote ponds like the Carters are now stocked by helicopter.

There are several good points around the Upper Pond for a swim. The water is chilly but profoundly refreshing. Don't dive in blindly, as there are rocks under the water, too. Washing is forbidden in this public water supply.

## Lower Carter Pond

A rocky walk of 100 feet through stunted firs brings you to the NW shore of the Lower Pond, a diminutive pool with an hourglass shape. Here, too, the rocks seem ready to snuff out the pond's existence. The far (south) shore is walled in by a line of boulders. Looming above is the jagged line of the Rampart, immense chunks of rock torn from the cliffs of Carter Dome and strewn in a tumbled confusion of stone and scrub. Because this barrier blocks the outlet end of the pond, the water that eventually feeds the Wildcat River must filter underground through the rocks.

As you look left across the water, the eastern battlements of Carter Notch take center stage. The craggy west ridge of the Dome slants to the sky, with the remarkable Pulpit Rock jutting out from its ragged edge. The cliff just to the left of Pulpit Rock is the bird's-eye outlook described below.

The trail splits by the side of the pond, rejoining a few yards beyond the shore for the short climb to the AMC hut and the fascinating Rampart beyond. The left branch leads to several sitting rocks, not so sunny as those at the larger pond, and shallow water where you can take a dunk rather than a full-fledged swim. Little minnows will nibble at your feet as you wade into the somewhat murky water.

*Bird's-Eye View:* If time and energy permit, return to the sign for Carter-Moriah Trail by the Upper Pond for the steep climb to the notch overlook. This side trip will add about 0.6 mile round-trip and 500+ feet of climbing to the hike. The ridge trail begins innocently enough, climbing moderately for about 0.1 mile. Suddenly it shoots up at a breath-stealing grade that should be approached with a steady, determined pace. Actually, the footing is rather easy for such a steep trail, thanks to the many rock steps wrestled into place by AMC trail crews.

After a long 0.2 mile, you cross two open ledges that preview the panorama to come. In 100 feet look for a rough side path on the right—unmarked, but well-worn—that climbs 100 feet to a magnificent ledgy perch atop the precipitous ridge. This sun-warmed outlook reveals the notch in all its grandeur. Pulpit Rock juts out close by on the left. At your feet a long train of scrub-grown boulders spills from the side of Carter Dome down to the rocky swell of the Rampart. Below are the ponds, serene and secure in their deep hollow beneath the shadowed face of Wildcat Mountain. To the south a wide view opens beyond the valley of Wildcat River. Around to the right are the Northern Presidentials. After enjoying the views, you have a knee-jarring descent back to Nineteen-Mile Brook Trail, unless you're continuing on to Carter Dome, 0.9 mile and 900 feet above.

A good view down at Lower Carter Pond is found at the east outlook on the summit of Wildcat Mountain, reached with a climb of 0.7 mile/1,000 feet up the Wildcat Ridge Trail from the height-of-land in Carter Notch.

*Winter:* Unheated Carter Notch Hut is open on a caretaker basis in winter. A day or overnight trip into the notch makes a fine adventure. The parking area on NH 16 is plowed, and the Nineteen-Mile Brook Trail usually has a good snowshoe track. (It's too steep for most skiers.) There's one icy spot on the brook bank that can be tricky to traverse. Either pond is spectacular on a bright winter day, with the surrounding rock-scenery frosted in its winter garb.

# NO-KETCHUM POND

◆

**Location:** Perkins Notch
**Hiking Facts:** 8.6 miles round-trip, 800-foot vertical rise, more difficult
**Map:** USGS 7½' Jackson
**Area:** 0.5 acre   **Elevation:** 2,550 feet
**Activities:** Hiking, camping (lean-to), fishing (possible native brook trout),
   birding

◆

To call this boggy channel a pond is a bit of a stretch, but it has borne its quaint name for many years. AMC explorers made note of this long, narrow pool back in 1880 during a reconnaissance of Perkins Notch, the gentle gap between Carter Dome and Black Mountain.

No-Ketchum Pond is the knot at the end of a string of spongy bogs forming the headwaters of the Wild River. It lies just north of the Wild River Trail, east of the Perkins Notch Shelter. The trail offers only branch-screened glimpses down to the water, which is guarded by a dense barrier of scrub and a shrubby bog mat. Hopeful anglers have beaten a couple of mucky paths out to the shore and a solitary rock perch. The reflected view of the Carter Dome massif encompasses Rainbow Ridge, the Dome proper (4,832 feet), and Mount Hight (4,675 feet).

The dark brown water—I'd boil this a *long* time before drinking—is home to beaver and, perhaps, small native brook trout (though the pond's name would indicate otherwise). Old AMC guidebooks noted that a beaver colony set up shop here in 1927. A dam can still be seen at the eastern outlet, where the pond is widest. Birders will find this area productive for bog and mid-elevation forest species. The insect population is large and aggressive.

## Access/Trails to No-Ketchum Pond

The easiest route to this interesting area is from the end of Carter Notch Road in Jackson via the muddy Bog Brook Trail (2.8 miles) and the link of Wild

River Trail through Perkins Notch (1.5 miles). Other approaches include Wild River Trail from the end of Wild River Road (14 miles round-trip, 1,400-foot vertical rise), or East Branch Trail and a short link on Wild River Trail from the end of East Branch Road (9.6 miles round-trip, 1,200-foot vertical rise). All are long, pleasant woods walks, but each has brook crossings that are potentially difficult in high water.

The upper Wild River valley is similar to the better-known Zealand Valley in the western White Mountains: mellow terrain with open forests of birch, spruce, and fir, peppered with beaver ponds and bogs. Both valleys burned in 1903 in the wake of logging operations, which explains the prevalence of white birches. Early AMC guidebooks noted that the Perkins Notch area "possesses a weird charm of its own." It still holds a strange

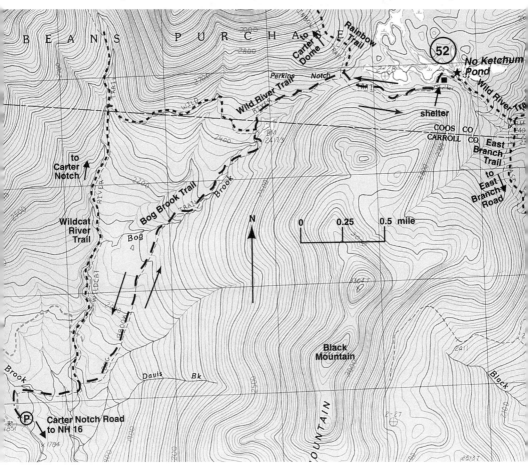

*No-Ketchum Pond and Carter Dome*

fascination for the backcountry explorer. Ambitious bushwhackers can seek out ledges on the surrounding ridges for interior views of this broad, remote valley. The Perkins Notch Shelter is a convenient overnight base; from a side path 100 yards east of the shelter there's a view over the bogs to Carter Dome. For a suggested five-day backpack in this region, see Daniel Doan's *Fifty More Hikes in New Hampshire.*

*Bird's-Eye View:* A raven's perspective on No-Ketchum Pond and its satellite bogs is found on the bare summit of Rainbow Ridge, a 4,274-foot spur of Carter Dome. This knob is one of the best viewpoints on the Carter Range. Access is via the Rainbow Trail, a stiff climb of 1,700 feet in 1.5 miles from the Wild River Trail in Perkins Notch, 0.8 mile west of the shelter.

*Winter:* Perkins Notch is an interesting area to explore on skis or snow-shoes, when the pools and bogs are frozen and snow-covered (though the ice of No-Ketchum Pond itself was unsafe when I visited). This is the best time to enjoy the views of Carter Dome rising over 2,000 feet to the west. Many of the access trails are cross-country trails in the Jackson Ski Touring Foundation system; snowshoeing is permitted. The best approach is via Bog Brook and Wild River Trails. Parking is very limited on Carter Notch Road; inquire at the JSTF center in Jackson village.

# CHAPTER 53

# BASIN POND

◆

**Location:** South of Evans Notch
**Hiking Facts:** Roadside; optional hike, 0.2 mile round-trip, easy
**Map:** USGS 7½' Wild River
**Area:** 23 acres   **Elevation:** 662 feet
**Avg./Max. Depth:** 9/15 feet
**Activities:** Camping, picnicking, canoeing, hiking, fishing (brook trout)

◆

When hikers ponder the great cirques of the White Mountains—those striking bowl-shaped ravines scooped from the mountainsides by Ice Age glaciers—the Basin does not often come to mind. Not to be confused with its more notorious namesake in Franconia Notch (a pothole scoured by glacial meltwater), New Hampshire's "other" Basin is a ravine of remarkable beauty carved into the eastern flank of the Baldface-Royce Range.

A wide-screen view of the Basin is found at Basin Pond, a reservoir created at the mouth of the cirque in 1969. The grassy picnic area beside the pond is one of the grandest lunching spots in the mountains. The Basin Trail provides a short, easy walk to more secluded shoreside haunts or a more challenging trek up to the Basin Rim and a heady view of pond and cirque.

### Access
The pond is located beside the road to the WMNF Basin Campground, which leaves NH/ME 113 18.9 miles north of US 302 and 2.5 miles south of the height-of-land in Evans Notch. The paved road leads west for 0.6 mile to a large parking lot on the right. The road continues into the 21-site campground, a fine base for exploring the area's network of uncrowded trails.

### At Basin Pond
The expansive view of the pond and its mountain bowl can be enjoyed from car, picnic table, or shore. On a clear day the water-forest-mountain vista is

so dazzling that you hardly notice the earthen flood control dam behind you that gave birth to Basin Pond. (Before the dam was built beavers had fashioned their own dams along the course of Basin Brook.) The airy amphitheater is embraced by a cliff-studded arm of West Royce Mountain (3,210 feet) on the north and the dark, spruce-clad mass of Mount Meader (2,782 feet) on the south. The ridge dips to a central headwall known as the Basin Rim (1,870 feet).

Amenities include a boat launch and a wheelchair-accessible fishing dock reached via a short paved path. Many visitors stroll over to the grass-grown top of the dam at the pond's east end.

On the west edge of the parking lot is a sign for the Basin Trail, which leads up the cirque, over the rim, and down to the Wild River valley be-

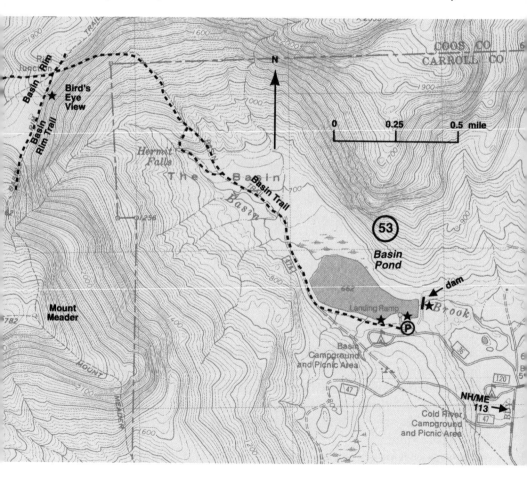

yond. The trail leads past rest rooms and slices through the hardwoods between campground and pond. Within 200 yards a side path cuts across; follow this a few yards right and down to a small gravelly beach with a superb view across the water, removed from the bustle of the parking lot. If this spot is occupied, continue 100 yards farther on the Basin Trail to a short side path leading right to a little grassy peninsula, a fine picnic spot. This is your turnaround point if you're out for an easy stroll.

*Bird's-Eye View:* More ambitious trampers may continue to the clifftop viewpoints on the Basin Rim, a 4.6 mile round-trip with 1,200 feet of climbing. Highlights include magnificent beech forests on the floor of the cirque, a loop side path to Hermit Falls, and a dramatically engineered ascent of the headwall beneath a great gray cliff. At the five-way Rim Junction turn left on Basin Rim Trail and proceed 0.1 mile to the outlook ledges on your left. The view down the cirque to the sparkling pond is even more impressive than the panorama you enjoyed from below—or maybe it just seems that way because you worked a little harder for it.

*Winter:* Though out-of-the-way, this is a wonderful short trip for the skier or snowshoer. NH 113 is plowed from the south up to the Basin Campground road, where there is ample parking. Proceed 0.6 mile up the winding side road to the pond and its splendid views. (Keep off the ice near the outlet structure by the dam.) Shuffling westward across the pond you gaze into the heart of the cirque. The trip can be easily extended along the Basin Trail into the fine hardwood forest on the cirque floor.

*Basin Pond and The Basin*

# CHAPTER 54

# SHELL POND

◆

**Location:** SE of Evans Notch
**Hiking Facts:** 1.4 miles round-trip, 200-foot vertical rise (outbound), easy
**Maps:** USGS 7½' Center Lovell, ME, Speckled Mountain, ME, and Wild
   River, NH
**Area:** 50 acres   **Elevation:** 590 feet
**Activities:** Hiking, birding, fishing, picnicking

---

Shell Pond, a broad triangle of shallow water, spreads beneath rugged cliffs fronting a southerly spur of Speckled Mountain. The WMNF Shell Pond Trail provides an easy approach from east or west, though it does not lead to the pond itself. From the trail a clear old logging road can be followed to an opening on the east shore with beautiful views westward over the water to the Baldfaces and Meader Ridge.

Private land surrounds the pond on all but its SE side. Please do not camp, litter, or otherwise jeopardize continued hiking access to this peaceful corner of the mountains, and pay heed to posted areas around the Stone House Farm, where the owners request that hikers stay on the trail.

## Access
The east end of Shell Pond Trail provides the shortest route. It leaves the gravel Deer Hill Road (FR 9) between North Chatham, NH, and Kezar Lake, ME. This road departs the east side of NH 113, 15.9 miles north of US 302 in Fryeburg, ME. Drive in 3.4 miles to the trailhead on the left, marked by a hiker symbol but no sign. A small parking slot is located 100 feet west of the trailhead. (You might consider a stop at Deer Hill Bog on the drive in. There's an observation blind overlooking this wildlife-rich impoundment on the right, 2.8 miles from NH 113.)

## The Trail To Shell Pond
From the road, the east link of Shell Pond Trail descends moderately through

second-growth hardwoods to a T intersection at 0.5 mile. The trail is mucky in places and not much used, but easy enough to follow. Keep straight where it crosses two old roads and a brook on the descent. A sharp left turn onto the old logging road heads you around the shore of Shell Pond.

An alternate approach is the west end of Shell Pond Trail, which begins at a gate 1.1 miles in from NH 113 on Shell Pond Road; this unmarked road leaves the east side of the highway 17.9 miles north of US 302, by a red house. Park on the right before the gate. The trail follows the road for 0.5 mile, passing the White Cairn and Stone House Trails to Blueberry Mountain (see below). It then traverses a large field/airstrip to bypass the Stone House, with views ahead to the cliffs of Rattlesnake Mountain and back to Mount Meader and the Baldfaces. In a swampy area you cross a bridge over

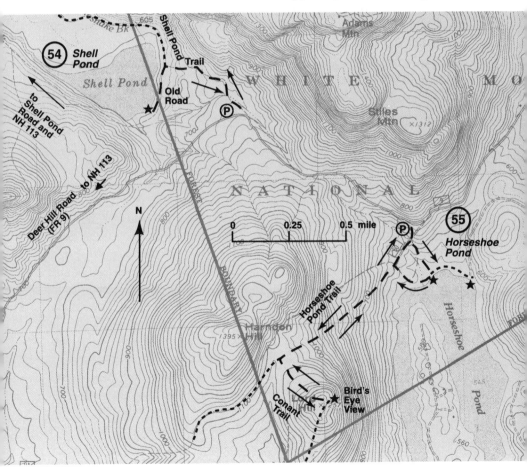

Rattlesnake Brook, which flows into the pond, and at 1.3 miles you reach the intersection with the old road that leads to the pond. Continue straight here.

## At Shell Pond

The logging road leads southward behind the east shore of the pond, briefly mucky, then rising gently to drier ground. At 0.1 mile or less a side path leads 100 yards right to several sitting rocks along the shore, with views across to the Meader-Baldface Range. The road curves right, crosses a streambed, and dips to a fork about 0.2 mile from the Shell Pond Trail junction. The right branch runs a few yards to a clearing on a brushy bank above the SE shore, suitable for a picnic. A wide view opens across the pond to the mountain rampart beyond: the Baldfaces on the left, Mount Meader in the middle, the low-slung Basin Rim on the right. The swampy north shore is lined with red maples; the south shore is backed by the steep wooded slope of Deer Hill (1,367 feet). The pond itself—an "interesting haunt of the great blue heron and bittern," according to earlier AMC guidebooks—is shallow and supports an abundance of aquatic vegetation. It's a good place to look and listen for water and marsh birds. One spring evening I saw a great blue heron, an osprey, and pairs of common goldeneyes and common mergansers, and heard Canadian geese and a barred owl—all in less than five minutes. The path descends to the shore for a wider view and a stab at some warm-water fishing, but there are no good seats at the water's edge.

*Bird's-Eye View:* A beautiful view of Shell Pond nestled in its forested basin is found atop the SE ledges of Blueberry Mountain (1,781 feet). For a scenic loop from Shell Pond Road, ascend the steep and rocky White Cairn Trail, with great views south and west, including a unique look at Basin Pond and The Basin. Turn right on Blueberry Ridge Trail and quickly right again on the Overlook Loop, which leads to open rock perches looking down at Shell Pond, the fields of the Stone House Farm, Harndon Hill behind the pond, and Pleasant Mountain in the distance. From the far end of Overlook Loop, descend the Stone House Trail to Shell Pond Road. The complete loop, including 0.2 mile between the trailheads, is 3.4 miles, with a 1,200-foot vertical rise (not including the walk to and from the pond).

*Winter:* Deer Hill Road is not plowed, so you'll have to approach from NH 113; this adds 1.1 miles each way to this western route. Roadside parking can be found by the entrance to Shell Pond Road, which is used by snowmobiles. Frozen Shell Pond provides spectacular views of the Baldface–Meader–Royce ridge to the west, Blueberry Mountain to the NW, and the cliffs of Rattlesnake Mountain overhanging the north shore.

# CHAPTER 55

# HORSESHOE POND

◆

**Location:** West of Kezar Lake, ME
**Hiking Facts:** 0.8 mile round-trip, 150-foot vertical rise (outbound), easy; add
  2.2 miles, 650 feet for Lord Hill
**Map:** USGS 7½' Center Lovell, ME (Page 259)
**Area:** 132 acres   **Elevation:** 545 feet
**Avg./Max. Depth:** 40 feet
**Activities:** Hiking, swimming, fishing (brook trout, brown trout, smallmouth
  bass, chain pickerel), picnicking, canoeing

◆

Sculpted in remarkable fashion by Ice Age glaciers, Horseshoe Pond curls amidst low wooded hills in western Maine. The short hike down Horseshoe Pond Trail to the north shore rewards with sunny, expansive water views and a chance to swim, fish, or lounge at this scenic spot. More ambitious trampers can fulfill climbing urges with a side excursion to an open ledge on Lord Hill (1,257 feet) featuring a unique view of the U-shaped pond.

Both the broad eastern arm and the narrow western prong of Horseshoe Pond stretch nearly a mile north and south. The north and west shores are bordered by National Forest land. The remainder of the shoreline is privately owned but undeveloped save for a handful of camps and houses on the long finger of land that splits the pond. Boats may be launched from the gravel Horseshoe Pond Road, which can be approached from ME 5 on the south and touches the south end of the western prong.

## Access

The Chatham Trail Association's Horseshoe Pond Trail leaves the south side of Deer Hill Road (FR 9) 4.4 miles east of NH 113. (See SHELL POND.) A parking spot opens on the right at a leftward curve; look for the small white CTA sign. The pull-off offers a peaceful vista of western Horseshoe Pond framed by the waving boughs of tall pines.

## The Trail To Horseshoe Pond

Following yellow blazes and markers, you descend the needle-cushioned trail through a fine grove of white pine. In 100 yards you pass a grave site where Olive W. Stiles, "Died Aug 1848, AE 51 Yrs., 7 M.," rests inside a square stone wall beneath a great spreading oak. Like many a New England hillside, this stand of pine was open pasture when Olive and her husband Jacob worked the land near Horseshoe Pond. Perhaps Jacob Stiles himself laid out the stone walls down-slope from the grave site.

At 0.1 mile the trail drops you onto a gravel logging road. Follow it right for 50 feet, then bear left back into the woods at a CTA sign and double yellow blaze. The steep downgrade continues until the path levels at a grassy clearing. You swing left, dip through a collapsed stone wall, and clomp across plank walkways through a lush, ferny swale. Cresting a hemlock-shaded rise, you catch sight of Horseshoe Pond ahead through the trees, 0.3 mile from Deer Hill Road.

## At Horseshoe Pond

The yellow-blazed trail makes a 90° degree right turn before reaching the north shore. The best viewpoints are found along a side path to the left, which quickly leads to a wide vista down the eastern pond under dangling pine boughs. A few steps back from the shore a latter-day pioneer has crafted an unusual bench seat notched between two towering white pines. It's a contemplative spot with a long water view.

Informal footways continue eastward behind the shore through shady hemlock and pine woods. They wind about to a clearing at the base of the old Chadbourne Road, a rough and circuitous access from Deer Hill Road. This opening at the water's edge is fine for picnicking and swimming. Lord Hill rises to the right, crowned with dark conifers and a patch of ledge. When you take your leave of this restful place, retrace your steps along the shore and back up to Deer Hill Road.

## Lord Hill

If you want to tackle the short but stiff climb to the overlook on Lord Hill, follow the westward loop of Horseshoe Pond Trail along the shore at the right-angle turn. After crossing a brook the yellow-blazed path swings right into a bushy area; to the left, past a line of red-blazed trees, you can make your way through open woods to the shore and an unusual look at the bend of the horseshoe. An elegant silver maple arches overhead.

The loop trail winds upward 0.2 mile through thick brush. This devas-

*Horseshoe Pond from Lord Hill*

tated area, extending far up the side of Lord Hill, is recovering from the windstorm of December 1980 and subsequent timber salvage operations. In a grassy logging yard bear left at a junction and follow cairns up open, grass-grown skid roads, a hot climb in midsummer. Higher up you ascend through spruce and pine to the ridge crest and junction with the Pine Hill–Lord Hill Loop Trail (formerly the Conant Trail) 1 mile from the pond. Turn left for the final 0.2 mile scramble to the summit of Lord Hill, where a path leaves right for an old mine site.

Stay on the main trail, dipping steeply left to the rough, slanting ledges overlooking Horseshoe Pond. Nearly the entire two-mile "U" of water can be seen, perhaps the most remarkable *bird's-eye view* of a White Mountain pond. More distant views include Speckled Mountain, Red Rock Ridge, Albany Mountain, and other mountains of western Maine.

On the return trip bear left at the junction in the logging yard at the base of the descent. This branch shortly leads to a gravel logging road. Turn left here and left again in 0.2 mile to follow the Horseshoe Pond Trail up to Deer Hill Road and your car. The entire loop hike to Horseshoe Pond and Lord Hill is 3 miles with a vertical rise of 800 feet.

*Winter:* This makes a pleasant 9-mile ski tour or hike from the west in combination with Shell Pond. Take Shell Pond Trail to its east end, then follow Deer Hill Road 1 mile over a height-of-land to Horseshoe Pond Trail. (Skiers may want to continue on the road to a logging road that descends less steeply.) The pond receives some use from snowmobilers and ice anglers. You can ski or snowshoe a mile southward along the broad east arm, with views of the nearby hills and a glimpse northward to the high ridges of Speckled Mountain.

# CHAPTER 56

# VIRGINIA LAKE

◆

**Location:** Stoneham, ME
**Hiking Facts:** Roadside; optional hike, 1 mile round-trip, minimal vertical rise, easy
**Map:** USGS 7½' East Stoneham, ME
**Area:** 128 acres   **Elevation:** 820 feet
**Max. Depth:** 28 feet
**Activities:** Canoeing, fishing (brook trout, horned pout, chain pickerel, white perch), hiking, swimming, picnicking

◆

Though the jigsaw puzzle of White Mountain National Forest lands is nearly complete, new parcels are periodically added as acreage and funds become available. Beautiful Virginia Lake, purchased in 1987, is one of the finest recent acquisitions. Its 128 acres of clear water stretch for a mile north and south amidst the hills of western Maine. The lake's shores are wooded and undeveloped save for one private summer home on the east side.

Virginia Lake is car-accessible via a short dirt road, but its out-of-the-way location keeps it a quiet, uncrowded place. A boat launch at an eastern cove opens canoeing and fishing opportunities. Walkers can enjoy a short stroll along an old road to a small sand beach at the south shore, with good swimming and a nice view up the lake to the low line of mountains beyond.

## Access

The road approach to Virginia Lake follows ME 5 south from Bethel or north from Fryeburg. In Stoneham, at the SW corner of Keewaydin Lake, turn north onto Bartlettboro Road. (This corner is 3.2 miles west of the junction of ME 5 and ME 35 and 10.5 miles north of the intersection of ME 5 and ME 93.) In 0.4 mile bear left at a fork onto Virginia Lake Road. Enter the National Forest at 0.8 mile, and at 1 mile from ME 5 bear left onto a gravel road, FR 308. (The right fork leads to the private Virginia Lake Farm.)

This access road to the lake is rough but usually passable for conventional vehicles. (If the first short pitch is washed out, park off the road at the corner and walk; it's a short and pleasant stroll.) It winds about through pastures and patches of woods, passing an older road left at 0.2 mile and an old driveway on the left at 0.3 mile. In another 200 yards the road dips to cross the lake's outlet brook at a narrow eastern cove. Here you'll find the gravel boat launch and roadside parking for a couple of cars. (For alternate parking, use the driveway.) The road is gated and posted as private property beyond this point.

## At Virginia Lake
The boat launch leads to the water at the tip of a hidden eastern finger of the

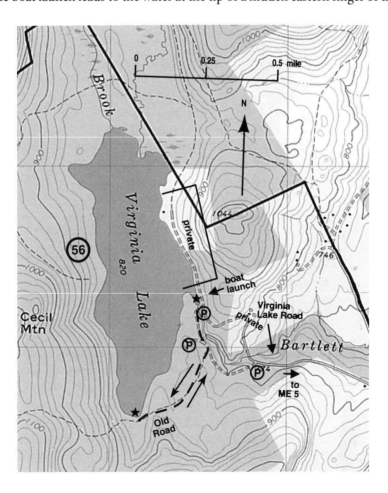

lake. From the edge there's a nicely framed view NW across the water to the mountains around little-known Miles Notch. The prominent ridge in the center is Miles Knob (2,090 feet). The vista here is pretty, but you have to canoe out of the cove to take in the full sweep of the lake. (Motorized boats are not allowed.)

You can get a full view from the beach on the south shore. From the boat launch, walk back along the access road past the former driveway and turn right onto the old road (shown as a trail on the USGS map) that runs along the west edge of a pasture. The track soon bears right across a weedy clearing and winds through thin, brushy woods. At the top of a slight rise clumps of sweet fern guard the roadside. You descend past tall bunches of bracken to a sharp left turn.

At the corner walk across a parking slot on the right and swing left on a well-worn path that dips to the SE corner of Virginia Lake. Two side paths lead right to limited shoreline viewpoints. The main footway cuts through an alder thicket to the shallow, sandy end of the lake. Pick your way along the sand strip and hop or wade across a tiny inlet brook to reach the secluded beach.

The sand extends perhaps 200 feet across and 12 feet back from the water. It faces north up the length of the lake towards the long, level ridge line between Miles Notch (left) and Albany Notch (right). From the west end you can look NE to the ledgy hump of Albany Mountain (1,930 feet). Like most of the lakeshore, this lovely spot is shaded by oaks and red maples. The water is shallow with a sandy, gently inclined bottom.

Retrace your steps from "Virginia Beach" to your car back by the boat launch. The round-trip to the beach is about a mile, with minimal climbing.

*Winter:* Virginia Lake is used mainly by snowmobilers, but it's a pleasant short outing for skiers or snowshoers as well. Virginia Lake Road is plowed, though the side road to the lake is not. There's limited parking at the junction. Stay off the cove by the outlet and boat launch—the ice there is dangerous. The traverse of the mile-long lake can be quite enjoyable, with views northward to the mountains around Miles and Albany Notches.

# CHAPTER 57

# BROKEN BRIDGE, CROCKER, AND ROUND PONDS

◆

**Location:** Albany, ME, east of Albany Mountain
**Hiking Facts:** Roadside (Broken Bridge and Crocker Ponds); 2 miles round-trip, 200-foot vertical rise, easy (Round Pond)
**Map:** USGS 7½' East Stoneham, ME

|  | Broken Bridge Pond | Crocker Pond | Round Pond |
|---|---|---|---|
| **Area:** | 18 acres | 13 acres | 11 acres |
| **Elevation:** | 794 feet | 824 feet | 790 feet |
| **Avg./Max. Depth:** | 14/25 feet | 9/14 feet | 21/29 feet |

**Activities:** Hiking, camping, fishing (brook trout in all three ponds), canoeing, picnicking

◆

The Albany region of western Maine is one of the quiet corners of the White Mountain National Forest. The relatively low terrain is far from spectacular, but the rolling hills and serene ponds have a charm all their own. The WMNF Crocker Pond Campground is a convenient base for exploring the trio of trout ponds—Broken Bridge, Crocker, and Round—strung along the eastern base of Albany Mountain. If you yearn for an overlook, a trail leads to ledges at the 1,930-foot summit.

## Access
Crocker Pond Campground can be reached via Forest Service roads from north and east. From the north, follow US 2 to the village of West Bethel, ME. Turn south by the Mountain View Country Store, following WMNF camping signs. Keep straight at 2.5 miles (surface becomes gravel) and 2.9 miles. At 4 miles the road narrows and enters the National Forest as FR 7. A leftward curve leads to a junction at 5.4 miles; turn right here on FR 18, which

passes Broken Bridge Pond and ends at the campground at 6.9 miles.

The east approach is made from ME 5, where WMNF camping signs mark a road heading west just south of Songo Pond. Becoming FR 7, this leads to the junction with FR 18 in 2.7 miles; turn left for the campground.

## Broken Bridge Pond

From FR 18, two short side roads drop to the west shore of Broken Bridge Pond, a horseshoe of placid water. In either case, I recommend parking on the shoulder of the main road and walking down to the pond. The first side road departs 1 mile south of the junction of FR 7 and FR 18. Stony and washed-out, it dips steeply for 200 feet to a fork. The right branch leads to a clearing near the NW finger of the pond. From here a path, partly blazed

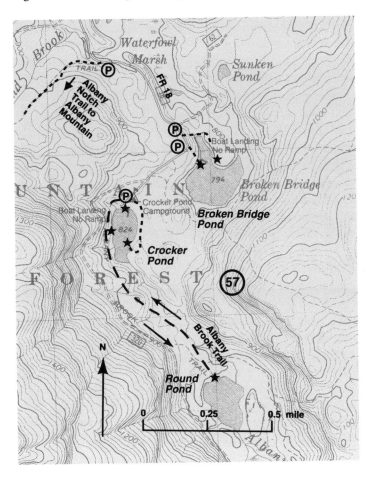

in dark red, skirts the east edge of the finger with fine views of the main body of the pond. It ends at a beaver lodge piled against the shore.

The second side road leaves sharp left 1.1 mile from the junction and drops 200 feet to a large clearing amidst tall hemlocks. Paths on either side lead down to the water's edge for pretty views of the pond in its simple wooded setting. With a short carry, you could launch a canoe here for an exploration of the pond's farther reaches.

## Crocker Pond

Beyond Broken Bridge Pond, FR 18 passes a side road left to several campground sites and ends at a turnaround at the north end of Crocker Pond, once known as Papoose Pond. (This is the trailhead for the Albany Brook Trail to Round Pond.) A needle-carpeted spur, suitable for launching a canoe, dips to the shore for a nice water view. The oblong pond is rimmed with pine and birch and hemmed in by the wooded slopes of Albany Mountain. A great flat-topped whitish rock rises from the water near the west shore—a Crocker Pond landmark.

The campground's seven sites are arrayed along the side road by the pond's east shore. Open year-round, they offer a peaceful camping experience quite different from the mini tent cities at Dolly Copp or along the Kancamagus Highway. From the loop at this road's end, a path leads south between sites #5 and #6. It dips briefly, rises over a hemlock-covered knoll, then swings right across glacier-scratched ledges fronting a finger-like cove. In another 100 feet it comes to a large outcrop overlooking the south half of the pond, a great sunning spot. A lower ledge to the right affords a full view of the pond. This is the premier picnic spot at Crocker Pond.

## Round Pond

Back at the trailhead by the north end of Crocker Pond, the Albany Brook Trail departs westward at a WMNF sign. This easy, pleasant walk begins with a dip and a swing left around a swampy swale. You rise into a corridor of birches and follow a wide, level footway on a bank above the west shore of Crocker Pond. The trees open for a close look at the big white boulder out in the water, a miniature Rock of Gibraltar. In another 100 feet a side path, easily missed, leads 50 feet to a good sitting rock. Cushioned by pine needles, the main trail takes you past a beaver lodge.

At 0.2 mile a stiff 100-yard climb lifts you into slender hardwoods and away from Crocker Pond. The trail rolls over low ridges and crosses several small streams that feed into Albany Brook, down-slope and out of sight to your left. At 0.9 mile you cross an old logging road, with a clearing on the right. Follow the yellow blazes ahead and descend gently through hemlocks and beeches to the north shore of Round Pond at 1 mile.

Round Pond is a secluded beauty that opens wide from this hemlock-shaded viewpoint. Rooty seats allow you to relax and enjoy the vista. Hemlocks, white pines, and red maples rim the shoreline. A line of dark, pine-topped cliffs guards the pond on the left (east). This lovely spot—by far the best at Round Pond—is the end of the Albany Brook Trail. Old roads and overgrown paths can be followed to other points around the pond, of interest chiefly to anglers.

## Albany Mountain

If you're staying at Crocker Pond Campground, consider a hike to Albany Mountain via the Albany Notch and Albany Mountain Trails (3.8 miles round-trip, 1,100-foot vertical rise). An east-facing ledge at the trail's end near the summit offers a *bird's-eye view* of Broken Bridge Pond far below in the forest. A semi-bushwhack south along the ridge leads 0.25 mile to open ledges with superb views S and SW, including a look down at Virginia Lake. The Albany Notch Trail leaves the west side of FR 18 0.9 mile north of the campground; parking is limited and the trail sign is hidden at the back of a clearing. (See John Gibson's *50 Hikes in Southern and Coastal Maine.*)

For the less ambitious, the Forest Service has developed a self-guided "Patte Brook Auto Tour" that includes stops at Broken Bridge and Crocker Ponds and at Waterfowl Marsh, an artificial pool and marsh with good birding possibilities. An interpretive leaflet is available.

*Winter:* The road from US 2 in West Bethel is usually plowed for 4 miles, leaving a 2.9 mile ski/walk to Crocker Pond. The roads are also snowmobile trails, and the ponds receive some traffic. If you don't mind the road slog, this is a fine area to explore in winter. The entire three-pond excursion is a mellow 8 miles.

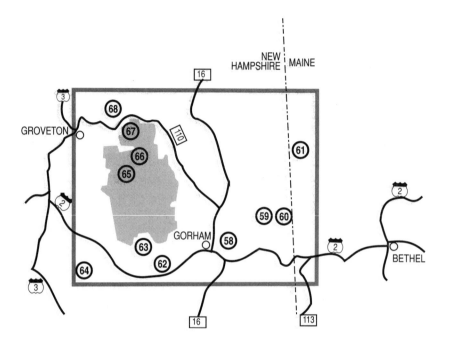

*South Pond and Long Mountain*

# V. NORTHERN
# WHITE MOUNTAINS

◆

SOME OF THE LOVELIEST PONDS in the White Mountains are found amidst the less-frequented peaks and valleys north of the main ranges. If you delight in visiting remote, spruce-shadowed ponds, the northern Whites will provide you with many pleasurable excursions.

North of US 2 and east of NH 16 is the Mahoosuc Range, a line of gnarly knobs and peaks far more rugged than their modest elevations would suggest. The lower southern Mahoosucs shelter a quartet of pretty ponds along the ridge-crest Appalachian Trail: Page Pond, Dream Lake, Moss Pond, and Gentian Pond. Mascot Pond, set at the base of a former lead mine, is located on a side trail at the south end of the range. Speck Pond, reputed to be the loftiest pond in Maine, resides on the shoulder of 4,180-foot Old Speck Mountain at the higher north end of the Mahoosucs.

To the west, just north of US 2 and the Northern Presidentials lies Durand Lake, whose manicured shores provide fine views of the big peaks. Nearby, the legendary Pond of Safety nestles on the flank of the 3,200-foot Crescent Range. The two Cherry Ponds, rich in wildlife and Presidential Range views, rest on the broad plains of Jefferson, SW of 4,006-foot Mount Waumbek and the Pliny Range.

The detached northern sector of the National Forest is bordered on the west by the Pilot Range, including 4,170-foot Mount Cabot, the highest New Hampshire peak north of the Presidentials. The Pilots and the rolling upland to the east form the alluring backcountry region known as The Kilkenny. Drained by the Upper Ammonoosuc River and traversed by the 20-mile Kilkenny Ridge Trail, this area has a wonderfully secluded feel to it. The Kilkenny was logged for spruce at the turn of the century. In 1903— that most disastrous year for White Mountain forests—over 25,000 acres were burned. Today an open birch and fir forest encloses Unknown Pond, a restful spot at the foot of the region's finest peak, the Horn. Nearby is the tiny hidden tarn known as Bishop's Pond. To the NE, overlooked by the granite face of Rogers Ledge, is boggy little Kilback Pond. At the northern edge of the Kilkenny lies South Pond, a large recreation-rich pond accessed via a side road off NH 110.

A recent addition to New Hampshire's public wild lands is the Nash Stream Forest, saved from the hand of developers by an intensive conservation effort in 1988. Two ponds with a true North Country flavor—Little Bog and Whitcomb—are easily visited from a side road in the Nash Stream forest. Far from any road or trail is Long Mountain Pond, a wild oval of water tucked in the saddle between the two summits of its massive namesake mountain.

# CHAPTER 58

# MASCOT POND
# (LEADMINE POND)

◆

**Location:** Gorham, at SW end of Mahoosuc Range
**Hiking Facts:** 2.6 miles round-trip, 250-foot vertical rise, easy
**Map:** USGS 7½' Berlin
**Area:** 6 acres   **Elevation:** 1,050 feet
**Avg./Max. Depth:** 6/16 feet
**Activities:** Hiking, picnicking

◆

The short hike into Mascot Pond, close by the roaring traffic and smoke-belching mills of the Gorham-Berlin highway, could hardly be classified as a wilderness journey. It's an interesting walk nonetheless and is certainly unique among White Mountain pond excursions. The pond is cradled between craggy Leadmine Ledge and a wooded knob that fronts the great eastward bend of the Androscoggin River. At trail's end the shore opens to a nice water-and-mountain view. Experienced hikers can go on to explore a ledgy viewpoint above.

## Access
Your ticket to Mascot Pond is the Mahoosuc Trail, for most of its length one of the wildest trails in the Whites. At its south end, though, it gets off to an inglorious start in a setting that will remind you more of metropolitan New Jersey than northern New Hampshire. From the stoplight at the western junction of NH 16 and US 2 in Gorham Upper Village, drive 0.4 mile north on NH 16 to a green railroad bridge that spans the busy four-lane highway. Stay in the right lane and make a quick right turn into a gravel pull-off just past the bridge. There may or may not be a sign for the Mahoosuc Trail here.

## The Trail To Mascot Pond
You duck under an iron girder (a sign warns of "Low Head Clearance") and

cross the Androscoggin River on a plank walkway under the Boston and Maine trestle. The broad, stony river is sluggish here as it approaches its curve towards the distant coast. To your right, downstream, you see the peaks of Mounts Moriah, Imp, and North Carter.

Across the bridge, turn right and follow blue blazes along a dirt road beside the river's east bank. In 0.4 mile bear left at a fork and cross a canal via the top of a dam. Turbines rumble from the bowels of the red brick powerhouse on your right. Be sure to heed the high voltage warning signs! (The 1920 edition of the AMC *Guide* cautioned that this crossing was occasionally closed to trampers "because certain gardens on the east bank have suffered depredations." An alternative was to apply at a nearby house for ferry passage across the river.)

Once across the canal, bear left (north) and uphill at another split in the road. In 100 yards the Mahoosuc Trail bears right (east) into the woods at an AMC trail sign. At 0.8 mile you climb steeply across a power line swath, then more gradually beside a small brook. Leaving the industrial world behind, the trail becomes a pleasant woods walk through a spindly hardwood forest adorned with white birches. At 1.1 miles from your car a sign shows the side trail to Mascot Pond. Bear right and descend gently for 0.2 mile, glimpsing the pond to the right through the trees. The yellow-blazed path curls right and drops you by the pond's north shore amidst low mounds of gravel.

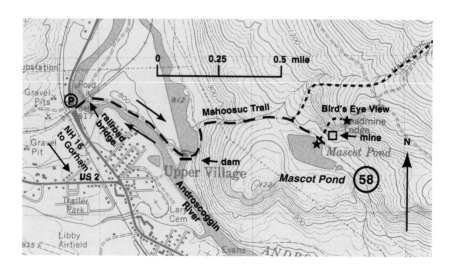

## At Mascot Pond

Across the water the rocky crowns of Mounts Madison (5,366 feet) and Adams (5,799 feet) tower over the antennaed crest of Pine Mountain (2,410 feet) and a nearby wooded hill. To your left you can sight down the shore to Moriah and North Carter. The mountain beauty found at Mascot Pond is a surprise, given the hike's inauspicious start. This is a good place to enjoy lunch or a snack. By following an old road a short distance east, you'll find a woodsy picnic spot in a pretty hemlock grove behind the shore.

The dark-water pond is fringed with mucky sedge-meadows, leather-leaf, and a mixed forest of conifers and hardwoods. Old lodges and blackened stumps testify to former beaver activity. Unfortunately, swimming and fishing are uncertain propositions in the murky water of Mascot Pond. A 1952 biological survey reported no fish present here; one theory is that the water is contaminated with lead from the old mine.

## Leadmine Ledge

If you look behind you while standing on the open shore, you may be startled to see a great dark crag breaching the forest, with a steep slope of broken rock spilling down almost to the water's edge. You're facing Leadmine Ledge, where once miners blasted into a vein of lead reportedly 10-20 feet wide and extending 200 vertical feet.

According to Paul Doherty's *Smoke From a Thousand Campfires*, local legend holds that the vein of lead was discovered by a trapper who slipped while climbing down a steep ledge above the pond. In desperation he drove his tomahawk into the rock. His quick thinking saved his life and brought him face-to-face with an outcropping of pure lead.

The trapper never returned, but the vein was rediscovered in 1870 by a Dr. Rowe who was strolling along the shore of what was then called Pollywog Pond. In 1880 several entrepreneurs organized the Mascot Mine Company. They quickly built a road, blasted two shafts into the cliff, and started shipping ore back to Boston. At its height the company employed sixty men and produced six tons of ore per day. The help lived in a two-story house on the north side of the pond, which was renamed Mascot Pond.

The mine was played out by 1886 and the operation was dismantled in February 1887. The house was accidentally burned some years later. The lower mine shaft is still visible from the shore of the pond, above the manmade scree slope. The tunnel is an important hibernation site for bats and is closed to hikers.

A *bird's-eye view* of Mascot Pond is your reward for a short but very

*Mascot Pond from Leadmine Ledge*

steep climb around to the top of the ledge, high above the mine. This side trip is recommended for experienced hikers only. From the gravel mounds, backtrack on the Mascot Pond side trail for 200 feet and cut sharp right into the woods across an old embankment. A dim path angles up to the left behind the ledge, becoming more distinct—and much steeper—higher up. The last pitch is a strenuous scramble amidst white pines and slick, lichen-glazed ledges.

The best view is from a mid-level crag that shows the pond and the nearby village of Gorham set amidst a great mountain amphitheater comprised of the Carter-Moriahs, the Presidentials, and the Crescent Range. The climb up to the ledge and back adds 0.4 mile and 200 feet of climbing to the hike. Use caution on the steep descent from the ledge. Your return to your car is made by the same route.

*Winter:* Mascot Pond is an easy and interesting winter excursion. The parking area by the railroad bridge is often plowed. The frozen pond offers nice views of all three Moriah summits not easily obtained in summer.

CHAPTER 59

# DREAM LAKE AND PAGE POND

◆

**Location:** Southern Mahoosuc Range
**Hiking Facts:** 10.1 miles round-trip, 3,100-foot vertical rise (2,300 in, 800 out), more difficult
**Maps:** USGS 7½' Shelburne

|  | Dream Lake | Page Pond |
|---|---|---|
| **Area:** | 15 acres | 12 acres |
| **Elevation:** | 2,610 feet | 2,230 feet |
| **Avg./Max. Depth:** | 4/4 feet | 1/2 feet |
| **Activities:** | Hiking, picnicking | |

The wild, spruce-clad ridges of Bald Cap Mountain (3,065 feet), the highest summit in the southern Mahoosucs, are flanked on either side by a picturesque mountain pond. On the east is Dream Lake, whose boggy shore offers a long, spellbinding view across the water to the Presidentials on the horizon. To the west, beyond a pair of spur ridges, lies shallow Page Pond, an enchanting place where sun-soaked ledges beckon for a midday siesta.

The hike in to Dream Lake on Peabody Brook Trail is a moderately strenuous affair, with the added delight of Giant Falls along the way. The two ponds are linked by a roller-coaster stretch of the Mahoosuc Trail—a section completed in 1924—leading through beautiful conifer forests and past a fine rock outlook at Wocket Ledge.

The return trip on the Mahoosuc Trail from Page Pond to Dream Lake entails a discouraging 800 feet of climbing. This difficulty of access ensures a certain degree of solitude at Page Pond; it's visited mostly by backpackers trudging between shelters/campsites. Note that camping is prohibited in the Mahoosucs except at the designated sites, so no tenting at either pond.

## Access
From the eastern junction of US 2 and NH 16 in Gorham drive east on US 2. In 3.3 miles turn left (north) onto North Road, which crosses the Androscoggin River at 0.3 mile and makes a sharp right at 0.5 mile. At 1 mile from US 2 the road crosses Leadmine Brook. Park in a pull-off on the left just beyond; there is *no* parking at the trailhead. Walk 0.25 east along the road and look for the AMC sign for Peabody Brook Trail on the left.

### The Trail To Dream Lake
The trail starts as an old logging road between a wood-shingled house on the left and a stone-cobbled house on the right. Please respect the owners' rights to privacy and quiet. Walk past a log gate to a fork at 0.1 mile. (The left fork is the unmarked Sinclair Trail, an overgrown and obscure logging road that eventually leads to Page Pond. It is sometimes used by mountain bikers in summer and snowmobilers in winter but is not recommended for summer hiking.)

Bear right on the blue-blazed trail and cross Peabody Brook on step stones. On the east bank swing left on a logging road leading upstream through hemlock forest. Bear right at a fork at 0.5 mile and left at 0.8 mile; signs and blue blazes mark the way. The footway narrows and the ascent steepens as you pass under an imposing crag on the right. Moderate climbing through attractive hemlocks leads to the side trail left to Giant Falls at 1.2 miles. (See Bruce and Doreen Bolnick's *Waterfalls of the White Mountains.*)

The trail becomes rocky and rough as it slabs the ravine high above the brook. You cross a belt of red pines and scale a ladder at 1.6 miles. The steady ascent continues up through birches and mixed hardwoods above the tumbling brook. At 2.1 miles you bear left to cross the stream where a branch drops in on the left. With the main brook now on your right, you climb up the wild, tangled ravine, thick with young conifers. At 2.4 miles you recross the dwindling brook. The grade eases as you approach the swampy flat that holds Dream Lake. The footing along this boggy, bushy plateau is mucky in places, especially after a rain. Many of the bog bridges are disintegrating with age and dampness.

### At Dream Lake
At 2.8 miles the Peabody Brook Trail bears left and slightly downhill at a sign. Side paths lead a short distance left to the boggy southeast shore of Dream Lake. These first northwoodsy views look across the pond to the dark conifer

spires on the northwest shore. Continuing on the main trail, you pass the Dryad Fall Trail on the right at 3 miles and swing left and down to the northeast shore and longer views. The first good look is from a short side path to the left, with Mount Adams rising over the east shore in the distance.

For the prettiest vista, walk another 100 feet along Peabody Brook Trail to an exposed ledge on the right. A rough side path left drops to the shrubby, fir-shadowed shore. If this were a perfect world, a sun-warmed sitting rock would await. The reality is that there are no good seats at the shore of Dream Lake. But the view SW down the broad, sparkling sheet of water is exceptional. Graceful twin peaks cut the horizon: Mount Washington on the left and Mount Adams on the right, with the lower crest of Mount Clay between. In good light Mount Madison can be seen in front of Adams. On either side the shores are lined with spearlike spruce and fir. The low, spired knoll on the left is Bald Cap Peak (2,795 feet). (The original trail to the pond, long abandoned, was cut over this knob in 1877.) The whole scene is dreamily beautiful on a clear day.

Your reverie at Dream Lake might be broken by the sight of a moose dipping its mighty head into the water. Although I have not seen beaver here, the pond's outlet is shored up by a long, bush-grown beaver dam. Resident bird life includes the rusty blackbird and other northwoods species. But don't bring your fishing rod. Although stocking has been attempted in the past, both Dream Lake and Page Pond are deemed too shallow to support trout.

### The Trail To Page Pond

From the side trail, follow Peabody Brook Trail another 200 feet to the Mahoosuc Trail. You'll walk this white-blazed path (part of the Appalachian Trail) 1.7 miles west to Page Pond. Turn left and skirt the northernmost corner of Dream Lake. After you cross the inlet brook, a short path leads left to a clearing under the firs, a shady picnic spot with a screened view of the water.

Soon the trail bears right and climbs steeply above Dream Lake into beautiful conifer forest. A 220-foot ascent places you atop the first of the two ridges you cross en route to Page Pond. You dip 200 feet through woods ravaged by blow-down, cross the small, mossy west branch of Peabody Brook, and climb another 200 feet to the scrubby top of Wocket Ledge. Views are limited here, but as you drop down the far side a short side path right (sign) leads 50 feet to a superb outlook ledge. The view west and SW includes the Carter-Moriah Range, the Presidentials, the nearby southern Mahoosuc peaks (low but very rugged), and many mountains in New Hampshire's north country.

You've now come 1.1 miles from Dream Lake. Ahead you face a rugged descent of 500 feet in 0.6 mile to Page Pond. You scramble down two precipitous rocky pitches separated by a spruce-wooded terrace. A more moderate grade eases you down to the pond's narrow basin, clasped between Wocket Ledge and a set of peaks known as the Trident.

## At Page Pond

You pass an AMC trail sign (the terminus of the overgrown Sinclair Trail) and emerge in a shrubby clearing overlooking Page Pond on your right. The long oval of shallow water stretches northward between spruce-fringed shores. Continue on the Mahoosuc Trail through a patch of woods and across an ancient beaver dam at the pond's outlet.

A side path leads a few yards right to flat, whitish ledges at the pond's SW edge. When the sun is high this is a nice place to relax and gaze at the water and the dark ridge of Wocket Ledge to the east. The only sign of man may be a sulfur-laden breeze wafting up from Berlin. There were no paper mills in the area when a hunter named "Yager" Page hewed out a clearing from the vast woods of Success in the early 1800s. The pond was presumably named in this pioneer's honor.

The water of Page Pond is very shallow—hardly six inches deep in front of the ledges. Swimming would be a physical impossibility. The level was down in 1992, exposing some muck along the edges but also making a jumble of rocks at the south end more accessible. This vantage point opens an excellent view down the length of the pond.

The traverse back over the ridges to Dream Lake is a tiring 1.7 miles with 800 feet of ascent, followed by a 3.1 mile descent back down Peabody Brook Trail.

*Winter:* The Peabody Brook Trail is a difficult winter route to Dream Lake due to the treacherous sidehill above Giant Falls. It's easier to come across the ridge from Gentian Pond. The Presidential views from frozen Dream Lake are magnificent. Following the Mahoosuc Trail to Page Pond can be a challenge, especially the steep pitch below Wocket Ledge. If you're good at route-finding, you can snowshoe up the Sinclair Trail, which is sometimes used by snowmobiles. There's a bonus view of North Carter from the north end of Page Pond. The best winter parking is at the Centennial Trail 0.7 mile west of the Peabody Brook trailhead.

# CHAPTER 60

# GENTIAN AND MOSS (UPPER GENTIAN) PONDS

♦

**Location:** Southern Mahoosuc Range
**Hiking Facts:** 5.6 miles round-trip, 1,600-foot vertical rise, moderate
**Map:** USGS 7½' Shelburne (Page 280)

|  | Gentian Pond | Moss Pond |
|---|---|---|
| **Area:** | 4 acres | 2 acres |
| **Elevation:** | 2,150 feet | 2,530 feet |
| **Avg./Max. Depth:** | 6/7 feet | n/a |
| **Activities:** | Hiking, camping (lean-to), picnicking | |

♦

*We soon came upon a small sheet of water, partially filled
with lily pads, and surrounded by beds of moss.... The
outlet led us... to a lower terrace, where another surprise
awaited us. This was an exquisite pond, larger than the
other.... Having gathered some bottle-gentian by the
shore, we ventured to bestow the name of Gentian Pond.*
—Mrs. L.D. and Miss Marian M. Pychomska
"Baldcap Mountain," *Appalachia,* 1880.

Among the prominent members of the fledgling Appalachian Mountain
Club were Lucia and Marian Pychowska, a dynamic mother and daughter
hiking team from Hoboken, New Jersey. In the 1870s this intrepid duo
poked around the trailless Mahoosucs, exploring these two tarns, as well as
Bald Cap Mountain, Dream Lake, Dryad Fall, Giant Falls, and other
features.

Soon enough logging roads were thrust from Shelburne up to Gentian
Pond, and by 1924 AMC trail builders had run the Mahoosuc Trail along
the ridge past both Gentian and Moss Ponds. A peeled log shelter was raised
beside the shore of the former.

*Gentian Pond*

You can acquaint yourself with these two high, wild water bodies in a moderate day of hiking from Shelburne. Scenic Gentian Pond, a favorite stop for Appalachian Trail hikers, is perched on a wooded shelf rimmed by steep, ledgy ridges. Diminutive Moss Pond lies hidden on a higher terrace amidst ridge-top evergreens. Hikers with energy to burn can fashion an extended loop to take in Dream Lake and Dryad Fall. Note that camping is allowed only at the shelter and tent sites at Gentian Pond.

### Access

The blue-blazed Austin Brook Trail runs 3.5 miles from North Road in Shelburne to Gentian Pond. In recent years a gravel logging road has been drivable to a point 1.4 miles up the trail. From US 2 in Shelburne, 5.4 miles east of the eastern NH 16 junction in Gorham, turn north onto Meadow Road, marked by a sign for Philbrook Farm Inn. After crossing the Androscoggin River, Meadow Road reaches a T-junction 0.9 mile from US 2. Bear left onto North Road, then right in 100 feet onto the unmarked Mill Brook Road. (Mill Brook and Austin Brook are one and the same.)

A sign posted by Boise Cascade, owner of much of this woodland, alerts hikers to ongoing logging operations. Stay straight at a fork 1.6 miles from North Road and park at a pull-off on the right just before a brook crossing.

Boise Cascade requests that hikers park safely off the road here and drive no farther.

If the Mill Brook Road is closed or impassable when you arrive, the Austin Brook Trail starts 0.5 mile farther west on North Road. There is limited parking on the south side of the road. The blue-blazed trail spins through a wooden turnstile and follows old logging roads, with one relocation to the left. After crossing Austin Brook, the trail reaches Mill Brook Road in 1.1 miles, 0.3 mile below the parking pull-off. This would add 2.8 miles and 200 vertical feet to the listed hiking facts.

## The Trail To Gentian Pond

Proceeding on foot from the pull-off on Mill Brook Road, bear right at a fork in less than 0.1 mile and climb gradually up the road. You pass the Dryad Fall Trail on the left at 0.5 mile. At 0.7 mile, just before a steep pitch, signs and blue blazes point you left off the gravel road onto a wide new logging road.

Swinging left off Mill Brook Road, the Austin Brook Trail climbs steadily up the newer road through recently logged hardwood forest. In about 0.5 mile you make a sharp right turn. Soon the trail merges with a skid road beside a clear-cut slope on the right. Follow the muddy road 0.1 mile, then bear right off it at a point marked by blue blazes and surveyor's tape. Swinging left, the trail crosses another skid road. Following markings carefully, you zigzag through a spruce grove on the fringe of the cuttings and cross dwindling Austin Brook, the outlet for Gentian Pond. Log bridges lead you across a boggy plateau in the shadow of lofty wooded cliffs.

Beyond the bogs (1.8 miles from your car) you swing left to angle up a steep hardwood slope, the hardest climbing of the day. Higher up the trail hooks right for the final ledgy ascent through a wild, needle-blanketed spruce forest. A glimpse of the shelter ahead assures you that the end of the short but steep grind is at hand. The lean-to clearing opens a view south down the valley to the Royces, the Moriah ridge, and the high Carter Range. You're 2.1 miles and 1,200 vertical feet above your car.

## At Gentian Pond

First, an abstract of the trails that radiate from Gentian Pond Shelter: On the south side of the lean-to (the side toward the road), the northbound Mahoosuc Trail heads sharp right past several tent sites toward Mount Success. On the north side of the shelter (the pond side), the southbound Mahoosuc Trail angles right and downhill; this section was relocated several years ago to bypass a difficult scramble at the pond's outlet. Straight ahead, a side path drops 75 feet to flat shoreline ledges at the SE tip of Gentian Pond, a delightful spot with good afternoon sun exposure.

The view presented by the waterfront rocks is "a picturesque combination of water, ledges and mountains." So wrote Karl P. Harrington, the AMC trailmaster who helped string the Mahoosuc Trail in the 1920s. The little tea-colored pond is bordered by shapely softwoods and guarded by high mountain walls. The ridge directly across bears a slanting line of cliffs. Behind and to the right is a higher ledge-spotted ridge. The southbound Mahoosuc Trail curls left through the fold between these buttresses, shadowing a brook up to Moss Pond.

Close by on the left, across the outlet, is a steeply inclined ledge that confounded backpackers until the recent relocation. If you enjoy a short rock scramble, cross the outlet on logs and scale the ledge via good footholds and handholds. This sunny perch has a great view north down the length of the pond. Look for an overgrown old beaver lodge by the bushy bog at the far end.

### The Trail To Moss Pond

Climb back up toward the shelter and turn sharp left on the southbound Mahoosuc Trail, marked by a sign for Peabody Brook Trail, US 2, and Gorham. The white-blazed path dips and rolls through wild spruce-fir woods above the east shore and crosses a small brook. White birches and feathery ferns appear as you skirt the bog at the pond's north end. You curve left to approach the inlet brook, then bear right to follow it upward into a lovely birch-glade ravine.

The trail swings left and steepens amidst yellow birches. You pass by a big stub chiseled by pileated woodpeckers, then tackle a rugged, bouldery pitch. The sun gleams off cliff faces glimpsed to the right through the trees. The grade eases as you step back and forth across the mossy little brook. Beyond a squared-off boulder you see open sky ahead, a time of anticipation whenever you approach a pond in the mountains. The trail tunnels through conifers and emerges at the NE corner of Moss Pond, 0.7 mile from Gentian Pond Shelter.

### At Moss Pond

Moss Pond is a tiny, spruce-robed gem. From this waterside vantage point—which captures sun through early afternoon—you gaze across the east half of the pond to the serried ranks of conifers lining the south shore. There are no good sitting rocks, but you can enjoy lunch beside the trail under an AMC sign that names the pond. Traffic is light here, so unless it's Appalachian Trail through-hiking season (late summer), you may have Moss Pond to yourself.

For a full view of the pond, step out onto the fern-feathered beaver dam that blocks the outlet a few yards to the left.

On one visit my friend Mike and I heard a snort from the boggy west end of the pond. We looked over to see a huge bull moose neck-deep in the water. Joined by two AT hikers, we spent a half hour watching the majestically antlered bull swim, feed, and cavort in the pond.

The trail does not make another close approach to Moss Pond, and the shores are fragile, so enjoy this little pearl of the Mahoosucs from here before retracing your steps to your car. If you're burning with ambition, you can continue southward on the Mahoosuc Trail through beautiful evergreen forest to the Peabody Brook Trail and Dream Lake, looping back to Mill Brook Road on the steep Dryad Fall Trail. The distance is 4.1 miles, with 300 feet of climbing, compared with 2.8 miles via a direct return.

*Winter:* These wild ponds are seldom visited in the season of snow and ice. Parking is very limited on North Road; it may be best by the junction with the unplowed Mill Brook Road. The steep sidehill approaching Gentian Pond can make for difficult snowshoeing. Moss Pond is especially lovely in winter, hemmed in by snow-laden conifers and overlooked by northern cliffs out of view from the summer trail.

CHAPTER 61

# SPECK POND

◆

**Location:** Mahoosuc Range
**Hiking Facts:** 8.3 miles round-trip, 2,500-foot vertical rise, more difficult
**Maps:** USGS 7½' Old Speck Mountain (ME), Success Pond (NH)
**Area:** 9 acres   **Elevation:** 3,430 feet
**Max. Depth:** 36 feet
**Activities:** Hiking, camping (lean-to), fishing (brook trout), picnicking, swimming

◆

Speck Pond, the crown jewel of the Mahoosuc Range tarns, is said to be the highest water body in Maine. It is assuredly one of the most beautiful. Clear and deep, it snuggles into a fir-forested bowl enclosed by Mahoosuc Arm (3,790 feet) and Old Speck Mountain (4,180 feet, the fourth highest peak in Maine).

This northern Mahoosuc region was little known to hikers before AMC trail builders strung the rugged Mahoosuc Trail across the ridge in 1918–21. For years Speck Pond inspired some exaggeration among its admirers. The 1916 AMC *Guide* sized it at 40 acres (it's actually nine), and until 1972 the guidebook noted a reputed depth of 250 (!) feet. A recent survey established the bottom at 36 feet, still an eye-opening figure for a small high-country pond.

The hike into Speck Pond utilizes three paths—Speck Pond Trail, May Cutoff, and Mahoosuc Trail—for a scenic loop over the bare summit of Mahoosuc Arm, around the pond, and back up to a parting bird's-eye view. The pond itself beckons for its remoteness, beauty, and superb trout fishing. By the north shore is the AMC's Speck Pond Campsite, which is busy with backpackers through the summer and fall. It's the only legal camping place along the route of this hike.

## Access
The Speck Pond Trail begins from the James River Company's gravel Success

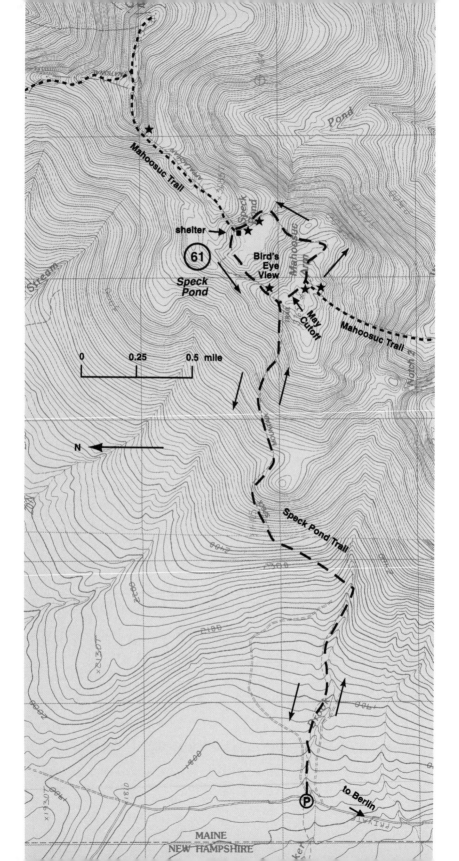

Mahoosuc Trail

shelter

(61)

Speck Pond

Bird's Eye View

May Cutoff

Mahoosuc Arm

Mahoosuc Trail

0    0.25    0.5 mile

N

Speck Pond Trail

P

to Berlin

MAINE
NEW HAMPSHIRE

Pond Road on the west side of the Mahoosuc Range. Finding this logging artery can be an adventure in itself. From the junction of NH 16 and US 2 in Gorham Upper Village, continue north on NH 16 through downtown Berlin. At 6.7 miles turn right at a stoplight where there are Off-Highway Recreational Vehicles Parking and Hospital signs. Cross the Androscoggin River and in 0.2 mile turn right onto Hutchins Street. In another 0.4 mile jog left 100 feet on Bridge Street to skirt the James River mill complex. Turn right again on Hutchins Street for 0.3 mile to signs that read: "OHRV Parking—1 mile" and "Success Pond."

Turn left here onto Success Pond Road, which climbs past logging yards. After a teeth-chattering first mile the surface is generally better but occasionally rough. Keep an eye out for logging trucks; they have the right-of-way and will claim it. You'll pass branching logging roads and several trailheads. Bear right at a fork 11.1 miles from Hutchins Street, and at 11.9 miles look for the small white AMC sign for Speck Pond Trail on the right. Park in a clearing off the left side of the road.

### The Trail To Speck Pond

The blue-blazed trail enters the woods just to the right (south) of a branch logging road. For the first 1.4 miles it meanders through second-growth woods beside a small brook. Passing a small pool, you climb more steeply and bear left, away from the brook. The trail crosses an old logging road and traverses a sidehill slope sprouted to hardwood saplings.

Soon you veer right at a steeper grade through wilder woods of spruce, fir, and birch. The pitch eases as you skirt a minor knob. You twist through an area wracked by blow-down, then stroll through an open stand of hoary moss-draped firs. From here up it's a steep pull over a rough and eroded footway. A ladder helps you surmount one steep ledge. At 3.1 miles you emerge into scrubby firs and reach the junction with May Cutoff. You've climbed over 2,000 feet to this 3,700-foot level.

Swing right to follow the windings of May Cutoff across the summit ridge of Mahoosuc Arm. This 0.3-mile path is a Mahoosuc Range sampler of scrub, ledge, and heath meadow. The thin, mucky, acidic soil of these Mahoosuc bogs supports such interesting flora as leatherleaf, broom crowberry, and Labrador tea. (*Please* stay on the trail—the bogs are fragile.)

Within ten minutes you arrive at the Mahoosuc Trail. A rock knob a few yards right (south) looks north to Old Speck—identified by its fire tower and ledgy shoulder—and a sweep of lake-and-mountain country. The large water body with scalloped shores is Lake Umbagog, where bald eagles have nested in recent years.

For an even better panorama walk about 0.2 mile south to where the trail commences a steep drop towards Mahoosuc Notch. A double-decker ledge on the left opens a spectacular view of the sharply-cut notch, the Mahoosuc summits stretching to the south, and many distant peaks in Maine and New Hampshire.

Retrace your steps and continue northward on the Mahoosuc Trail beyond May Cutoff. The range trail winds downward through alpine meadows, black spruce scrub, and ledges with varying views, then drops steeply to the pond, 0.8 mile from May Cutoff.

## At Speck Pond

The Mahoosuc Trail emerges from the woods by the SE corner of Speck Pond, where Pond Brook begins its plunge to the Bull Branch valley. Hop out to some waterfront rocks for an expansive view of the tarn and its enclosing forest bowl. The water is a sparkling sky-blue on a fine summer day. The shores are woven with a tangled tapestry of balsam fir, the hardy tree best suited to the rigors of life at this 3,400-foot elevation. One early 1900s adventurer deemed these woods around Speck Pond "the most trying scrub I have ever encountered."

Rock seats invite you to linger here at the pond's quieter side, removed from the hubbub of the campsite across the water. This is a favored spot to cast a line for a Speck Pond trout. According to Al Raychard's *Remote Trout Ponds in Maine*, good fishing is found here from late May through September. During the warm summer months the trout retreat to the cooler, deeper reaches.

The Mahoosuc Trail crosses the outlet on a small rock dam (look for an old beaver dam on the right) and swings left past two openings along the north shore. You climb into the fir woods, then dip to a vantage looking SW over the water to the ragged slope of Mahoosuc Arm. The rocky footway again leads up and away from the pond and back down to the shore. Tent platforms appear on the right; a side path left departs for a rocky point.

You soon arrive at the lean-to, a favorite with Appalachian Trail through-hikers—and resident Canada jays, who will happily partake of your lunch. The shelter is tucked in the woods away from the pond by a trail junction; a fee is charged for camping here in summer and fall. To the right the Mahoosuc Trail leads 1.4 miles (and 800 feet up) to the summit of Old Speck. To the left is the Speck Pond Trail, your return route. From the latter trail, just past the shelter, a side path leads left to shoreline rocks offering good swimming and a superb view down the pond.

To make your way homeward, continue SW on Speck Pond Trail. You pass the AMC caretaker's tent and a side trail right to a spring. The trail skirts a shallow, lily-dotted cove and soon begins the climb out of the pond's basin. Near the top of the 0.5 mile, 350-foot ascent look back over the firs for a striking *bird's-eye view* of Speck Pond nestled in the forest under the rounded hulk of Old Speck. Take a last look at the tarn and the wild North Country view beyond, then forge ahead a short way to the junction with May Cutoff.

Keep straight here on Speck Pond Trail for the descent. You might pause to admire a view west through the trees to Success Pond, its shores dotted with camps and cabins. Enjoy the varied forest on the 3.1-mile trek back down to your car.

*Winter:* Hidden in its high forest bowl, Speck Pond sees few winter visitors. The Success Pond Road is usually closed in winter, so the best access is over Old Speck Mountain via Old Speck Trail and Mahoosuc Trail from Grafton Notch, a rugged but exhilarating outing for experienced snowshoers. Roadside parking is available in the notch. The trail along the open west shoulder of Old Speck often requires crampons; it is steep, icy, and exposed to face-numbing NW winds. The frozen pond offers a sense of solitude often lacking in summer and fall. Beyond the southern outlet huge snowdrifts lift you to views SE. Canada jays will likely make your acquaintance at the shelter.

*Speck Pond and Old Speck Mountain*

# CHAPTER 62

# DURAND LAKE

---◆---

**Location:** Randolph, near Appalachia
**Hiking Facts:** 0.8 mile loop, 50-foot vertical rise, easy
**Map:** USGS 7½' X 15' Mount Washington; AMC/Washburn Mount Washington and Presidential Range (Page 218)
**Area:** 10 acres   **Elevation:** 1,268 feet
**Activities:** Hiking, picnicking, fishing (brook trout, horned pout)

---◆---

You can enjoy a perfectly civilized stroll around this artificial pond just north of US 2, enjoying grand views of the Northern Presidentials and other peaks along the way. The area around Durand Lake is maintained as a park and wildlife refuge by the town of Randolph. (Durand was the original name for Randolph, applied by colonial Gov. John Wentworth to honor John Durand, a business associate from London.) Around the turn of the century Abel and Laban Watson, proprietors of the Ravine House hotel, created Durand Lake by diverting and damming part of the Moose River's flow.

## Access
Park in the hikers' lot at Appalachia, on the south side of US 2, about 1 mile west of the Pinkham B (Dolly Copp) Road and 2 miles east of Lowe's Store. Cross the highway and pass through a gap in a fence at signs for Durand Lake and the Bee Line trail. Descend a short distance on a grassy road to a T-junction near the south shore of the pond.

## At Durand Lake
Ahead, a path descends a short distance to an opening on the south shore of the pond, with a view left to Mount Randolph (3,180 feet) and its rocky viewpoint, Lookout Ledge (2,240 feet). The main trail turns left (west) at an arrow onto a grass-grown road. As you emerge into a weedy field, turn right at a sign for Bee Line. This trail skirts the west shore, cuts through a patch of woods on a narrow footway, then bears right again on another road near the NW corner.

Walk east along the open, grassy north shore of Durand Lake and take in the water-and-mountain views. Pine Mountain, Mount Moriah, and Imp Mountain are to the east. South across the pond the gaunt rocky summits of Mount Madison and Mount Adams tower 4,000+ feet above you, buttressed by wooded foreground ridges. This side of the pond is good territory for picnicking or fishing for the stocked trout that reside in the water. Swimming is not allowed.

The Bee Line leaves left halfway along the north shore; keep straight to continue the loop. Follow the road as it curves right around the east shore, crossing the outlet and a small inlet brook. At the SE corner swing right again well behind the south shore, skirting a field that slopes down from Route 2. A weedy swath leads 100 feet right to a mammoth beaver lodge that has sprouted several small birches on its crown. At the loop junction, turn left and climb gently back to US 2 and your car.

*Bird's-Eye View:* Durand Lake is prominent in the northern view from the summits of Adams and Madison. The wide path wraps a light green ribbon around the shore, giving the pond a manicured look.

For a closer bird's-eye view, climb the Randolph Mountain Club's Ledge Trail, leading 1.3 miles and 950 vertical feet from Durand Road to Lookout Ledge. The trailhead, located at the site of the former Ravine House hotel, can be reached from the north shore of Durand Lake by following the Bee Line a short distance north to Durand Road, then walking 0.1 mile left (west) to the Ledge Trail. This rocky viewpoint—the best on the Crescent Range—affords a memorable view across the Randolph Valley to the Northern Presidentials, with Durand Lake below to the left.

*Winter:* The loop around the lake is an easy and attractive ski tour or winter walk. The Appalachia parking area is plowed.

CHAPTER 63

# POND OF SAFETY

$\blacklozenge$

**Location:** Randolph, between Crescent and Pliny Ranges
**Hiking Facts:** 6.4 miles round-trip, 700-foot vertical rise, moderate
**Map:** USGS 7½' X 15' Pliny Range
**Area:** 12 acres   **Elevation:** 2,190 feet
**Avg./Max. Depth:** 4/8 feet
**Activities:** Hiking, fishing (brook trout, horned pout), picnicking

---

Pond of Safety has long been a watery mountain haven for man and beast. It's well known to hunters, anglers, and snowmobilers, but less so to hikers. Nestled between the Pliny Range on the west and the Crescent Range to the east, its 12 placid acres form the source of the Upper Ammonoosuc River. The nearby woodlands have been extensively logged, but the spruce-rimmed pond is a backcountry gem.

Pond of Safety owes its name to one of the most intriguing of White Mountain legends. Several versions have been advanced by various historians. Though the authenticity of the story has been questioned, local town histories tell it this way: Four soldiers of the Continental Army—Benjamin Hicks, James Ryder, William Danforth, and Lazarus Holmes—were captured by the British during the Revolutionary War. They were soon paroled and returned to their regiment, sworn never again to take up arms against the redcoats. However, their superiors declared their papers to be fraudulent and ordered the quartet to rejoin the ranks. Being men of their word, they refused.

Catching wind of their imminent arrest as deserters, they fled north into the wilderness and sought refuge at a pond hidden in the mountainous recesses of Durand (today's Randolph). For three years they lived off the land, "undiscovered and perhaps forgotten," in the words of town historian George N. Cross. At war's end they surfaced from their backwoods asylum and moved into the nearby settlement of Dartmouth (now Jefferson), becoming pillars of the community. It seems the army forgave and forgot—in

1826 all four men were listed as Revolutionary pensioners.

Though anglers' paths undoubtedly existed, the first official trail to Pond of Safety was cut in 1881, at a time when Randolph was blossoming as an early center of hiking. In the 1880s a logging village and steam saw-mill sprang up on the shore. In the early 1900s the AMC *White Mountain Guide* devoted several pages to describing trails that converged on the pond. A noted landmark, visible from many summits, was an acre-large pile of sawdust deposited by the saw-mill near the pond. The pulpy heap was wryly dubbed "Mount Sawdust" on AMC maps.

Only a decade ago there were still three hiking routes open, but today there's only one—the Pond of Safety Trail, a series of logging roads/snow-mobile trails from the Forest Service's Bog Dam Road to the north. Four-

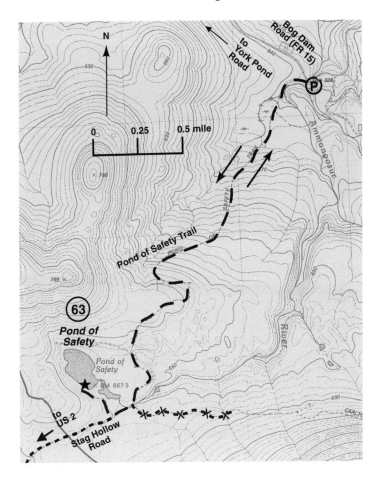

wheel-drive vehicles can motor almost all the way to the pond from the SW on the Stag Hollow Road from Jefferson.

## Access

From NH 16 in Berlin, follow NH 110 west for 7.1 miles and turn left (south) on the paved York Pond Road, the access to the Berlin Fish Hatchery. In 1.6 miles, just past the Kilkenny Guard Station, bear left onto the east link of the gravel Bog Dam Road (FR 15), which makes a 14.6-mile loop around the boggy lowlands of the Upper Ammonoosuc River. Drive south through the woods for 7.6 miles. The trailhead for Pond of Safety Trail, marked by a WMNF sign, is on the left as the road makes a sharp right turn at its southern tip. There's room for several cars to park.

## The Trail To Pond of Safety

The Pond of Safety Trail follows a succession of logging roads up and over a low ridge to the pond. It's a rather easy walk, attractive in its first two miles but less so as you reach the logged areas near the pond.

You start out on an old logging road (FR 236) running level through spruce woods. In 0.1 mile you cross a tributary of the Upper Ammonoosuc. At 0.5 mile, just before reaching a clear-cut area, turn right on another old road; a Forest Service arrow points the way. The old road winds gradually upward through open hardwoods, wet and soft in spots but providing generally pleasant walking. There are no blazes; occasional orange diamonds mark the route as a snowmobile trail.

At 1.7 miles you cross the National Forest boundary and come to an angled T-intersection, marked by snowmobile trail signs. Bear left (SE) here on a well-worn road and descend for 0.1 mile. The road swings right, rises slightly, then curves right again and levels, running SW across the crest of the low ridge.

Becoming more gravelly, the road descends into the logged country and passes a dilapidated shed on the right at 2.5 miles. At 2.9 miles you enter a large, weedy clearing and cross the small outlet brook from Pond of Safety—the infant Upper Ammonoosuc River.

At the far edge of the opening, 3 miles from your car, an unmarked spur road leaves on the right for Pond of Safety. Rough and churned out by four-wheel-drive vehicles, the road passes an open bog on the right and rises slightly to its end at a clearing in 0.2 mile. An unmarked footpath on the right drops down a bank into the woods and leads 200 feet to an opening on the south shore of the pond.

*Pond of Safety*

*Alternate Approach:* You can reach Pond of Safety by foot or four-wheel-drive vehicle up Stag Hollow Road from the SW. From the junction of US 2 and NH 115, drive west on US 2 for 0.4 mile. Turn right (north) on Ingerson Road and proceed 1 mile to a fork where the main road bears left. Continue straight on Stag Hollow Road, which has been drivable for most vehicles for at least 2.3 miles in recent years. (Avoid branching roads by bearing left at 1.4 miles and right at 2 miles.) It is steeper and rougher beyond, and many drivers may want to park off the road here and hoof it the rest of the way. Swing left at a T-intersection at 3 miles and you'll reach the spur road to the pond on the left at 3.6 miles.

## At Pond of Safety

The footpath from the spur road ends at a muddy, rock-studded opening at the water's edge. In contrast to its cutover environs, the spruce-girt pond has a lovely wilderness look to it. The peaceful vista across the water is northward to the hardwood slope of Pond Hill. It's easy to see why the soldiers would seek out this high-country refuge.

Wildlife is much in evidence at Pond of Safety. I've seen moose, deer, and beaver, watched a kingfisher plunge for a finny meal, heard a duet of barred owls hooting across the pond, and stopped in my tracks at the sight of a copious pile of bear scat. There are stocked brook trout in the waters and at times a reported overabundance of horned pout.

Pond of Safety was once famous for the gorgeous reflected vista of the Northern Presidentials seen from its north shore. Today this view is accessible only by boat or a semi-bushwhack along obscure paths behind the west shore, with views of Mounts Crescent and Randolph en route. Most visitors will be content to fashion a picnic at the opening on the south shore; there's one good rock seat available. Please note that Pond of Safety's shores are owned by James River Co. Public recreational use is welcome but camping and fires are not allowed.

*Bird's-Eye View:* The secluded north outlook on 3,230-foot Mount Crescent has a fine view over the Kilkenny region, with the Pond of Safety off to the west, shimmering beneath the wooded cone of Mount Pliny. The summit is attained via a 1.7-mile, 1,400-foot climb up the Mount Crescent Trail from Randolph Hill Road. The pond also sparkles in the northerly view from Mounts Adams and Madison.

*Winter:* Pond of Safety is lovely inside its necklace of snow-speckled evergreens. The view of the whitened Northern Peaks is magnificent. Don't try the northern approach; Bog Dam Road is not open. Southern approaches can be made via Stag Hollow Road (difficult parking) or snowmobile trails over the ridge from Lowe's Store on US 2 in Randolph ($1 parking, free trail advice). In either case you may be breathing snowmachine fumes much of the way—weekend traffic can be heavy on this major through route, though less so on the pond itself. Watch for soft ice near the outlet.

# CHAPTER 64

# CHERRY PONDS

◆

**Location:** Jefferson, north of Cherry Mountain
**Hiking Facts:** 3.2 or 1.8 miles round-trip, minimal vertical rise, easy
**Maps:** USGS 7½' X 15' Bethlehem and Lancaster

|  | Cherry Pond | Little Cherry Pond |
|---|---|---|
| **Area:** | 87 acres | 25 acres |
| **Elevation:** | 1,109 feet | 1,099 feet |
| **Avg./Max. Depth:** | 3/4 feet | n/a |

**Activities:** Hiking, birding, canoeing, fishing (horned pout, chain pickerel, yellow perch), picnicking

◆

Though the Cherry Ponds lie outside the National Forest, any compendium of White Mountain ponds would be remiss if it didn't include this National Natural Landmark. Abundant wildlife, unusual bog vegetation, and a unique waterfront view of the Presidentials combine to make this one of the most interesting pond excursions in the region.

These two shallow ponds lie amidst an extensive wetland plateau NW of the Presidentials and Cherry Mountain. Easily accessible Cherry Pond is an 87-acre oval encircled by a bog mat and fringes of cattail marsh. Nearby is Little Cherry Pond, a boggy 25-acre pool thick with aquatic vegetation.

As "Great Ponds," these water bodies are the property of the state, while 305 surrounding acres of heath bog and tamarack–black spruce forest are owned by the Audubon Society of New Hampshire. The area is managed by ASNH and the New Hampshire Fish and Game Department as the Pondicherry Wildlife Refuge. Dave Govatski of Jefferson, the ASNH volunteer refuge manager who is involved in many aspects of caring for this special area, notes that efforts are under way to protect significant additional acreage around and between the ponds.

The name Pondicherry was applied to the region as early as 1772, possibly by French Canadian explorers in reference to the capital of French India. The area soon became known for its wealth of game, especially

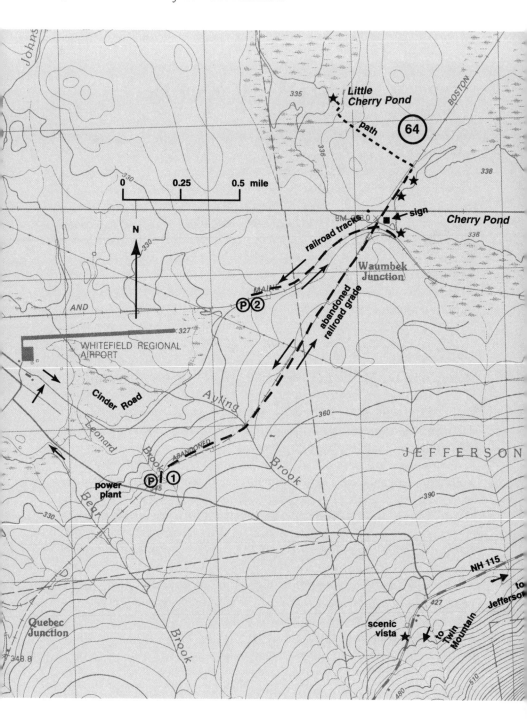

moose. In 1784 the historian Dr. Jeremy Belknap described Cherry Pond as a spot "where ye moose at this season go to bathe to get clear of ye flies, & are sometimes shot in ye water." Lucy Crawford wrote of an early settler named Stanley who mowed down five moose with his rifle in one Cherry Pond outing, "a good day's work."

Chances of spotting a moose at Pondicherry are good to excellent today. (The only shooting allowed in the refuge is of the photographic variety.) The boggy flat is also home to beaver, otter, mink, muskrat, coyote, deer, and black bear. The Cherry Ponds are birding hot spots, offering a rich blend of water, marsh, bog, and boreal species. Cherry is one of the few White Mountain ponds where you can hear the wild yodels of nesting loons. Unusual summer residents recorded at Pondicherry include ring-necked duck, green-winged teal, blue-winged teal, pied-billed grebe, American bittern, northern harrier, Virginia rail, common snipe, marsh wren, Canada jay, boreal chickadee, rusty blackbird, Wilson's warbler, and Lincoln's sparrow.

### Access
Take NH 115 north from its junction with US 3 in Twin Mountain. In 3.8 miles pull off at a scenic vista on the left for a sneak preview of Cherry Pond, reposing below on a broad plain with the Pliny, Pilot, and Sugarloaf ranges arrayed in the distance. At 0.4 mile beyond the overlook turn left onto a road marked by a small green airport sign. Changing from pavement to dirt, the road descends to the Mount Washington Regional Airport in 2.2 miles. Depending on your vehicle, current road conditions, and beaver flooding, you can choose from two access routes.

1) Down 1.4 miles from NH 115 is a rough dirt road on the right that follows an abandoned railroad bed to the present railroad tracks, a stone's throw from Cherry Pond. Park off the main road and walk the easy 1.5 miles to the pond. The side road, rough at the start, quickly curves left and picks up the straight and level railroad grade. It ends across from a sign welcoming you to Pondicherry Wildlife Refuge. There are plans to acquire and upgrade this refuge access route.

2) Continue down the main road, past a power plant. At a T-intersection, begin a series of quick jogs on airport roads: right, left, right onto Joe Astle Lane, and in 200 feet right again onto a cinder road between Hangar A on the left and two trailers on the right. This old Boston and Maine right-of-way, shown as a road on the USGS Bethlehem quadrangle, is narrow but has been drivable for conventional vehicles. However, it gets rougher every year, and small half-fallen trees may obstruct the way. If you can negotiate

passage, drive 1.2 miles to a pull-off on the left just before a power line. Walk 0.1 mile to the road's end and turn right (NE) along the railroad tracks.

Trains pass by once a day, and you should be alert to the possibility. Trains have rumbled around Cherry Pond since the 1870s, when Brown's Lumber Company of Whitefield thrust its narrow-gauge John's River Railroad—among the first of the White Mountain logging lines—into the virgin coniferous forest. After 0.7 mile of tie-hopping you reach a split in the tracks known as Waumbek Junction. The refuge sign is a few yards down the right-branching track. (Plans call for the section of track from here to Gorham to be converted to a recreation trail, providing a new access to Cherry Pond from the east.)

## At Cherry Pond

Whichever access you use, take a moment to read the refuge entrance sign. Note that the area is reserved for hiking, nature study, canoeing, and fishing. Hunting, trapping, camping, motorized vehicles, and fires are prohibited.

Canoeists may put in at the end of a path that leaves left about 100 yards down the SE-branching tracks. Paddlers should take care not to disturb nesting loons.

Hikers should proceed down the left-branching (north) tracks past a B&M mileage marker ("P102," 102 miles to Portland, ME; "B53," 53 miles to Beecher Falls, VT). You cross a bridge over the Johns River, which joins the ponds. Just beyond, an unsigned but obvious path departs sharply right and leads directly to the shore. Here paths left and right provide secluded shoreline walking along a small ridge formed by ice pressure from the pond. There are gorgeous views across to the Presidentials and ample opportunities for wildlife viewing. The right branch ends at the outlet, while the left fork leads to a National Natural Landmark plaque and then back to the railroad tracks.

Continuing north along the tracks you break into the open, looking across a cattail marsh and the pond to the Presidentials. I was once startled here by the sight of a black bear ambling along the tracks some distance ahead. For a heart-pounding minute I watched through binoculars as the bruin, unaware of my presence, poked among the trackside bushes before melting into the forest.

At the end of the open area look carefully for an unmarked footpath leading down through the grass on the right. The overgrown path runs 100 yards through shrubby woods to a grassy shoreline clearing supplied with

The view from this premier picnic spot is a Panavision sweep of water and mountain. To the left are the Pliny Range and the low waves of the Crescent Range. The rock-strewn Presidentials take center stage, rising nearly a vertical mile above you. Left to right are Madison, Adams, and Jefferson, Clay and Washington, and craggy Monroe peering over the Dartmouth Range. The right-hand view is dominated by shapely Cherry Mountain (3,573 feet), with the sharp spur of Owl's Head jutting on the left. Farther right still are the high and distant peaks of South and North Twin Mountains. Photo buffs can poke around for the best camera angles. The shot is a stunner in fall, when golden tamaracks shine against the foliage-draped, snow-capped Presidentials.

When not scanning the ridges, you can train your binoculars on the watery expanse for loons, ducks, great blue herons, and many another possibility. Red-winged blackbirds and swamp sparrows call noisily from the marsh, while a chorus of songbirds enlivens the bordering woods. Add the nice sun exposure on this SE-facing shore, and you'll find that an hour or two will pass quickly at the side of Cherry Pond.

Return the same way you came.

## Little Cherry Pond

The boggy shore of Little Cherry Pond can be reached via an unmarked, wet, and sometimes obscure 0.8-mile path from the Boston and Maine tracks. This excursion is suitable only for experienced pond-explorers. The path leads through wild, mossy fir woods, then circles right and out to the bog that surrounds the pond. Behind its forest shield Little Cherry remains the bog primeval, teeming with life. A visit may well reward the adventurous birder and naturalist, but please tread lightly.

*Bird's-Eye View:* You can gaze down at Cherry Ponds from the sharp summit of Owl's Head (3,258 feet). The 1.9-mile, 2,000-foot climb from NH 115 via Owl's Head Trail is very steep in its upper section. The tree-framed vista of the ponds is found at the highest point rather than the open ledges to the south.

*Winter:* Best access is the old railroad bed from the road between NH 115 and the airport; roadside parking is available near the entrance to the power plant. The views from the big pond extend from the Pilot Range through the Presidentials to Franconia Ridge. Little Cherry, more accessible in winter, has a wilder and more intimate feel in its bog-forest setting. When exploring the Pondicherry area in winter take care not to trample delicate bog vegetation, and watch for soft ice in poorly-frozen boggy spots.

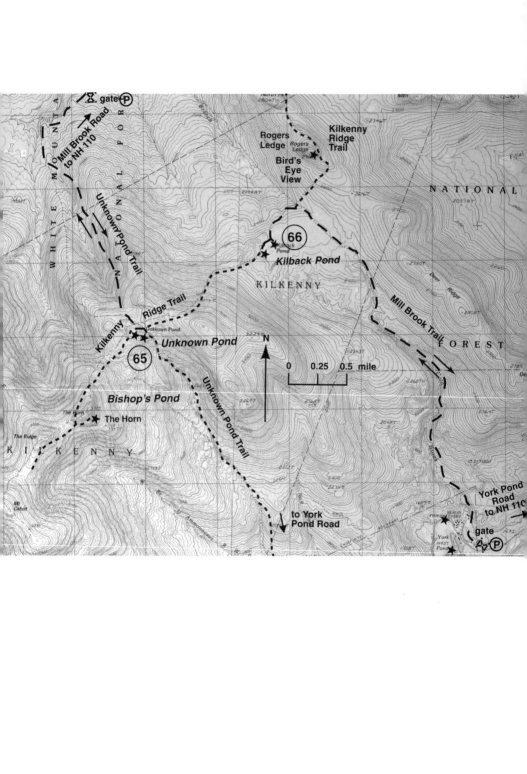

**Mill Brook Road to NH 110** gate ⚒ Ⓟ

**WHITE MOUNTA** NATIONAL FOR

Unknown Pond Trail

Kilkenny Ridge Trail

Rogers Ledge

Bird's Eye View

**66**
Kilback Pond

KILKENNY

Mill Brook Trail

NATIONAL

FOREST

Unknown Pond

**65**

Bishop's Pond

The Horn

The Bulge

KILKENNY

Unknown Pond Trail

N

0    0.25    0.5 mile

to York Pond Road

York Pond Road to NH 110

gate Ⓟ

York Pond

# CHAPTER 65

# UNKNOWN POND

◆

**Location:** Pilot Range, NE of The Horn
**Hiking Facts:** 6.2 miles round-trip, 1,400-foot vertical rise, moderate
**Map:** USGS 7½' Stark
**Area:** 5 acres   **Elevation:** 3,170 feet
**Avg./Max. Depth:** 7/13 feet
**Activities:** Hiking, backcountry camping, picnicking

◆

This remote, balsam-rimmed tarn rests on a high plateau overlooked by the ledge-capped Horn, the Kilkenny region's finest peak. True to its name, Unknown Pond is a northwoods mystery to many White Mountain hikers. It did not find its way into the AMC *Guide* until 1940, shortly after the Unknown Pond Trail was opened. Today there's a four-way trail junction and backcountry campsite by its shore, but seldom will you encounter more than a handful of fellow hikers.

Backpackers can visit the pond as part of a multi-day traverse of the Kilkenny Ridge Trail. For a day hike it's most easily reached via a moderate trek up the Unknown Pond Trail. Much of the climb is through a beautiful white birch forest. The trip can be extended to take in the wild panorama from the summit of the Horn.

## Access

The pond is set midway along the six-mile Unknown Pond Trail, permitting an approach from Mill Brook Road (FR 11) on the NW or York Pond Road (FR 13) on the SE. The latter has the disadvantage of a gate near the Berlin Fish Hatchery, which is locked from 4:00 P.M. to 8:00 A.M. Early starters and late finishers face an extra 2 miles of road walking on each end of the hike from that direction.

To reach the Mill Brook Road trailhead, drive east on NH 110 from US 3 in Groveton. In 6.7 miles you pass through the tiny village of Stark, shadowed by the dark precipice of Devil's Slide. About 0.4 mile east of

Stark Covered Bridge a hiker symbol marks the gravel Mill Brook Road on the right. Turn right and drive 3.6 miles south to a steel gate. Park here in a pull-off on the left, regardless of whether the gate is closed.

## The Trail To Unknown Pond

The hike begins with a 0.8 mile leg on the gravel road. You climb easily, then descend towards Mill Brook. Just before the road bridges the stream, a sign on the left marks the start of Unknown Pond Trail. Turn left here and enter the Kilkenny woods. The path, marked with blotches of yellow paint, parallels a branch brook at easy grades through a deep hardwood forest, rich in yellow birch and sugar maple. The walking is pleasant, save for an occasional patch of "Kilkenny muck."

About 1 mile from the road you pass a post marking the Stark/Kilkenny boundary line. White birches mix in with the other hardwoods, hinting at the forest beauty above. The grade steepens as you pass a birch-shaded swale, marking the beginning of a relentless 1-mile climb up the side of a ridge. As compensation for your toil, the trail takes you through an expansive stand of pure white birch, nature's eye-pleasing balm for the scourge of forest fire. Look right for leaf-screened glimpses of the Pilot Range, a chain of trailless wooded summits.

The pitch eases as the narrow footway approaches a height-of-land. You pass through a small, wet opening and cross a tiny brook. Up here, at an elevation over 3,000 feet, the woods take on the look typical of the Kilkenny ridges: a magical mix of heart-leaved birch (its bark showing a pinkish tint) and balsam fir, brimming with feathery ferns. In another 0.2 mile you crest the ridge and dip slightly to a junction with Kilkenny Ridge Trail near the NE corner of Unknown Pond, 2.2 miles from Mill Brook Road.

*Alternate Approaches:* Take Unknown Pond Trail from York Pond Road; 6.6 miles round-trip, 1,600-foot vertical rise. (As noted above, you may have to add 2 miles each way on York Pond Road from the gate at the fish hatchery.) This is a moderate ascent up the valley of Unknown Pond Brook, with fine northern hardwood and white birch forests. A grand tour of the Kilkenny—including both Kilback and Unknown Ponds—can also be made from this side along the Mill Brook, Kilkenny Ridge, and Unknown Pond Trails, and York Pond Road. Throw in a side trip to the great views atop Rogers Ledge, and you have a very rewarding 12.6-mile loop with 2,300 feet of climbing.

*Unknown Pond and The Horn*

## At Unknown Pond

For a picturesque view of the pond, follow the southbound Kilkenny Ridge Trail 25 feet right (SW) from the junction with Unknown Pond Trail. Bear left at a fork, then quickly right on a second path that angles into the woods, hooks left to a campsite, and dips through firs and bog shrubs to an opening on the north shore. This vantage point opens a memorable water-and-mountain view. The conifer-girt pond is a picture of serenity. Across the water rises the Horn, a shapely pyramid robed in birch and crowned with ledges—the quintessential wilderness peak. In late September it's awash in gold. This is a "stand-up" view; there are no good seats along this narrow path.

Retrace your steps to the junction of the Unknown Pond and Kilkenny Ridge Trails and turn right. The two trails coincide, running SE behind the shore. In 100 yards you pass a side path right that drops 50 feet to another watery vista toward the Horn. In a few more steps the northbound Kilkenny Ridge Trail splits left to climb the low ridge east of the pond. To the left is the unobtrusive Forest Service backcountry campsite. (The 20-mile Kilkenny Ridge Trail, opened in the 1980s, was designed to offer a deep-woods backpacking experience away from the crowds.)

Continue 100 feet SE on Unknown Pond Trail to a path that leads 40 feet right to a clearing and shoreline opening. Here a hiker or two can sit in the afternoon sun and gaze across the placid water, with the Horn glimpsed through a veil of tall conifers to the left. In early summer you'll be serenaded by a resonant chorus of white-throated sparrows, a fitting overture for this tarn cradled high in the Kilkenny wilds. One October day my friend Creston and I were surprised to see a flock of twenty Canada geese resting on the pond.

The other shores of Unknown Pond are inaccessible, and the pond is closed to fishing (it's the water source for the Berlin Fish Hatchery), so this is the place to linger for lunch. When you're ready, return to your car by the same route.

Gung-ho trampers can take the southbound Kilkenny Ridge Trail and a side trail up to the rocky crest of the Horn (3,905 feet) for wide views of the Kilkenny and many distant ranges. This ramble through the ferns and birches will add 4 miles round-trip and 800 feet of climbing.

*Winter:* The Kilkenny, with its open forests of birch and fir, is a snowshoer's delight. The Mill Brook Road is not plowed, but the road to the fish hatchery is up to the gate. Trail-breaking and sidehills may be difficult on the south leg of seldom-used Unknown Pond Trail. Out on the pond there are views of a nameless and trailless set of cliffs to the NE; their topmost ledge provides a spectacular view of the pond, the Horn, and distant ranges. For the experienced winter hiker, the trek to Unknown Pond is an appealing adventure in a setting of supreme wintry isolation.

# CHAPTER 66

# KILBACK POND

◆

**Location:** The Kilkenny, south of Rogers Ledge
**Hiking Facts:** 9.2 miles round-trip, 1,000-foot vertical rise, more difficult; add
1.2 miles, 450 vertical feet for Rogers Ledge
**Map:** USGS 7½' West Milan (Page 306)
**Area:** 1.5 acres **Elevation:** 2,490 feet
**Activities:** Hiking

◆

Along the northern leg of the Kilkenny Ridge Trail is a sheer face of pink granite known as Rogers Ledge (2,965 feet). From this high rock mantel you see the Kilkenny backcountry sprawling southward toward the sawtooth skyline of the Presidentials. This wild scene befits the ledge's honoree, Major Robert Rogers, whose brawling Rangers made a name for themselves during the French and Indian War.

The tableland at your feet is an ocean of birch that swells gently to 3,500-foot Unknown Pond Peak. At the base of that ridge, amidst a dark splash of conifers, look for a glimmer of water. You've stolen a glance at Kilback Pond, a tiny spruce-rimmed jewel of the North Country. To make its acquaintance you must devote a full day to walking through the Kilkenny woods. But it's well worthwhile if you have a taste for wild country, especially if a visit to Kilback is combined with the short side trip to Rogers Ledge.

## Access

Kilback Pond is located beside the Kilkenny Ridge Trail, 1.3 miles south of the ledge. The best approach is the Mill Brook Trail from the Berlin Fish Hatchery on York Pond Road, which leaves the south side of NH 110 7.1 miles west of NH 16 in Berlin. At 4.8 miles park in front of a gate (locked from 4:00 P.M. to 8:00 A.M.) and proceed up the road on foot. In 0.1 mile turn right on a side road (sign) and follow it to the left of a hatchery building. The road dead-ends at a sign for Mill Brook Trail; turn sharp right and walk

100 feet on an overgrown road, then bear left on a clear old logging road leading NW into the woods.

## The Trail To Kilback Pond

The Mill Brook Trail leads at easy grades through pleasant hardwoods up the valley of Cold Brook. At 1.7 miles you pass a post marking the Berlin/Milan town line. In another 0.5 mile, the trail swings right and climbs away from the brook into conifers and white birch. At 2.7 miles you cross the Milan/Kilkenny boundary, and at 3.1 miles the trail levels on a high plateau. The next 0.5 mile is an exhilarating stroll through a white birch forest carpeted with ferns and hobblebush. Beyond, you descend gently through firs to the junction with Kilkenny Ridge Trail at 3.8 miles (4.0 miles from your car). Turn left (SW) here. A rolling 0.6 mile walk through this upland of birches, firs, and bogs delivers you to the north shore of Kilback Pond.

The pond can also be reached from South Pond via Kilkenny Ridge Trail (10.6 miles round-trip, a 2,300-foot vertical rise), which entails climbing Rogers Ledge in both directions.

## At Kilback Pond

Kilback Pond is a northwoods beauty, encircled by a bushy bog and an outer ring of dagger-tipped conifers. The bog-bridged trail offers several views, the first looking over the shrub mat and dark water to birch-cloaked Unknown Pond Peak rising 1,000 feet above the tableland. (The Kilkenny Ridge Trail climbs over a col on this ridge en route to Unknown Pond.) Beyond a small knoll you cross the pond's small outlet, sometimes dammed by beavers. Water level permitting, you can find modest sitting rocks on either side of the outlet—nice spots to soak up the sun and savor the remoteness.

To enjoy those grand views from Rogers Ledge, return to the junction with Mill Brook Trail and continue straight (north) on Kilkenny Ridge Trail past a designated backcountry campsite. A 0.6-mile, 450-foot climb will hoist you to the sun-washed granite shelf and its *bird's-eye* glimpse of Kilback Pond. The sweep of mountains includes the Mahoosuc, Carter, Crescent, Presidential, and Pilot Ranges.

Upon your return to the fish hatchery area, a 0.2-mile walk west on York Pond Road will lead you to *York Pond* (21 acres, elevation 1,493 feet, avg./max. depth 9/17 feet). The road—once a branch of the Upper Ammonoosuc logging railroad—cuts a tight curve around the north and west shores of the pond. A small picnic area and boat launch, originally developed by the Civilian Conservation Corps in the 1930s, are found by

*Kilback Pond*

the pond's north end. Mount Weeks and the tops of Mounts Adams and Madison can be seen across the hardwood-fringed water. To protect the hatchery, fishing is prohibited at York Pond. Anglers can take pleasure in a tour of the hatchery (open 8:00 A.M.—4:00 P.M. daily), where 140,000 pounds of trout and salmon may be produced in a typical year.

*Winter:* Kilback Pond is a pleasant all-day snowshoe or ski outing from the fish hatchery. York Pond Road is plowed and you'll find room to park by the gate. The northwoods isolation of the pond is accentuated in winter, with views of Unknown Pond Peak and Rogers Ledge.

# CHAPTER 67

# SOUTH POND (PERCY POND)

◆

**Location:** Stark, south of NH 110
**Hiking Facts:** Roadside; optional short hikes
**Map:** USGS 7½' West Milan (Page 306)
**Area:** 124 acres   **Elevation:** 1,115 feet
**Avg./Max. Depth:** 40/105 feet
**Activities:** Swimming, picnicking, canoeing, hiking, fishing (lake trout, rainbow trout, horned pout, chain pickerel, yellow perch)

◆

Sprawling between wooded hills at the northern fringe of the National Forest is one of the finest aquatic playgrounds in the White Mountains. The South Pond Recreation Area has something for everyone: swimming off a sand beach, picnicking, deep-water fishing, boating, and a mellow lakeside trail through the forest, accessible for wheelchairs.

Large, deep, and mostly undeveloped, South Pond is the centerpiece of a crescent of ponds clasped between Mill Mountain (2,517 feet) on the west and Location Hill (1,990 feet) on the east. Adjacent ponds include North Pond (private and heavily developed) above and trailless Rocky Pond below.

### Access
The 1.8 mile access road to South Pond leads south from NH 110, 10 miles east of US 3 in Groveton and 14.4 miles west of NH 16 in Berlin. The junction is well marked with WMNF signs. The paved road winds upward, changes to gravel, and reaches a fork at 0.7 mile. Bear right here back onto asphalt; the left branch is a private road.

Just beyond is a steel gate that may be open or closed, depending on the season. South Pond is a day-use facility and schedules may vary with the vagaries of the Forest Service budget. Usually it's open from 9:00 A.M. to 8:00 P.M. July Fourth through Labor Day, with shorter hours in spring and fall. Check with the Androscoggin Ranger District (603-466-2713) for cur-

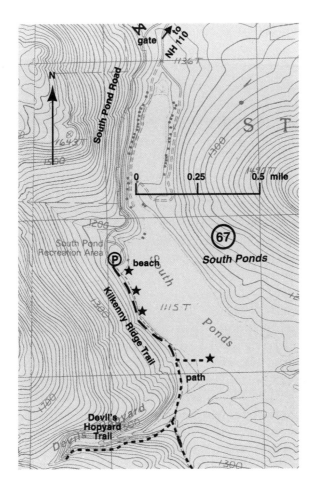

rent information. If the gate is shut, you'll have to pull into a parking slot on the left and walk the last 1.1 mile to the pond—uphill at the start, downhill at the end. Drive on if the gate is open but be prepared to pay an entrance fee at the gate house by the parking area.

## At South Pond

Beside the roomy parking lot is a grassy, picnic ground caressed by cool breezes off the water. You can choose from nearly two dozen picnic tables with views of the expansive pond. The sand beach and roped-off swimming area are just a few yards away. The water is shallow near shore, ideal for a family swim. The area is equipped with rest rooms, water fountains, and other rustic amenities.

South Pond is one of the few water bodies in the National Forest upon which motorboats are allowed. This is a drawback if you're looking for true peace and quiet. The public boat launch is not accessible by vehicle, so all boats must be carried a short distance to the water. Anglers should find it worth the trouble, as the fishing is varied and excellent, with a rare (in the White Mountains) chance to hook a lake trout. Summer boaters should take pains not to disturb loon nests.

South Pond also serves as the northern terminus of the 20-mile Kilkenny Ridge Trail. If you want to escape the bustle near the parking lot, seek out the brown trail sign and follow the yellow-blazed path southward beside the pond. The first 300 yards has been graded and graveled for wheelchair accessibility, with several pull-outs for fishing and enjoying views across the water. Overhead is a cool canopy of hemlock and yellow birch.

About 0.3 mile from the picnic ground you pass a spring that pours into the pond from a hose. Soon the trail starts to pull away from the pond. At 0.5 mile a side path leaves sharp left, leading 0.2 mile through the woods to a view of massive Long Mountain (3,661 feet) from the south shore.

## Devil's Hopyard

A side trail to a fascinating diversion called the Devil's Hopyard lies 0.2 mile ahead on the Kilkenny Ridge Trail. Turn right (west) at a sign for Devil's Hopyard Trail and follow the path's meander into this remarkable gorge, a mini Mahoosuc Notch. The Hopyard is strewn with tumbled, mossy boulders and walled in by overhangs of fractured ledge. The brook that drains the moist ravine gurgles underground for much of its course. Early visitors fancied a resemblance between this gloomy defile and a vine-draped haunt of the devil, hence the name.

Use caution on the slick, mossy rocks along this rather rough trail. The footway ends under a sheer cliff in a rugged natural amphitheater, 1.3 miles from the South Pond parking lot with 200 feet of climbing. "This wild and picturesque gorge should be visited by more trampers," opined earlier editions of the AMC *White Mountain Guide*. A walk into Devil's Hopyard is a refreshing way to top off a visit to South Pond.

*Winter:* This is an easy half-day exploration on snowshoes or skis. South Pond Road is plowed to the fork at 0.7 mile, where there may be room for two cars to park, or you can park at the NH 110 junction. The snowy expanse of South Pond, popular with snowmobilers, offers views of Mill Mountain, Long Mountain, the back side of Rogers Ledge, and a glimpse of distant Goose Eye Mountain. Trip options include an excursion into Devil's Hopyard, an easy bushwhack traverse of the three smaller ponds to the east, or an afternoon of ice fishing.

# CHAPTER 68

# LITTLE BOG AND WHITCOMB PONDS

◆

**Location:** Nash Stream Forest, north of NH 110
**Hiking Facts:** Little Bog Pond, roadside; Whitcomb Pond, 1.4 miles round-trip,
230-foot vertical rise, easy
**Map:** USGS 7½' Percy Peaks

|  | Little Bog Pond | Whitcomb Pond |
|---|---|---|
| **Area:** | 37 acres | 20 acres |
| **Elevation:** | 2,042 feet | 2,273 feet |
| **Avg./Max. Depth:** | 10 feet (Max.) | 6/7 feet |

**Activities:** Hiking, canoeing (Little Bog), fishing (brook trout in both ponds),
picnicking

◆

The Nash Stream Forest—a sharply cut valley ringed by wooded, mostly trailless mountains—is the true North Country, akin to the vast timberlands of northern Maine in look and mood. For many decades no one paid much attention to it except for the timber companies who owned the land, the loggers who worked the woods, and the locals who came here to hunt and fish.

But in May 1988 there was a rude awakening for this hideaway north of the notches. Diamond International, longtime owner of the Nash Stream Valley, abruptly sold a 67,000 acre tract to Rancourt Associates, a down-state development firm. The prospect of subdivision, condos, and restricted access galvanized conservation groups, government agencies, local sportsmen, and other concerned parties.

Complex negotiations with Rancourt ensued, involving the State of New Hampshire, the Federal government, the Nature Conservancy, and the Society for the Protection of New Hampshire Forests. Action was swift and decisive. By October 1988 the title to the core parcel of 45,000 acres was in the state's hands. The price tag was a cool $12.75 million.

The Nash Stream crisis catalyzed a broader effort to assure a stable future for the Northern Forest Lands—the millions of privately-owned acres that sprawl across the northern tier from New York to Maine. A multitude of interests—government, conservation, timber, recreation, landowner— have come together to tackle what has become one of the big environmental issues of the '90s.

Outside of the trails to the Percy Peaks and Sugarloaf Mountain, hikers have seldom set their boots on the duff of the Nash Stream woods. But New Hampshire's newest state forest does offer other enticing possibilities for the tramper. As Bruce and Doreen Bolnick relate in their *Waterfalls of the White Mountains*, the falls on Pond Brook are among the most scenic in the White Mountain region. And the ice-cold water that feeds those cascades flows down from a series of picturesque ponds in the high valley to the east, between Long and Whitcomb Mountains. Two of these, Little Bog and Whitcomb Ponds, afford a pleasant and easy walk with a real northwoods flavor. Rock-rimmed Whitcomb is an especially good spot for a picnic lunch. The ponds hike can be combined with an exploration of nearby Pond Brook Falls for an afternoon's sampler of Nash Stream woods and waters.

### Access

From US 3 in Groveton, drive 2.5 miles east on NH 110 and turn left (north) on Emerson Road. Bear right at 1.4 miles from NH 110, and at 2.1 miles veer left on the gravel Nash Stream Road as Emerson Road swings right. In 0.5 mile you'll come to a large wooden map beside the road, showing the road and trail layout of the forest. Your driving route to the ponds is shown on the map

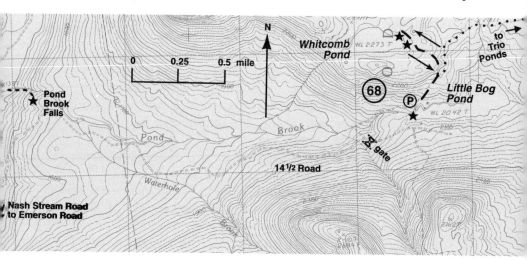

as "14½ Road," named after an old logging camp. (The sign also informs you that camping and fires are not allowed in the forest.) Drive on, but slowly, for Nash Stream Road is rough and washboarded in places.

At 4.9 miles from Emerson Road, turn right onto the 14½ Road, marked by a sign. This recently upgraded road is sound and has been passable for conventional vehicles. It is narrow, winding, steep, and rough in places. There's a left turn at 2.6 miles, and the drivable road ends at a parking area on the left, 3 miles from Nash Stream Road.

## Little Bog Pond

Park your car and walk 100 feet right to a wooden boat ramp and the bouldery outlet of Little Bog Pond, also known as 14½ Pond. There's a small private camp on either side of the outlet and a handful of others around the pond. (The camps' owners have long-term leases to retain use of their property. Please respect their rights and do not disturb the camps.) Still, this long, narrow, spruce-rimmed pond keeps its backwoods beauty. The best views are from sitting rocks on either end of a weedy earthen dam. Little Bog Pond was created many years ago to provide water storage for log drives down in the valley. The river drives have passed into history, but the pond remains, to the delight of the canoeist and trout enthusiast.

## Whitcomb Pond

The walking route to Whitcomb Pond follows a grassy, rocky road from the north edge of the parking area. This rough old roadway bears right and climbs steadily for 0.3 mile. At a junction marked only by a "Prevent Forest Fires" sign, turn left on a side road. (Ahead, the main road continues another 1.1 mile to the Trio Ponds, ending at a cluster of private camps. The fishing is excellent, but this is not recommended as a hiking excursion.) You climb for another 0.1 mile, then swing left (west) on an easy grade through a wild forest of spruce, fir, and birch, with one looping bypass to the right.

At 0.7 mile from your car the road forks. Follow the main branch to the left. (The right fork is a path that leads to the only private camp on Whitcomb Pond, tucked away in a cove on the north shore. Please respect the owners' privacy.) Bear left again through a screen of conifers to the NE corner of the pond, which bursts open in dramatic fashion. A small state forest sign gives the name.

Whitcomb is a northwoods gem, hemmed in by rockbound shores and a wild-looking forest of spruce and fir. The shallow east edge of the pond is a field of low-lying granite boulders. Hop out from the trail's end and choose a sitting rock that suits you. My favorite is a low shelf about 150 feet out. It has good sun exposure and a wide view westward over the pond, backed by a ragged spur of Whitcomb Mountain. There's another good perch at the SE corner. This is a peaceful place for a picnic, where your only company may be a spotted sandpiper bobbing and weaving among the rocks. When you're ready to depart, you should be back to your car within 20 minutes.

If you're exploring the Nash Stream area, you might consider a side trip by car to see beautiful *Christine Lake* (170 acres, elevation 1,203 feet, avg./ max. depth 27.5/60 feet) near the village of Percy. From NH 110 at Stark village, drive north through the covered bridge and bear right in 0.1 mile. In 2.2 miles an unmarked paved road splits left (north) and steeply uphill. Bear left in 0.3 mile (the right fork is private) to a public parking area at the east end of this long sheet of water. A thousand acres around the lake have been protected with conservation easements negotiated by the Society for the Protection of NH Forests. There's a small sand beach, a marvelous grove of white cedars to the left, and a long view down the lake with South Percy Peak (3,234 feet) looming on the right. With binoculars you can spot some lavish summer homes at the far end of the lake. The lake offers canoeing, swimming, and fishing for stocked brown trout. Fine sitting rocks with views of both Percy Peaks (North Percy Peak 3,410 feet) can be found to the left by rock-hopping the shore or following a snowmobile trail through the cedars.

*Whitcomb Pond*

# A NOTE ON BUSHWHACKING

◆

*...A young forest looks poetic in the distance...But attempt to go through one, where no path has been bushed out, and your admiration will be cut down, as Carlyle would say, "some stages"...the poetry of wild forest-clambering turns out pretty serious prose. It is about like fighting a phalanx of porcupines.*
—Thomas Starr King
*The White Hills,* 1859

Bushwhacking, or hiking off-trail through the mountain woods, can be exhilarating, miserable, or anything in between. It's definitely not for everyone, but those few hikers who do venture off the dashed lines on the map will discover a world of adventure and freedom. Bushwhacking enthusiasts can choose from a sparkling constellation of White Mountain ponds off the beaten path, and some unique bird's-eye viewpoints, too. Off-trail trips can range from fairly easy jaunts through open woods to day-long epics beset with blow-down, blackflies, and vast thickets of close-growing conifers.

Bushwhacking requires, among other skills, proficiency with map and compass. It is not a recommended pastime for novice hikers. The only sensible way to learn is to accompany veteran bushwhackers on relatively easy treks. The normal safety precautions are doubly important when moving off-trail, as mishaps can have serious consequences.

In addition to taking care of yourself, you must take extra pains to minimize your impact on the mountain environment when bushwhacking, both en route to your destination and at the pond or viewpoint itself. The roomy woods of the White Mountains can absorb a small number of bushwhackers each year and show little or no trace of their passing—*if* they are aware of, and practice, low-impact techniques. (See *Soft Paths,* by Bruce Hampton and David Cole, and *Backwoods Ethics,* by Laura and

Guy Waterman.) A few pointers:

- Limit the size of your group to four to six persons.
- Spread out and walk abreast rather than single file.
- Place your steps for the lowest impact, choosing rocks or other durable surfaces over delicate vegetation wherever possible, and avoiding steep erodible slopes.
- Use special care at the shore of an off-trail pond. Avoid trampling plants along the water's edge.
- Don't camp beside a bushwhack pond; day hikers leave far less evidence of their visit.
- Don't mark off-trail routes.
- Never walk off-trail above tree line unless you're on bare rock.
- Though it requires more equipment, effort, and technique, winter bushwhacking has less impact and can be supremely rewarding. You can easily pass over terrain that's impossible in summer, and views are more easily obtained.

The *Gazetteer* includes capsules of the named bushwhack ponds in the White Mountains. No route descriptions are included. Charting your own course is one of the great rewards of bushwhacking. Blow-by-blow narrations could encourage inexperienced trampers to get in over their heads (sometimes literally!) and might foster the development of "herd paths."

By studying the USGS topo maps or scanning summit views, you may find many more ponds without names—a sliver of water amidst the birches of Zealand Notch, a pair of somber ponds high on the west ridge of Mount Field, a jewel of a beaver pond glimpsed in the Sawyer River valley from South Hancock, another in the northern shadow of Mount Osceola. Or you might seek out a secluded ledge offering a unique bird's-eye view of a more familiar lakelet. Such trailless vantage points are found near Peaked Hill Pond, Beaver Pond, Ethan Pond, Province Pond, Round Pond, Unknown Pond, and other ponds described in this book. Your bushwhack options are limited only by your time and imagination.

*Flat Mountain Pond*

# APPENDIX

◆

# KEY TO POND AND LAKE EXPLORATIONS

◆

**B** - Birding hot spot
**C** - Campground/site, shelter,
       or AMC hut
**F** - Fishing

**H** - Hiking
**L** - Boat launch
**P** - Shoreside picnic spot
**S** - Swimming

## ROADSIDE PONDS

3) Mirror Lake  F-L-P-S
5) Oliverian Pond  F-L-P
6) Long Pond  F-L-P
9) Beaver Pond  F-H-L-P
15) Profile Lake  F-H-L-P
16) Echo Lake (Franconia)  F-H-L-P-S
17) Russell Pond  C-F-H-L-P-S
21) Upper Hall Pond  F-L
23) Kiah Pond  F-L-P
26) Chocorua Lake  F-L-P-S
27) White Lake  B-C-F-H-L-P-S

28) Echo Lake (North Conway)
    F-H-P-S
29) Red Eagle Pond  F-P
40) Lily Pond  F
41) Saco Lake  F-H-L-P
53) Basin Pond  C-F-H-L-P
56) Virginia Lake  F-H-L-P-S
57) Broken Bridge Pond  F
57) Crocker Pond  C-F-H-L-P
67) South Pond  F-H-L-P-S
68) Little Bog Pond  F-L-P

## EASY POND HIKES

2) Peaked Hill Pond  B-F-H-P
7) Elbow Pond North  B-F-H-P
11) Mud Pond (Easton)  F-H-P
20) Atwood Pond  F-H-P
26) Heron Pond  H-P
30) Falls Pond  F-H-P
38) Sawyer Ponds  C-F-H-P-S
39) Church Pond  B-F-H-P
42) Ammonoosuc Lake  F-H-P
48) Province Pond  C-F-H-P

49) Mountain Pond  C-F-H-P-S
50) Lost Pond  H-P
54) Shell Pond  B-F-H-P
55) Horseshoe Pond  F-H-P-S
57) Round Pond  F-H-P
58) Mascot Pond  H-P
62) Durand Lake  F-H-P
64) Cherry Pond  B-F-H-P
68) Whitcomb Pond  F-H-P

## MODERATE POND HIKES

1) Three Ponds  C-F-H-P
4) Wachipauka Pond  F-H-P-S
7) Elbow Pond South  B-F-H-P
8) Tunnel Brook Ponds  B-F-H-P
13) Lonesome Lake  C-F-H-P-S
18) Little East and East Ponds  F-H-P-S
19) Greeley Ponds  F-H-P-S
22) Lower and Middle Hall Ponds  F-H-P

31) Black Pond  F-H-P
35) Ethan Pond  C-F-H-P
44) Hermit Lake  C-H-P
47) Shingle Pond  H
60) Gentian and Moss Ponds  C-H-P
63) Pond of Safety  F-H-P
65) Unknown Pond  C-H-P

## MORE DIFFICULT POND HIKES

10) Gordon Pond  F-H-P
12) Harrington Pond  H
14) Kinsman Pond  C-F-H-P
24) Guinea and Black Mountain Ponds  B-F-H-P-S
25) Flat Mountain Pond  C-F-H-P
32) Eagle Lake  C-H-P
33) Garfield Pond  H-P
34) Zealand and Zeacliff Ponds  B-C-F-H-P
36) Shoal Pond  F-H

37) Nancy and Norcross Ponds  B-H-P
43) Lakes of the Clouds  C-H-P
45) Star Lake  C-H-P
46) Spaulding Lake  H-P
51) Carter Ponds  C-F-H-P-S
52) No-Ketchum Pond  C-F-H
59) Dream Lake and Page Pond  H-P
61) Speck Pond  C-F-H-P-S
66) Kilback Pond  H

# WHITE MOUNTAIN PONDS AND LAKES AT A GLANCE

◆

## BEST FAMILY HIKES

Three Ponds
Peaked Hill Pond
Tunnel Brook Ponds
Lonesome Lake
Profile Lake
Echo Lake (Franconia)
East Pond
Greeley Ponds
Heron Pond
White Lake
Echo Lake (North Conway)

Falls Pond
Black Pond
Sawyer Pond
Saco Lake
Ammonoosuc Lake
Province Pond
Mountain Pond
Lost Pond
Crocker/Round Ponds
Durand Lake
South Pond

## AWAY FROM THE CROWDS

Peaked Hill Pond
Wachipauka Pond
Elbow Pond South
Tunnel Brook Ponds
Gordon Pond
Mud Pond (Easton)
Harrington Pond
Atwood Pond
Lower/Middle Hall Ponds
Heron Pond
Shoal Pond
Shingle Pond

Province Pond
No-Ketchum Pond
Shell Pond
Virginia Lake
Mascot Pond
Dream Lake/Page Pond
Moss Pond
Pond of Safety
Cherry Ponds
Unknown Pond
Kilback Pond
Whitcomb Pond
Any bushwhack pond

# HIGHEST ELEVATION

| | |
|---|---|
| Storm Lake | 5,200 feet |
| Lakes of the Clouds | 5,050/5,025 feet |
| Star Lake | 4,896 feet |
| Red Pond | 4,400 feet |
| Spaulding Lake | 4,228 feet |
| Eagle Lake | 4,180 feet |
| Garfield Pond | 3,860 feet |
| Hermit Lake | 3,857 feet |
| Kinsman Pond | 3,740 feet |
| Zeacliff Pond | 3,700 feet |
| Ponds near West Peak, Mount Field | 3,460 feet |
| Pond between Mount Nancy and Mount Bemis | 3,460 feet |
| Speck Pond | 3,430 feet |
| Long Mountain Pond | 3,410 feet |
| Harrington Pond | 3,380 feet |
| Bear Pond | 3,340 feet |
| Carter Ponds | 3,290/3,280 feet |
| Carrigain Pond | 3,180 feet |
| Unknown Pond | 3,170 feet |
| Norcross Pond | 3,120 feet |
| Bishop's Pond | 3,110 feet |
| Nancy Pond | 3,100 feet |
| Duck Pond | 3,060 feet |

# LARGEST

| | | | |
|---|---|---|---|
| Stinson Lake | 346 acres | Cherry Pond | 87 acres |
| Chocorua Lake | 222 acres | Lower Trio Pond | 65 acres |
| Forest Lake | 192 acres | Elbow Pond | 56 acres |
| Christine Lake | 170 acres | Ellsworth Pond | 56 acres |
| Upper Kimball Pond | 136 acres | Shell Pond | 50 acres |
| Jericho Lake | 135 acres | Sawyer Pond | 47 acres |
| Horseshoe Pond | 132 acres | Bog Pond | 43 acres |
| Virginia Lake | 128 acres | Russell Pond | 39 acres |
| Long Pond | 124 acres | Mirror Lake | 37 acres |
| Mountain Pond | 124 acres | Hildreth Pond | 36 acres |
| South Pond | 124 acres | Flat Mountain Pond | 30 acres |
| White Lake | 123 acres | Campton Pond | 30 acres |

# DEEPEST

| | | | |
|---|---|---|---|
| South Pond | 105 feet | Elbow Pond | 32 feet |
| Sawyer Pond | 100 feet | Black Mountain Pond | 32 feet |
| Russell Pond | 78 feet | Ellsworth Pond | 32 feet |
| Stinson Lake | 75 feet | Wachipauka Pond | 30 feet |
| Loon Pond | 65 feet | Mirror Lake | 30 feet |
| Christine Lake | 60 feet | Round Pond | 29 feet |
| Middle Hall Pond | 56 feet | Cone Mountain Pond | 28 feet |
| White Lake | 45 feet | Little Sawyer Pond | 28 feet |
| Horseshoe Pond | 40 feet | Chocorua Lake | 28 feet |
| Upper Hall Pond | 39 feet | Carrigain Pond | 28 feet |
| Echo Lake (Franconia) | 39 feet | Virginia Lake | 28 feet |
| Speck Pond | 36 feet | East Pond | 27 feet |
| Black Pond | 34 feet | Upper Greeley Pond | 27 feet |

# BEST SITTING ROCKS

| | |
|---|---|
| Upper Three Ponds | Black Pond |
| Peaked Hill Pond | Zeacliff Pond |
| Beaver Pond | Ethan Pond |
| Gordon Pond | Sawyer Pond |
| Lonesome Lake | Church Pond |
| Kinsman Pond | Hermit Lake |
| Profile Lake | Star Lake |
| Russell Pond | Spaulding Lake |
| Atwood Pond | Lost Pond |
| Middle Hall Pond | Upper Carter Pond |
| Kiah Pond | Crocker Pond |
| Flat Mountain Pond | Page Pond |
| Falls Pond | Gentian Pond |
| Whitcomb Pond | |

# BEST SWIMMING

| | |
|---|---|
| Mirror Lake | Echo Lake (North Conway) |
| Lonesome Lake | Sawyer Pond |
| Echo Lake (Franconia) | Upper Carter Pond |
| Russell Pond | Horseshoe Pond |
| East Pond | Virginia Lake |
| Upper Greeley Pond | Forest Lake |
| Black Mountain Pond | South Pond |
| Chocorua Lake | Christine Lake |
| White Lake | Jericho Lake |

# BEST FISHING

Consult your local oracle.

# BEST SHORELINE VIEWS

Tunnel Brook Ponds (Tunnel Brook Notch)
Beaver Pond (Kinsman Notch)
Lonesome Lake (Franconia Ridge, Kinsmans)
Kinsman Pond (North Kinsman Mountain)
Profile Lake and Echo Lake/Franconia (Eagle Cliff)
Greeley Ponds (Mad River Notch)
Black Mountain Pond (Black Mountain)
Flat Mountain Pond (Mount Tripyramid, Mount Whiteface)
Chocorua Lake (Mount Chocorua)
Echo Lake/North Conway (White Horse Ledge)
Black Pond (Bond Range)
Ethan Pond (Mount Willey, Twin Range)
Shoal Pond (Mount Carrigain, Zealand Notch)
Norcross Pond (Twin Range)
Sawyer Pond (Mount Tremont, Owl's Cliff)
Lakes of the Clouds (Mount Washington, Mount Monroe)
Hermit Lake (Tuckerman Ravine)
Star Lake (Mount Adams, Mount Madison)
Spaulding Lake (Great Gulf)
Mountain Pond (Doubleheads, Baldfaces)
Lost Pond (Mount Washington)
Carter Ponds (Carter Notch)
Basin Pond (The Basin)
Shell Pond (Baldface Range)
Dream Lake (Mount Washington, Mount Adams)
Gentian Pond (lower Mahoosucs)
Cherry Pond (Presidential Range)
Unknown Pond (The Horn)

# BEST BIRD'S-EYE VIEWS

Wachipauka Pond from Webster Slide Mountain
Tunnel Brook Ponds from South Peak, Mount Moosilauke
Lonesome Lake from outlooks on Hi-Cannon Trail
Kinsman Pond from North Kinsman
Echo Lake (Franconia) from Artist's Bluff

Upper Greeley Pond from slide on Mount Osceola Trail
Black Mountain Pond from Black Mountain
Echo Lake (North Conway) from White Horse Ledge
Sawyer Ponds from Mount Tremont
Lakes of the Clouds from Mount Monroe
Star Lake from Mount Adams
Spaulding Lake from Gulfside Trail
Shingle Pond from Kearsarge North
Mountain Pond from North Doublehead
Carter Ponds from Pulpit Rock Outlook
Basin Pond from Basin Rim Trail
Shell Pond from Blueberry Mountain
Horseshoe Pond from Lord Hill
Mascot Pond from Leadmine Ledge
Speck Pond from Speck Pond Trail

# CAMPING FACILITIES

(numbers indicate capacity)

Middle Three Ponds (WMNF shelter/10)
Lonesome Lake (AMC hut/46)
Kinsman Pond (AMC shelter/12; tent platforms/25)
Russell Pond (WMNF campground/87 sites)
Black Mountain Pond (SLA shelter/8; slated for removal)
Flat Mountain Pond (WMNF shelter/8)
White Lake (NH State Parks campground/170 sites)
Eagle Lake (AMC hut/34)
Zealand Pond (AMC hut/36)
Ethan Pond (AMC shelter/8; tent platforms/20)
Sawyer Ponds (WMNF shelter/8; tent platforms/20)
Saco Lake (AMC hostel/40)
Lakes of the Clouds (AMC hut/90)
Hermit Lake (AMC shelters/86)
Star Lake (AMC hut/50)
Province Pond (WMNF shelter/5)
Mountain Pond (WMNF shelter/8)
Carter Ponds (AMC hut/40)
No-Ketchum Pond (WMNF shelter/6)
Basin Pond (WMNF campground/21 sites)
Crocker Pond (WMNF campground/7 sites)
Gentian Pond (AMC shelter/14; tent platforms/16)
Speck Pond (AMC shelter/10; tent platforms/20)
Unknown Pond (WMNF backcountry campsite)

# ACCESS FOR THE PHYSICALLY CHALLENGED

**Mirror Lake:** Gravel parking area beside south shore.

**Long Pond:** Gravel parking lot and picnic area on NE shore.

**Beaver Pond:** Small parking area at north end of pond.

**Profile Lake:** Paved path from designated parking area to NE shore and view of Old Man of the Mountain.

**Echo Lake (Franconia):** Short gravel ramp to small beach at SW corner of pond; longer downhill gravel ramp to beach at north end.

**Russell Pond:** Paved path from parking area to wheelchair-accessible fishing dock.

**Upper Hall Pond:** Small gravel parking area at NE corner of pond (rough road).

**Kiah Pond:** Gravel parking area at SE corner of pond (rough road).

**White Lake:** Gravel parking area close to beach on south shore.

**Chocorua Lake:** Gravel parking area and picnic grove at south end of lake.

**Echo Lake (North Conway):** Downhill gravel path from parking area to beach on east shore.

**Saco Lake:** Gravel parking area on SW shore of pond.

**Basin Pond:** Paved parking area, grass picnic area beside SW shore of pond. Paved path to wheelchair-accessible fishing dock.

**South Pond:** Paved parking area and grass picnic area close to beach. Wheelchair-accessible trail extends 300 yards along shore with fishing and viewing pull-offs.

# INDEX AND GAZETTEER OF WHITE MOUNTAIN PONDS AND LAKES

——————◆——————

NOTES:

- Ponds and lakes described in the text are indicated by chapter number.
- Other ponds listed are within the boundaries of the White Mountain National Forest (though not necessarily on National Forest land) or are on land just outside the Forest that is open to public use.

Elevation: 3,110 feet.

Comment: Jewel-like pond at base of the Horn, surrounded by beautiful birch-fir forest. Crystal-clear water and impressive close-up of the ledgy peak. Local name is reference to the Right Reverend Robert McConnell Hatch, who delighted in exploring Kilkenny region when not attending to duties as Suffragan Bishop of Episcopal Diocese of Connecticut. He wrote about adventures in *Appalachia*. Pond mentioned in 1970s AMC guides as key to ascent of the Horn, then a bushwhack peak.

**Black Pond**, Chapter 31.

**Black Mountain Pond**, Chapter 24.

**Black Spruce Ponds**, Chapter 27.

**Bog Pond (Lincoln)**

Location: East of Kinsman Ridge.

Access: Snowmobile trails/bushwhack

Map: USGS 7½' Lincoln.

Area: 43 acres.

Elevation: 2,317 feet.

Avg./Max. Depth: 3/4 feet

Comment: Sprawling centerpiece of swampy plateau between Mount Wolf and South Kinsman Mountain. Curving eastern pool and broad western lobe are linked by shallow channel. A scene of "utter desolation and loneliness," wrote Karl P. Harrington in 1926; still remote and wild despite power line that cuts across the channel. Once accessed via Georgiana Falls on WMNF Bog Pond Trail; path abandoned in 1950s. In 1970s Bog Pond area was considered as alternative corridor to Franconia Notch for I-93. Today snowmobile trails (wet in summer) lead to eastern pond from Hanson Farm Road in Lincoln, 12+ miles round-trip. Best views are from waterside ledges near east end of trailless western pond—darkly wooded Mount Wolf from north shore; South Kinsman, spreading for miles from stem to stern, from south shore. May harbor native brook trout. Good bird's-eye views of pond from Kinsman Ridge Trail. A delight to explore in winter; views of Franconia Ridge from frozen eastern pond.

**Bog Pond, Little**, Chapter 68.

**Breeding Pond**, Chapter 15.

**Broken Bridge Pond**, Chapter 57.

**Campton Pond**

Location: Campton.

Access: Roadside, NH 49 north of NH 175 junction.

Map: USGS 7½' Plymouth.

Area: 30 acres.

Elevation: 650 feet

Avg./Max. Depth: 2/10 feet

Comment: Artificial pond/marsh formed by dam in Mad River. Fishing for brook trout, horned pout, chain pickerel, yellow perch. USFS Campton Campground is just to north.

**Carrigain Pond**

Location: Between Mounts Carrigain and Hancock.

Access: Bushwhack.

Map: USGS 7½' Mount Carrigain.

Area: 4 acres.

Elevation: 3,180 feet.

Avg./Max. Depth: 14/28 feet.

Comment: Small and lovely pond secluded in a northern fold of the rough Carrigain-Hancock ridge, just NE of nubble called "the Captain." (The line that runs along this ridge on topographic maps is a town boundary and not a trail.) Source of Carrigain Branch. Stocked with trout—fishing pressure light! Earlier AMC guides noted that pond could be approached from summit of Carrigain by "1½ hours of strenuous beelined descent without trail." Carrigain Pond was reportedly discovered by Louis Morrison, one of J.E. Henry's loggers. Woods around pond devastated by clear-cutting in early 1900s (see *Appalachia*, June 1954), but have since made recovery to near-primeval appearance.

**Carter Pond, Lower,** Chapter 51.

**Carter Pond, Upper,** Chapter 51.

**Cherry Pond,** Chapter 64.

**Cherry Pond, Little,** Chapter 64.

**Chocorua Lake,** Chapter 26.

**Christine Lake,** Chapter 68.

**Church Pond,** Chapter 39.

**Church Pond, Little (Little Deer Pond, Sugar Pond)**

Location: Albany Intervale.

Access: Bushwhack.

Map: USGS 7½' Mount Carrigain.

Area: 6 acres.

Elevation: 1,260 feet.

Avg./Max. Depth: 2/10 feet.

Comment: "A sense of utter loneliness and desolation sweeps over one as he gazes upon this tiny sheet of water so completely buried in the great wilderness," wrote Charles Edward Beals, Jr., in 1916. Encircled by bogmeadow and conifer forest, with a marvelous view across the water to Green's Cliff from south end. Winter is the best time to visit, but avoid ice by outlet and inlet. Bushwhackers will find a stellar bird's-eye view of Little Church Pond, Albany Intervale, and Sandwich Range from a sun-soaked granite slab on SW ridge of Green's Cliff.

**Clouds, Lake of the, Lower,** Chapter 43.

**Clouds, Lake of the, Upper**—Chapter 43.

**Cone Mountain Pond (Cone Pond)**

Location: Thornton, south of Cone Mountain.

Access: Bushwhack.

Map: USGS 7½' Waterville Valley.

Area: 11 acres.

Elevation: 1,580 feet.

Avg./Max. Depth: 16/28 feet.

Comment: A pretty oval of clear green-tinted water nestled on flank of Cone Mountain in swath of National Forest land. Fringed with pine, spruce, hemlock; good view from glacier-scoured ledge on SW shore. Cone Mountain Pond is one of most acidic water bodies in White Mountains; trout stocking was discontinued in 1968. Currently the pond's low pH and high concentration of aluminum would preclude re-introduction of game fish. Forest Service's Northeastern Forest Experiment Station is conducting long-range study of acidification and acid deposition here; *do not disturb* outdoor laboratory area. Part of pond can be seen from summits of Welch and Dickey Mountains to north; these ledgy peaks are visible near outlet of pond.

**Crocker Pond,** Chapter 57.

**Deer Lake**

Formerly a tiny pond, now a bog, beside Beaver Brook Trail at head of Jobildunc Ravine between Mount Moosilauke and Mount Blue. Elevation 4,300 feet. Source of Baker River. Sweetser's guidebook described it as "a little sheet of water 'about as large as a man's hand.'"

**Desolation Pond**

Former pond, shown on 1946 USGS 15' Crawford Notch quad in small SE-facing cirque between Mount Eisenhower and Mount Monroe. Still shown on some current trail maps. Elevation 3,830 feet. All that's left today is a spot of bog and muck amidst the tangled firs.

**Dream Lake,** Chapter 59.

**Duck Pond**

Location: Nancy Range.

Access: Bushwhack.

Map: USGS 7½' Mount Carrigain.

Area: 2 acres.

Elevation: 3,060 feet.

Comment: Rocky, very shallow saucer of water, source of Whiteface Brook. Cupped in fir-forested hollow shadowed by Mount Anderson (3,740 feet) and Mount Lowell (3,740 feet), trailless wooded peaks with fine outlooks over eastern Pemi Wilderness. Good view of pond and its wooded mountain bowl from red-tinted rocks sprinkled around east shore. Nearby Duck Pond Mountain (3,330 feet) supports stand of old-growth spruce and fir.

**Durand Lake**, Chapter 62.

**Eagle Lake**, Chapter 32.

**East Pond**, Chapter 18.

**East Pond, Little**, Chapter 18.

**Echo Lake (Franconia)**, Chapter 16.

**Echo Lake (North Conway)**, Chapter 28.

**Elbow Pond**, Chapter 7.

**Ellsworth Pond**

> Location: Ellsworth.
> Access: Roadside, 5.0 miles from US 3.
> Maps: USGS 7½' Mount Kineo and Woodstock.
> Area: 56 acres.
> Elevation: 1,116 feet.
> Avg./Max. Depth: 12/32 feet.
> Comment: South and east shores privately owned; north and west shores are National Forest land. Boat launch at east end off Ellsworth side road. Fishing for chain pickerel, horned pout, yellow perch. No hiking trails.

**Ethan Pond**, Chapter 35.

**Failing Water Pond**

> Aptly named tarn on east side of Kinsman Ridge Trail on north ridge of Mount Wolf. Sometimes called Falling Water Pond. Shown but not named on USGS 7½' Mount Moosilauke quad, elevation 3,180 feet. Now a wide, circular bog mat, dotted with pitcher plants, holding only a tiny pool of water at east edge. South Kinsman rises to the north. The nameless pond shown to the SW on the USGS map (no trail) is a strange and lonesome place spiked with dead trees.

**Falls Pond**, Chapter 30.

**Flat Mountain Pond**, Chapter 25.

**Forest Lake**

> Location: Dalton and Whitefield.
> Access: Roadside, Forest Lake Road, 1.9 miles off NH 116 to State Park.
> Map: USGS 7½' X 15' Bethlehem.
> Area: 192 acres.
> Elevation: 1,079 feet.
> Avg./Max. Depth: 13/20 feet.
> Comment: Heavily developed, but Forest Lake State Park has nice swimming beach and birch-shaded picnic area. View across water to Twins, Garfield, Lafayette, Cannon, Kinsman. Warm-water fishing. One of New Hampshire's 10 original state parks, created in 1935.

**Foxglove Pond**, Chapter 1.

**Garfield Pond**, Chapter 33.

**Gentian Pond**, Chapter 60.

**Gordon Pond**, Chapter 10.

**Great Hill School Pond (Hemenway Pond, Duck Pond)**

    Location: Hemenway State Forest, Tamworth.

    Access: Short spur off gravel Hemenway Road leads to outlet.

    Map: USGS 7½' Mount Chocorua (pond not named).

    Area: 15 acres.

    Elevation: 980 feet.

    Avg./Max. Depth: 4/8 feet.

    Comment: Man-made pond at foot of Great Hill (trail to fire tower, good views of Sandwich Range). Huge boulder on SE shore offers interesting view across pond and its shrub-island to Mount Whiteface. Fishing limited to horned pout.

**Greeley Pond, Lower**, Chapter 19.

**Greeley Pond, Upper**, Chapter 19.

**Guinea Pond**, Chapter 24.

**Hall Pond, Lower**, Chapter 22.

**Hall Pond, Middle**, Chapter 22.

**Hall Pond, Upper**, Chapter 21.

**Harrington Pond**, Chapter 12.

**Heath Pond**

    Location: Ellsworth.

    Access: Old logging roads/snowmobile trails.

    Map: USGS 7½' Woodstock.

    Area: 2 acres.

    Elevation: 1,220 feet.

    Comment: Small, boggy, wild pond on private land, between Peaked Hill Pond and Ellsworth Pond. More accessible in winter.

**Hermit Lake**, Chapter 44.

**Heron Pond**, Chapter 26.

**Hildreth Pond**

    Location: Warren.

    Access: Roadside, NH 25. Map: USGS 7½' Warren.

    Area: 36 acres.

    Elevation: 834 feet.

    Comment: Long, curving man-made lake created by large flood control dam on Baker River. Dirt road leads across dam from NH 25 and down to crude boat launch on east shore. Old road/path leads to picnic ledges on west shore. Stocked with brook trout. Views of Webster Slide Mountain, Carr Mountain.

**Horseshoe Pond**, Chapter 55.

**Ice Pond,** Chapter 31.
**Jericho Lake**
>    Location: Berlin.
>    Access: Roadside, Jericho Lake Road off NH 110.
>    Maps: USGS 7½' X 15' Pliny, 7½' West Milan.
>    Area: 135 acres.
>    Elevation: 1,350 feet.
>    Comment: Artificial lake created in 1970 by large flood control dam on Jericho Brook. Area is operated as "Jericho Lake Park" by Berlin Receation and Parks Department. From NH 16 in Berlin drive 3.6 miles west on NH 110 to Jericho Lake Road (sign for park), which leads left (south) 1.3 miles to toll booth and parking lot. Facilities include fine sand beach, bathhouse, picnic area, playground, paved boat launch (motors prohibited). Lake is attractively fringed with spruce, fir, birch; best views are from rocky points on either side of beach. Crescent and Pilot Ranges can be seen across the water. Stocked with brook trout.

**Jericho Pond**
>    Location: Landaff, SW of Cooley Hill.
>    Access: 2.5 mile walk to east up logging road, starting on road 0.2 mile south of Chandler Pond.
>    Maps: USGS 7½' Sugar Hill and Lisbon.
>    Area: 4 acres.
>    Elevation: 1,490 feet.
>    Comment: Beaver pond on National Forest land at western boundary; unnamed on maps. Stocked with brook trout. Surrounding area heavily logged. Man-made Chandler Pond (20 acres, elevation 1,099 feet, avg./max. depth 3/6 feet) offers warm-water fishing, view of South Kinsman.

**Judson Pond**
>    Location: Southern Mahoosucs.
>    Access: Bushwhack.
>    Map: USGS 7½' Shelburne.
>    Area: 1 acre.
>    Elevation: 1,350 feet.
>    Comment: Small, muddy pond in shallow hardwood basin SE of Mount Ingalls. Formerly reached by Judson Pond Trail, now accessible only by bushwhack through logged areas on timber company land. "Attractive because of its secluded location," according to earlier AMC guidebooks.

**Kiah Pond,** Chapter 23.
**Kilback Pond,** Chapter 66.
**Kimball Pond, Upper**
>    Location: South Chatham.
>    Access: Roadside, off Green Hill Road.

Map: USGS 7½' North Conway East.

Area: 136 acres.

Elevation: 428 feet.

Max. Depth: 23 feet.

Comment: Good canoeing pond with extensive marshes and abundant bird life. Carry-in boat launch by dam at north end. Some development along east shore. Warm-water fishing. Nearby Lower Kimball Pond is more heavily developed. Both can be seen from summit of Kearsarge North.

**Kinsman Pond**, Chapter 14.

**Lily Pond**, Chapter 40.

**Lombard Pond**

Location: Stoneham, ME.

Access: Bushwhack.

Map: USGS 7½' East Stoneham, ME.

Area: 2.5 acres.

Elevation: 810 feet.

Comment: Shrubby, swampy pond south of Albany Mountain and visible from its south ledges.

**Lonesome Lake**, Chapter 13.

**Long Pond**, Chapter 6.

**Long Mountain Pond**

Location: Nash Stream State Forest.

Access: Bushwhack.

Map: USGS 7½' Percy Peaks.

Area: 2.5 acres.

Elevation: 3,410 feet.

Comment: One of the highest and wildest ponds in NH, a striking oval bound by dense weave of firs. Hidden in high saddle between two main summits (both 3,661 feet) of trailless Long Mountain, a massive wooded ridge. Good view of pond from rocky SE shore. Relics from old logging camp strewn in woods north of pond.

**Loon Pond (Big Loon Pond)**

Location: Loon Mountain.

Access: Service roads from ski trails/bushwhack.

Map: USGS 7½' Lincoln.

Area: 18.5 acres.

Elevation: 2,418 feet.

Max. Depth: 65 feet.

Comment: A spruce-rimmed beauty just 0.1 mile from trails of New Hampshire's busiest ski area, but seldom visited by hikers. In earlier days it was a popular hiking destination, and Loon Mountain (3,065 feet) was known as Loon Pond Mountain. Led by Lincoln guide Dura Pollard, an

AMC party visited the pond in September 1880. Lucia Pychowska described it as "a beautiful sheet of water ... quite deep, very clear, still holding trout, and bordered by wooded or rocky shores." In 1890 writer Julius Ward acclaimed Loon Pond as rival to Lonesome Lake in beauty and charm. For many years access was gained by WMNF Loon Pond Trail; footway abandoned in 1960s. Today Loon Pond is better known as utilitarian pond, providing drinking water for town of Lincoln and snowmaking source for Loon Mountain Ski Area; has been a source of controversy in ski area expansion. Is no longer stocked with trout and appears to be devoid of fish life, perhaps due to high acidity. Service roads lead to small dam at outlet and to maintenance building on opposite shore. Best spot at pond is sun-soaked ledge atop cliff that drops 30 feet to north shore, reached by short bushwhack from nearby ski trails; view over pond to wooded South Peak (2,807 feet) of Loon Mountain. Beautiful bird's-eye view of pond from deck of snack bar at top of gondola lift and nearby observation tower. (The gondola operates year-round.) Ski trails and pond are in National Forest. Many ski trails are open for hiking. Visitors should take care to protect purity of water supply; no swimming or camping in area. Ice is unsafe in winter due to snowmaking drawdowns.

### Loon Pond, Little
Location: Loon Mountain.
Access: Bushwhack.
Map: USGS 7½' Lincoln.
Area: 2 acres.
Elevation: 2,220 feet. Comment: Boggy, lily-dotted pool downstream from Big Loon Pond. In 1880 AMC explorer Lucia Pychowska called it "a rock-set gem." Bushwhackers can seek out a line of cliffs that drop to water along NW shore; nice views of pond in its dark forest hollow. Other ledges a few yards north offer vista to Cannon-Kinsman range.

### Lost Pond, Chapter 50.
### Mascot Pond, Chapter 58.
### Mead Pond
Location: Rumney, east of Stinson Lake.
Access: USFS logging road.
Map: USGS 7½' Rumney.
Area: 10 acres (est.).
Elevation: 1,620 feet.
Comment: Large, shrubby beaver pond in saddle south of wooded knoll known as Eagle Cliff (1,940 feet). From junction at SW corner of Stinson Lake, head SE on Cross Road, turn left at 0.7 mile, and drive 0.3 mile farther to gated Forest Service road on right (not shown on USGS map; it

is shown on Pemi Ranger District's excellent mountain biking map). Park off Cross Road and walk in to pond on the logging road (a mountain bike/snowmobile trail); 2.6 miles round-trip, 200-foot vertical rise. Beyond bridge over outlet brook, path leads down to fine sitting rock on NW shore, a good spot for birding and wildlife watching. There are other sitting rocks farther east along the north shore.

**Mirror Lake (Woodstock)**, Chapter 3.

**Moose Pond (Albany)**

> Location: North of Blue Mountain, a northern spur of Mount Chocorua.
> Access: Bushwhack.
> Map: USGS 7½' Silver Lake.
> Area: .25 acre.
> Elevation: 2,100 feet.
> Comment: A petite oval surrounded by leatherleaf and spruces. Named on 1958 USGS 15' Mount Chocorua quad and AMC Chocorua/Waterville map, but not on new USGS quad. In 1940s the long-abandoned Blue Mountain Trail passed by it.

**Moose Pond (Shelburne)**

> Location: South side of US 2, 2.4 miles east of Shelburne village.
> Access: Roadside with short loop trail.
> Map: USGS 7½' Shelburne.
> Area: 5 acres.
> Elevation: 690 feet.
> Avg./Max. Depth: 2/2 feet.
> Comment: Swampy pond choked with lily pads by midsummer. Encircled by a 0.5 mile trail, a pleasant walk through varied woods. Interesting views of Bear Mountain range (eastern Mahoosucs) from south shore. May harbor horned pout, chain pickerel. Lumberyard nearby.

**Moss Pond**, Chapter 60.

**Mountain Pond**, Chapter 49.

**Mud Pond (Easton)**, Chapter 11.

**Mud Pond (Jefferson)**

> Location: North of Cherry Ponds.
> Access: Bushwhack.
> Map: USGS 7½' x 15' Lancaster.
> Area: 2 acres.
> Elevation: 1,131 feet.
> Comment: A tiny teardrop hidden needle-in-haystack style amidst the boggy conifer forest of the Pondicherry region. Best explored in winter.

**Mud Pond (Lincoln)**

> Location: Franconia Notch.
> Access: Bushwhack.

Map: USGS 7½' Lincoln.

Area: 2.5 acres.

Elevation: 2,420 feet.

Comment: Boggy, snag-fringed pond nestled in spruces at base of steep eastern spur of South Kinsman Mountain. SW shore affords picturesque view of Franconia Ridge, more easily obtained in winter. Mud Pond can be spotted from Mounts Lafayette and Lincoln.

**Mud Pond (Thornton),** Chapter 2.

**Mud Pond (Tunnel Brook, Benton),** Chapter 8.

**Nancy Pond,** Chapter 37.

**No-Ketchum Pond,** Chapter 52.

**Norcross Pond,** Chapter 37.

**Norcross Pond, Little,** Chapter 37.

**Number 8 Pond**

Location: Stoneham, ME, south of Albany Notch.

Access: Snowmobile trail from Albany Notch Trail.

Map: USGS 7½' East Stoneham, ME.

Area: 1 acre.

Elevation: 1,050 feet.

Comment: A Forest Service ranger described it as "just a mudhole"—an accurate assessment of this puddle fringed with flooded hardwoods. A place for wood ducks, frogs, and mosquitoes.

**Oliverian Pond,** Chapter 5.

**Page Pond,** Chapter 59.

**Peaked Hill Pond,** Chapter 2.

**Profile Lake,** Chapter 15.

**Province Pond,** Chapter 48.

**Pudding Pond**

Location: North Conway.

Access: Pudding Pond Nature Trail or Maine Central Railroad tracks, from end of Locust Lane, 0.2 mile off NH 16.

Map: USGS 7½' North Conway East.

Area: 14 acres.

Elevation: 530 feet.

Avg./Max. Depth: 3/8 inches.

Comment: Long, narrow, swampy pond, not long for this world. The 1½ mile loop nature trail is a pleasant stroll through woods and ferns and past interesting wetlands, though views of the pond are limited.

**Ray's Pond**

Location: Southern Mahoosucs.

Access: Short blazed path from summit of Mount Ingalls (2,242 feet).

Map: USGS 7½' Shelburne.

Area: .25 acre.

Elevation: 2,190 feet.

Comment: A dark and lonely little pool in the spruce forest. Called "Roy's Pond" in current AMC *Guide*, unnamed on USGS map. Round-trip hike is 6.2 miles, 1,950-foot vertical rise from Philbrook Farm Inn on North Road, via Blue Trail or Red Trail to Mount Cabot (1,512 feet, view SW), short link on Judson Pond Trail, and upper Scudder Trail along ridge to Mount Ingalls (good views SW from ledges, but trail very obscure; lower Scudder Trail from Mill Brook Road disrupted by logging in 1992.) Steep ledge on north shore provides best look at Ray's Pond.

**Red Pond**

A boggy pool stashed amidst the ledges at NE base of Mount Eisenhower's summit cone, between Mount Eisenhower Loop and Crawford Path. Elevation 4,400 feet. Shown on AMC/Washburn Mount Washington map. Sweetser called it "a dull puddle of bad water," said that it was named for the red moss in the area and that in times of abundant rain it drained into both the Ammonoosuc and Saco Rivers.

**Red Eagle Pond,** Chapter 29.

**Rocky Pond**

Location: Stark.

Access: Bushwhack.

Map: USGS 7½' West Milan.

Area: 12 acres.

Elevation: 1,110 feet.

Comment: Trailless satellite of South Pond. Forest Service logging road approaches east end. Pond is long, narrow, shallow, and sedgy, dotted with boulders, rimmed with shrubs and red maples that light a ring of fire around water in September. String of rocks at eastern outlet provides view down pond towards Mill Mountain (2,517 feet). Gnarled white cedars cling to boulders near outlet. Two nameless shallow ponds lie between Rocky Pond and South Pond. A neat area to explore in winter.

**Round Pond,** Chapter 57.

**Russell Pond,** Chapter 17.

**Saco Lake,** Chapter 41.

**Safety, Pond of,** Chapter 63.

**Sawyer Pond,** Chapter 38.

**Sawyer Pond, Little,** Chapter 38.

**Shell Pond,** Chapter 54.

**Shingle Pond,** Chapter 47.

**Shoal Pond,** Chapter 36.

**South Pond,** Chapter 67.

**Spaulding Lake,** Chapter 46.

**Speck Pond,** Chapter 61.

**Star Lake,** Chapter 45.

**Stinson Lake**

Location: Rumney.

Access: Roadside, Stinson Lake Road from NH 25.

Maps: USGS 7½' Rumney and Mount Kineo.

Area: 346 acres.

Elevation: 1,303 feet.

Avg./Max. Depth: 39/75 feet.

Comment: Largest water body within National Forest boundary, but shore is privately owned and heavily developed. Private boat launch at SW corner; fee. Good fishing—brook, rainbow, and lake trout, smallmouth bass, chain pickerel, horned pout. Nice bird's-eye view of lake from NW outlook at summit of 2,900-foot Stinson Mountain; 3.6 miles round-trip, 1,400-foot vertical rise via Stinson Mountain Trail (see Daniel Doan's *Fifty Hikes in the White Mountains*).

**Storm Lake,** Chapter 45.

**Sunken Pond**

Location: Albany, ME.

Access: Bushwhack.

Map: USGS 7½' East Stoneham, ME.

Area: 1.5 acres.

Elevation: 810 feet.

Comment: A perfect little bog pond in a kettle hole rimmed with spruce, pine, and hemlock. Located just north of Broken Bridge Pond; best visited in winter.

**Three Ponds, Lower**

Location: NE of Carr Mountain.

Access: Bushwhack.

Map: USGS 7½' Mount Kineo.

Area: 2.5 acres.

Elevation: 1,740 feet.

Avg./Max. Depth: 5/14 feet.

Comment: Smallest and deepest of the Three Ponds lies on shelf east of Three Ponds Trail. A saucer of water guarded by ring of leatherleaf and beaver-felled trees. Large beaver lodge on north shore. Stocked with brook trout. View up to Carr Mountain; is much easier to get to in winter.

**Three Ponds, Middle,** Chapter 1.

**Three Ponds, Upper,** Chapter 1.

**Tunnel Brook Ponds,** Chapter 8.

**Unknown Pond,** Chapter 65.

**Virginia Lake,** Chapter 56.

**Wachipauka Pond,** Chapter 4.
**Whitcomb Pond,** Chapter 68.
**White Lake,** Chapter 27.
**Wildlife Pond**

> Small man-made pond in gravel area off USFS Zealand Road, between Mount Oscar to east and Sugarloaves to west. Shown as sand pit on USGS 7½' X 15' Bethlehem Quad; elevation 1,644 feet. Accessed by 0.2 mile road/trail (USFS sign, "Wildlife Pond") leaving east side of Zealand Road across from parking area for Sugarloaf Trail, 1.0 mile from US 302. Easy walk leads to open east shore, where there is impressive view across water to cliffs of Middle Sugarloaf (2,539 feet). Across road, Sugarloaf Trail leads to the ledgy summit (2.8 miles round-trip, 900-foot vertical rise) and panoramic views, including Wildlife Pond below.

**Willey Pond**

> Small artificial pond created on floor of Crawford Notch each spring by damming Saco River; drained in fall. Located on east side of US 302, across from Willey House Historical Site. Elevation 1,300 feet. Popular picnic spot, with striking views of Webster Cliffs and Mounts Willey, Avalon, and Willard. Short loop trail leads across dam and along east shore. Willey Pond is also old name for Ethan Pond.

**York Pond,** Chapter 66.
**Zeacliff Pond,** Chapter 34.
**Zealand Pond,** Chapter 34.

# BIBLIOGRAPHY

---◆---

## 1. Trail Guides, Maps, and Recreation

Allen, Linda Buchanan. *Short Hikes and Ski Trips Around Pinkham Notch.* Boston: Appalachian Mountain Club, 1991.

Appalachian Trail Conference. *Appalachian Trail Guide to New Hampshire-Vermont,* 7th ed. Harper's Ferry, WV, 1992.

Bolnick, Bruce and Doreen. *Waterfalls of the White Mountains.* Woodstock, VT: Backcountry, 1990.

Buchsbaum, Robert N. *Nature Hikes in the White Mountains.* Boston: AMC, 1995.

Chatham Trails Association. *Map of Cold River Valley and Evans Notch.* 1992.

Chocorua Lake Conservation Foundation. *A Guide to the Chocorua Conservation Lands.* Chocorua, NH, 1987.

Daniell, Eugene S., III, ed. *AMC White Mountain Guide*, 25th ed. Boston: Appalachian Mountain Club, 1992. Several earlier editions were consulted; the first was published in 1907.

DeLorme Mapping Company. *The Maine Atlas and Gazetteer.* Freeport, ME: DeLorme, 1984.

DeLorme Mapping Company. *The New Hampshire Atlas and Gazetteer.* Freeport, ME: DeLorme, 1988.

DeLorme Publishing Company. *Trail Map and Guide to the White Mountain National Forest.* Freeport, ME: DeLorme, 1987.

Doan, Daniel. *Fifty Hikes in the White Mountains*, 4th ed. Woodstock, VT: Backcountry, 1990.

Doan, Daniel. *Fifty More Hikes in New Hampshire*, 3rd ed. Woodstock, VT: Backcountry, 1991.

Dunn, John M. *Winterwise: A Backpacker's Guide.* Lake George, NY: Adirondack Mountain Club, 1988.

Ferguson, Gary. *Walks of New England.* New York: Prentice Hall, 1989.

Ford, Sally and Daniel. *Twenty-Five Ski Tours in the White Mountains.* Somersworth, NH: New Hampshire Publishing Co., 1977.

Gibson, John. *Fifty Hikes in Southern Maine.* Woodstock, VT: Backcountry, 1989.

346

Goodman, David. *Classic Backcountry Skiing*. Boston: AMC, 1989.

Gorman, Stephen. *AMC Guide to Winter Camping*. Boston: AMC, 1991.

Hampton, Bruce and David Cole. *Soft Paths*. Harrisburg, PA, Stackpole, 1988.

Lewis, Cynthia C. and Thomas J. *Best Hikes with Children in Vermont, New Hampshire, and Maine*. Seattle: The Mountaineers, 1991.

Maine Appalachian Trail Conference. *Guide to the Appalachian Trail in Maine*, 11th ed. Augusta, ME, 1988.

Micucci, Mike. *Mountain Biking in the Northern White Mountains*. Bethel, ME: Venture Project, 1991.

Pletcher, Larry. *The Hiker's Guide to New Hampshire*. Helena, MT: Falcon Press, 1995.

Prater, Gene. *Snowshoeing*, 3rd ed. Seattle: The Mountaineers, 1988.

Preston, Philip. *Squam Trail Guide*. Holderness, NH: Squam Lakes Association, 1991.

Preston, Philip, *Washington and Lafayette Trail Maps*. Ashland, NH: Waumbek Books, 1982.

Preston, Philip and Jonathan A. Kannair. *White Mountains West*. Ashland, NH: Waumbek Books, 1979.

Randolph Mountain Club. *Randolph Paths*. Randolph, NH, 1992.

Schweiker, Roioli, *Twenty-Five Ski Tours in New Hampshire*. Woodstock, VT: Backcountry, 1988.

Scudder, Brent E. *Scudder's White Mountain Viewing Guide*. Bellmore, NY: High Top Press, 1995.

Washburn, Bradford et al. *Mount Washington and the Heart of the Presidential Range*. Boston: AMC, 1988.

Waterville Valley Athletic and Improvement Association. *Map of Hiking Trails in Waterville Valley, NH*. Waterville Valley: 1985.

White Mountain National Forest. *Forest Service Map of WMNF*. Laconia, NH, 1984; plus various trail, campground, and recreation leaflets.

White Mountain National Forest. *Winter Recreation Map*. Laconia, NH, 1980.

White Mountain Snowmobile Club Trail Map (Lincoln/Woodstock Region).

Wilson, Alex. *Quiet Water Canoe Guide: New Hampshire/Vermont*. Boston: AMC, 1992.

Wilson, Alex and John Hayes. *Quiet Water Canoe Guide: Maine*. Boston: AMC, 1995.

Wonalancet Outdoor Club, *Trail Map and Guide to the Sandwich Range Wilderness*. Wonalancet, NH, 1991.

## 2. History and General Interest

American Guide Series. *New Hampshire: A Guide to the Granite State*. Boston: Houghton Mifflin, 1938.

Appalachian Mountain Club. *A Guide to Zealand Valley*. n.d.

Belcher, C. Francis. *Logging Railroads of the White Mountains*. Boston: AMC, 1980.

Bixby, Roland M. *History of Warren, NH*. 1986.

Brown, J. Willcox. *Forest History of Mount Moosilauke*. Hanover, NH: Dartmouth Outing Club, 1988.

Burt, F. Allen. *The Story of Mount Washington*. Hanover, NH: Dartmouth Publications, 1960.

Cross, George N. *Randolph Old and New: Its Ways and Its By-Ways*. Town of Randolph, NH, 1924.

Dickerman, Mike et al. *A Guide to Crawford Notch*. Littleton, NH: Bondcliff Books, 1997.

Doherty, Paul and Claude Brusseau. *A Visitor's Guide to Franconia Notch*. NH Division of Parks and Recreation, 1988.

Doherty, Paul T. *Smoke From a Thousand Campfires*. Berlin, NH: 1992.

Howarth, William. *Thoreau in the Mountains*. New York: Farrar, Straus, and Giroux, 1982.

Julyan, Robert and Mary. *Place Names of the White Mountains*. Hanover, NH: University Press of New England, 1993.

Kostecke, Diane, ed. *Franconia Notch: An In-Depth Guide*. Concord, NH: Society for the Protection of New Hampshire Forests, 1975.

Mudge, John T.B. *The White Mountains: Names, Places, and Legends*. Etna, NH: Durand Press, 1992.

Nyiri, Alan. *The White Mountains of New Hampshire*. Camden, ME: Down East, 1987.

Reifsnyder, William E. *High Huts of the White Mountains*. Boston: AMC, 1993.

Sandwich Historical Society. *Sixteenth Annual Excursion*. Sandwich, NH, 1935.

Sandwich Historical Society. *Sixty-Ninth Annual Excursion*. Sandwich, NH, 1988.

Sloane, Bruce. *New Hampshire's Parklands*. Portsmouth, NH: Peter Randall, 1985.

Waterman, Laura and Guy. *Backwoods Ethics*. Woodstock, VT: Countryman, 1993.

Waterman, Laura and Guy. *Wilderness Ethics*. Woodstock, VT: Countryman, 1993

Waterman, Laura and Guy. *Forest and Crag: A History of Hiking, Trail Blazing, and Adventure in the Northeast Mountains*. Boston: AMC, 1989.

Welch, Sarah N. *Franconia Notch History and Guide*. 1981.

## 3. White Mountain Classics

Atkinson, J. Brooks. *Skyline Promenades: A Potpourri.* New York: Alfred A. Knopf, 1925.

Beals, Charles Edward, Jr. *Passaconaway in the White Mountains.* Boston: Richard G. Badger, 1916.

Bolles, Frank. *At the North of Bearcamp Water.* Boston: Houghton Mifflin, 1893.

Drake, Samuel Adams. *The Heart of the White Mountains.* New York: Harper and Brothers, 1882.

Eastman, Samuel C. *The White Mountain Guide Book,* 7th ed. Boston: Lee and Shepard, 1867.

Harrington, Karl Pomeroy. *Walks and Climbs in the White Mountains.* New Haven: Yale University Press, 1926.

Hitchcock, Charles H. and Joshua H. Huntington. *The Geology of New Hampshire.* Concord, NH: Volume I, 1874. Volume II, 1877.

Kilbourne, Frederick W. *Chronicles of the White Mountains.* Boston: Houghton Mifflin, 1916.

King, Thomas Starr. *The White Hills: Their Legends, Landscape, and Poetry.* Boston: Crosby and Ainsworth, 1859.

Little, William. *The History of Warren, NH.* Manchester, NH, 1870.

Morse, Stearns, ed. *Lucy Crawford's History of the White Mountains.* Boston: AMC, 1978. (1st ed. 1846)

Packard, Winthrop. *White Mountain Trails.* Boston: Small, Maynard, 1917.

Spaulding, John H. *Historical Relics of the White Mountains.* Boston: Nathaniel Noyes, 1855.

Sweetser, Moses F. *The White Mountains: A Handbook for Travellers,* 4th ed. Boston: James R. Osgood, 1881.

Sweetser, Moses F. *Chisholm's White Mountain Guide.* Portland, ME: Chisholm Brothers, 1903.

Sweetser, Moses F., *A Guide to the White Mountains.* Boston: Houghton Mifflin, 1918.

Ward, Julius H. *The White Mountains: A Guide to Their Interpretation.* Boston: Houghton Mifflin, 1890.

Willey, Benjamin G. *Incidents in White Mountain History.* Boston: Nathaniel Noyes, 1856.

## 4. Natural History

Amos, William H. *The Life of the Pond.* New York: McGraw-Hill, 1967.

Appalachian Mountain Club. *AMC Field Guide to Mountain Flowers of New England.* Boston: AMC, 1977.

Audubon Society of New Hampshire. *A Brief Guide to the Natural History of the White Mountains.* Concord, NH, 1967.

Beecher, Ned. *Outdoor Explorations in Mt. Washington Valley.* Conway, NH: Tin Mountain Conservation Center, 1989.

Billings, Marland P. and Katherine Fowler-Billings. *Geology of the Gorham Quadrangle.* Concord, NH: New Hampshire Department of Resources and Economic Development, 1975.

Billings, Marland P. et al. *The Geology of the Mt. Washington Quadrangle.* Concord, NH: New Hampshire Department of Resources and Economic Development, 1979.

Bliss, L.C. *Alpine Zone of the Presidential Range.* Edmonton, Canada, 1963.

Caduto, Michael J. *Pond and Brook.* Hanover, NH: University Press of New England, 1990.

Casanave, Suki. *Natural Wonders of New Hampshire.* Castine, ME: Country Roads Press, 1994.

Cvancara, Alan M. *At the Water's Edge.* New York: John Wiley and Sons, 1989.

Godin, Alfred J. *Wild Mammals of New England.* Yarmouth, ME: DeLorme, 1981.

Johnson, Charles W. *Bogs of the Northeast.* Hanover, NH: University Press of New England, 1985.

Johnson, Charles W. *The Nature of Vermont.* Hanover, NH: University Press of New England, 1980.

Kulik, Stephen et al. *The Audubon Society Field Guide to the Natural Places of the Northeast.* New York: Pantheon, 1984.

Likens, Gene E., ed. *An Ecosystem Approach to Aquatic Ecology: Mirror Lake and Its Environment.* New York: Springer-Verlag, 1985.

Marchand, Peter J. *North Woods: An Inside Look at the Nature of Forests in the Northeast.* Boston: AMC, 1987.

Reid, George K. *Pond Life.* New York: Golden, 1967.

Rezendes, Paul. *Tracking and the Art of Seeing.* Charlotte, VT: Camden House, 1992.

Ridgely, Beverly S. *Birds of the Squam Lakes Region,* 2nd ed. Holderness, NH: Squam Lakes Association, 1988.

Silver, Helenette. *A History of New Hampshire Game and Furbearers.* Concord, NH: New Hampshire Fish and Game Department, 1957.

Snow, John O. *Secrets of Ponds and Lakes.* Portland, ME: Guy Gannett, 1982.

Steele, Frederic L. *At Timberline: A Nature Guide to the Mountains of the Northeast.* Boston: Appalachian Mountain Club, 1982.

Steele, Frederic L. and Albion R. Hodgdon. *Trees and Shrubs of Northern New England,* 3rd ed. Concord, NH: Society for the Protection of New Hampshire Forests, 1975.

Van Diver, Bradford B. *Roadside Geology of Vermont and New Hampshire.* Missoula, MT: Mountain Press, 1987.

White Mountain National Forest. *Checklist for Birds.*

Wulff, Barry L. *A Field Guide to Pinkham Notch.* Gorham, NH: AMC, n.d.

## 5. Pond and Lake Data and Fishing Information

NOTE:

Surface areas for ponds and lakes were obtained from the state biological surveys and pond inventories and the Trout Fishing folder issued by the WMNF. In some cases they were estimated from the 7½' USGS maps. Elevations for ponds and neighboring summits were taken from the 7½' USGS quads. Where no exact elevation was given, an estimate was made by taking the highest contour shown for the pond or peak and adding one-half of the contour interval. Average and maximum depths of water bodies came from the state surveys and the WMNF fishing folder.

Buso, Donald C. et al. *Potential for Acidification of Six Remote Ponds in the White Mountains of New Hampshire.* Durham, NH: Northeast Forest Experiment Station, Research Report No. 43, 1984.

Cowling, Derrill J. and Douglas Lash. *Characteristics of Lakes, Ponds, and Reservoirs of New Hampshire.* U.S. Geological Survey, 1975.

DeLorme Mapping Company. *Fishing Depth Maps, Maine Lakes and Ponds—Oxford County.* Freeport, ME: DeLorme, 1989.

Kologe, Brian R. *AMC Guide to Freshwater Fishing in New England.* Boston: Appalachian Mountain Club, 1991.

New Hampshire Department of Environmental Services. *Acidity Status of Remote High Altitude Ponds in New Hampshire.* Concord, NH: 1988.

New Hampshire Department of Environmental Services. *New Hampshire Lakes and Ponds Inventory.* Concord, NH. Vol. 2, 1981; Vol. 3, 1987; Vol. 4, 1988; Vol. 5, 1989; Vol. 6, 1990; Vol. 7, 1991.

New Hampshire Fish and Game Department. *Biological Survey of the Lakes and Ponds in Coos, Grafton, and Carroll Counties.* Concord, NH: 1972.

New Hampshire Fish and Game Department. *New Hampshire Freshwater Fishing Digest.* Concord, NH: annual.

North Country Angler. *New Hampshire Fishing Map.* North Conway, NH, 1982.

Northern Cartographic. *The Atlas of New Hampshire Trout Ponds.* 2nd ed. Burlington, VT: 1994.

Raychard, Al. *Remote Trout Ponds in Maine.* Unity, ME: North Country Press, 1984.

Scarola, John F. *Freshwater Fishes of New Hampshire.* Concord, NH: New Hampshire Fish and Game Department, 1973.

Swasey, Charlton J. and Donald A. Wilson. *New Hampshire Fishing Maps.* Freeport, ME: DeLorme, 1986.

White Mountain National Forest. *Trout Fishing in the White Mountain National Forest.* Laconia, NH: n.d.

## 6. Periodicals

*Appalachia.* The Journal of the Appalachian Mountain Club. Boston: Appalachian Mountain Club, 1876-date. Some articles of particular interest are:

Buchanan, Claire. "Life Forms in Lakes of the Clouds." December 1977, pp. 128–130.

Burt, Frank H. "The Nomenclature of the White Mountains." December 1915, pp. 359–390.

Godden, Jack A. "The Establishment of Wilderness, Scenic, and Natural Areas on the White Mountain National Forest." June 1965, pp. 403–413.

Hatch, Robert McConnell. "A Lean-To in the Mountains." December 1956, pp. 173–180.

Hatch, Robert McConnell. "Rogers Ledge." December 1965, pp. 581–586.

Likens, Gene E. "Mirror Lake: Its Past, Present, and Future?" December 1972, pp. 23–41.

Osborne, Maurice M. "Some Unconventional Walks in Livermore, 1912." June 1954, pp. 61–64.

Pychowska, Mrs. L.D. and Miss Marian M., "Baldcap Mountain," July 1880, pp. 121–129.

Pychowska, Lucia D. "Loon Pond Mountain," May 1881, pp. 284–286.

Wood, Richard G. "The Pond of Safety Legend." December 1949, pp. 409–414.


*Littleton Courier,* Littleton, NH

Dickerman, Mike. "Loon Pond: Controversial, Confusing." March 6, 1991.


*New Hampshire Spirit,* Tamworth, NH

Lawry, Nelson H. "Overland to Cone Pond: An Environmental Acid Trip." September-November 1988, pp. 25–29, 96.

Porterfield, John C. "North of the Notches." January-February 1989, pp. 34–39.

# Also from The Countryman Press and Backcountry Publications

The Countryman Press and Backcountry Publications, long known for fine books on travel and outdoor recreation, offer a range of practical and readable manuals.

## Related Books of Interest

*Backwoods Ethics*, by Laura & Guy Waterman
*Camp & Trail Cooking Techniques*, by Jim Capossela
*Canoe Camping Vermont and New Hampshire Rivers*, by Roioli Schweiker
*Earth Ponds* and *The Earth Ponds Sourcebook*, by Tim Matson
*50 Hikes in the White Mountains*, by Daniel Doan & Ruth Doan McDougall
*50 More Hikes in New Hampshire*, by Daniel Doan & Ruth Doan McDougall
*Look to the Mountain*, by LeGrand Cannon
*The Mountain Biker's Guide to Ski Resorts*, by Robert Immler
*New Hampshire: An Explorer's Guide*, by Christina Tree & Peter Jennison
*Our Last Backpack*, by Daniel Doan
*Reading the Forested Landscape*, by Tom Wessels
*30 Bicycle Tours in New Hampshire*, by Adolphe Bernotas with Tom & Susan Heavey
*25 Bicycle Tours in Maine*, by Howard Stone
*Waterfalls of the White Mountains*, by Bruce & Doreen Bolnick
*Wilderness Ethics*, by Laura and Guy Waterman

We offer many more books on hiking, walking, fishing and canoeing in New England, New York state, the mid-Atlantic states, and the Midwest—and many more books on bicycle touring, travel, nature and other subjects. Our titles are available in bookshops and in many sporting goods stores, or they may be ordered directly from the publisher. For ordering information or for a complete catalog, please contact:

The Countryman Press
c/o W.W. Norton & Company, Inc.
800 Keystone Industrial Park
Scranton, Pennsylvania 18512
or call our toll-free number: (800) 233-4830.
Check us out on-line at http://www.countrymanpress.com.